Silent Film's
Last Hurrah

ALSO BY DAVID MEUEL
AND FROM McFARLAND

Women Film Editors: Unseen Artists of American Cinema (2016)
The Noir Western: Darkness on the Range, 1943–1962 (2015)
Women in the Films of John Ford (2014)

Silent Film's Last Hurrah
The Remarkable Movies of the Long 1928

DAVID MEUEL

McFarland & Company, Inc., Publishers
Jefferson, North Carolina

ISBN (print) 978-1-4766-6895-6
ISBN (ebook) 978-1-4766-4859-0

LIBRARY OF CONGRESS AND BRITISH LIBRARY
CATALOGUING DATA ARE AVAILABLE

Library of Congress Control Number 2023004014

© 2023 David Meuel. All rights reserved

No part of this book may be reproduced or transmitted in any form or by any means, electronic or mechanical, including photocopying or recording, or by any information storage and retrieval system, without permission in writing from the publisher.

Front cover image of Buster Keaton (as William Canfield, Jr.) in *Steamboat Bill, Jr.*, 1928 (United Artists/Photofest); spotlight © Boris Rabtsevich/Shutterstock

Printed in the United States of America

*McFarland & Company, Inc., Publishers
Box 611, Jefferson, North Carolina 28640
www.mcfarlandpub.com*

*Once again,
to Kathryn*

*And this time,
to Jimmy, Annette, Henry, and August*

Acknowledgments

Although a book may only have one "official" author, numerous people help move a project from concept to completion, and I would like to thank several people in my life for their cogent insights on film, excellent listening skills, patience, and support as this book has taken shape. Specifically, these are Elliot Lavine, Bob and Melanie Ferrando, Jim Daniels, Peter Nelson, Natalie Varney, Bonnie Rattner, and Paul Bendix.

I would also like to acknowledge a great debt to the work of the scores of film critics and scholars whose various books, articles, and interviews were indispensable to this project. Their names are all listed in this book's bibliography.

Finally, I would like to extend a very special thanks to my long-time friend Mary Scott ("Scotty") Martinson for devoting both her expertise and many hours of her time to editing the manuscript. This is the fifth book of mine that she has edited, and her work is, as it always has been, highly valued and greatly appreciated.

Table of Contents

Acknowledgments	vi
Preface	1
Introduction: A Doomed Art's Glorious Last Days	5
1. At the Precipice: Mary Pickford and *My Best Girl*	17
2. "The maddest idea in the world": Gloria Swanson, Raoul Walsh, and *Sadie Thompson*	27
3. Tramp on a Tightrope: Charlie Chaplin and *The Circus*	40
4. "A lyricist of light and shadow": Josef von Sternberg, *The Last Command*, and *The Docks of New York*	51
5. "The highest reaches of the form": King Vidor and *The Crowd*	65
6. The End of an Amazing Run: Harold Lloyd and *Speedy*	77
7. In a Blaze of Windswept Glory: Buster Keaton and *Steamboat Bill, Jr.*	88
8. A Star Is Born: Joan Crawford and *Our Dancing Daughters*	100
9. "Astonishing elegance": William Wellman, Louise Brooks, Wallace Beery, and *Beggars of Life*	110
10. "Time was his; he owned it": Erich von Stroheim and *The Wedding March*	121
11. "I have a special confidence in you": Lillian Gish, Victor Sjöström, and *The Wind*	133
12. Partners in Perversity: Lon Chaney, Tod Browning, and *West of Zanzibar*	147

13. "To reach for the moon one last time": Douglas Fairbanks and *The Iron Mask* — 158
14. Twenty-Eight Other Notable U.S. Silent and Hybrid Films Released During the Long 1928 — 168

Afterthoughts: Requiem and Reemergence — 183
Where to Find the Films Featured in This Book — 187
Chapter Notes — 189
Bibliography — 195
Index — 199

Preface

The story of the ecstatic audience response to Warner Brothers' *The Jazz Singer* in October 1927 and the sound revolution it triggered in films has been told many times in articles, books, documentaries and even feature films such as 1952's *Singin' in the Rain*. Almost always, though, the emphasis has been on the transition to sound films and the enormous, often harsh, upheaval that occurred in the U.S. film industry as a result. Rarely has the main focus been on another, and quite remarkable, part of this story—the thunderous last wave of great silent films that flowed into U.S. movie theaters during a 16½-month period we'll call "the Long 1928." This period begins on October 6, 1927, the day *The Jazz Singer* premiered, and it ends on February 21, 1929, when *The Iron Mask*, Douglas Fairbanks's personal valedictory to the silent film, was released.

During the Long 1928, more than 1000 U.S.-produced films were released both around the country and the world. By far, the vast majority of these were silents. Today, many of these films have been lost or destroyed. Many more are also of dubious quality and, as such, of little or no interest to contemporary audiences. A surprisingly large number, however, range from very good to truly great and lasting works of cinema. Depending on the list, for example, numerous Hollywood releases during this 16½-month period have been ranked among the best 100 silent films ever made. These include such films as King Vidor's *The Crowd* and *Show People*, Raoul Walsh's *Sadie Thompson*, Victor Sjöström's *The Wind*, Charles Reisner's and Buster Keaton's *Steamboat Bill, Jr.*, Erich von Stroheim's *The Wedding March*, Charlie Chaplin's *The Circus*, William Wellman's *Beggars of Life*, Ted Wilde's and Harold Lloyd's *Speedy*, Josef Von Sternberg's *The Last Command* and *The Docks of New York*, Edward Sedgwick's *The Cameraman*, and Paul Leni's *The Man Who Laughs*. As a viable commercial product, the silent film was dying, but, as an art form, it was clearly at the height of its sophistication and accomplishment.

This book spotlights this paradoxical, tragic, and, in some ways, inspiring phenomenon, this "swan song" of the U.S. silent film. Each of the first 13 chapters focuses on one (or, in the case of Chapter 4, two) of these films as well as one or more of the principal creative figures behind each of them, their careers, their varying reactions to the changes that the sound revolution brought with it, and, ultimately, how their lives played out after the art form they had all supported and cultivated had died. Chapter 14 offers brief glimpses of 28 additional extant films that are also part of the Long 1928's impressive output. All of these selections, of course, are subjective and made for reasons ranging from the quality of the film to the particular silent film figures involved, many of whom were soon to face major turning points in their careers and lives.

Writing a single book about films released during a period in film history as fertile and varied as the late 1920s can be both exhilarating and frustrating. In many ways, it's like taking a first trip to Europe with only enough money to stay for a week. So, rather than being comprehensive, the aim here has been to be selective and delve more deeply into a fairly small group of films. One enormous challenge has been confining this book's discussion to only a limited number of U.S.-made films released during this 16½-month period. This leaves out, of course, exceptional European and Asian films that premiered during this time such as Carl Theodore Dreyer's *The Passion of Joan of Arc*, regarded by many film critics and scholars as one of the greatest films ever made. This also excludes several superb U.S.-made silent films, such as F.W. Murnau's *Sunrise* and William Wellman's *Wings*, which were released in 1927 just before *The Jazz Singer*'s premiere. Finally, this passes over the 1928 work of such major film directors as John Ford, Clarence Brown, Frank Borzage, Frank Capra, and Howard Hawks, whose films during this time, while good, were not among the Long 1928's very best. (Several of their films, though, are included in the list of 28 additional film recommendations in Chapter 14.)

* * *

The Long 1928 was part of what is arguably the most chaotic and wrenching period in U.S. film history. A dynamic and disruptive technology had managed to enthrall audiences, cause the death of a major international art form, and give birth to a new art that was—and is—vastly different from the old. Yet, in the midst of this rude rejection, and despite the difficult environment they had to work in, the practitioners of the dying art produced some of this art's most vibrant and enduring works. From a cinema studies perspective, their films, some of them greatly underappreciated, are absolutely worth learning more about. From a cultural studies perspective, the story of a doomed art's magnificent last hurrah, of how several of its most talented artists attempted to navigate through this turbulent time, and of why they were—or were not—able to adapt to the brave new world of the talkies remains timeless and irresistible.

Introduction

A Doomed Art's Glorious Last Days

> If I were teaching a master class in filmmaking, among the first things I'd assign would be a look at the pictures released in 1928.—Peter Bogdanovich[1]

Within the context of film history, perhaps the most prophetic line ever spoken on screen is Al Jolson's "You ain't heard nothin' yet" from 1927's *The Jazz Singer*.

In the clearest possible terms, these words announced that a new breed of movies, talking pictures, had arrived and would soon conquer. Suddenly, the only kinds of motion pictures people had ever known (the term "silent movies" hadn't yet been coined) were passé. Talk was in, and, for a while it seemed, talk was all that mattered. Within two years, these non-talking films had all but vanished.

There were exceptions, of course. Charlie Chaplin, one of the few silent filmmakers with the industry clout, financial resources, and personal stubbornness to resist the change, held out for nine more years, making his two great post-silent-era silent films, 1931's *City Lights* and 1936's *Modern Times*. Mostly because some non–U.S. filmmakers lacked the ability to adopt sound technology as quickly as Hollywood studios had, they continued to make silent films into the early and sometimes even the mid-1930s. Since then, occasional faux silent films such as Mel Brooks' 1976 *Silent Movie* and Michel Hazanavicius' 2011 *The Artist* have also paid fond tribute to the bygone era.

For all practical purposes, however, the release of *The Jazz Singer*, and audiences' almost euphoric reaction to its song and dialogue sequences, dealt the silent film a mortal blow. A major art form combining elements of theater, pantomime, photography, live music, and other arts to convey human experience through what many saw as its unique "universal language"—an art then at the height of its vitality, refinement, and achievement—was suddenly on its death bed. "Just when they had perfected it," Chaplin himself once observed, "it was all over."[2]

Although silent film was doomed commercially, it remained dominant in Hollywood for a period of about a year and a half, a period, which this book is calling "the Long 1928." It begins on October 6, 1927, the day *The Jazz Singer* first mesmerized audiences at the Roxy Theater in New York City, and extends to February 21, 1929, the day that *The Iron Mask*, Douglas Fairbanks's last silent film and grand farewell to the art that he loved, premiered.

During this time, both the major Hollywood studios and the smaller production companies operated on two, seemingly contradictory, tracks. One of these, of course, led to the future, as filmmakers struggled mightily with crude, cumbersome sound technologies and other challenges to make the talkies the new normal. The other track harkened back to the past, as silent film artists and others strove to achieve some notable last hurrahs for the dying art.

Usually, when this story is told, the emphasis is on the first track: the massive technological disruption that took place during this frenzied, uncertain, chaotic time. This book's main focus is instead on the less-well-known but nevertheless astonishing second track: the unusually large number of excellent-to-great silent films released during the Long 1928. In terms of both quality and output, many film critics and scholars have called this period one of the greatest ever in the long history of film, rivaled only by the peak pre–World War II years of 1939, 1940, and 1941. Coupled with the harsh reality that the art these filmmakers had devoted their professional lives to, nurtured, and cherished was facing extinction, their achievements become all the more remarkable and inspiring.

Before delving deeper into the wealth of silent film content released during the Long 1928, however, let's look briefly at the context: the events leading up to the destruction of one art form, the creation of a new one, and, ironically, a situation in which the film industry's obsession with sound contributed to the glory of the silent art's last days.

* * *

One myth about *The Jazz Singer* is that it came out of the blue and took the world completely by surprise when it premiered on October 6, 1927. The film, however, was more of a tipping point than a masterstroke: one in a long series of developments dating back three decades that, all totaled, would be instrumental in changing the essential nature of the film medium, the direction of the film industry, and the moviegoing expectations of the industry's hundreds of millions of customers.

Beginning the late 1890s, just as people were getting used to seeing

Jakie (Al Jolson) sings and then chats with his mother (Eugenie Besserer) in the scene from Warner's *The Jazz Singer* that riveted film audiences in 1927 and 1928 and helped to accelerate the transition to sound films (Warner Bros. Pictures/Photofest).

pictures that moved, efforts were also underway to get pictures to talk. Numerous people both in Europe and the U.S. were involved. In France, for example, inventor Leon Gaumont showed sound-synchronized pictures at his theater in Paris between 1900 and 1910. In the U.S., the Edison Company got into the act, producing sound-synchronized pictures of *Mother Goose Tales* and favorite nursery rhymes in 1912 and 1913.[3] During the rest of the 1910s, and throughout the 1920s, numerous other inventors joined the quest, proposing various solutions that employed processes ranging from sound on a record synchronized with film to sound recorded on an optical strip that used light (much like today's compact disc) to write and read the sound.[4] In the 1920s, short films with ambient sounds or music and/or talking sequences began to appear. Sometimes these talking sequences featured celebrities. Among those who appeared in them were playwright George Bernard Shaw, Italian dictator Benito Mussolini, and the "Father of Film"[5] himself, pioneer director D.W. Griffith.

The trouble with all these approaches and the ways they were executed, though, is that none was compelling enough to cause a major shift in thinking either within the film industry or among film audiences. Sound was seen merely as a gimmick or a novelty, not as an element that could completely transform the nature of medium.

One consequence of this long gestation period was that the silent film, which relied heavily on pantomime to communicate and live musical accompaniment to establish and intensify mood, continued to develop and mature at a rapid rate. Although the film industry hadn't yet mastered sound, it had, by the mid- to late 1920s, mastered virtually every other element of the medium. A generation of up-and-coming generation directors, many of whom had been inspired by Griffith, were creating increasingly accomplished and sophisticated films.[6] Actors were taking the silent film's unique brand of pantomime, the medium's universal language, to new heights as a communications vehicle. Writers, cinematographers, art directors, costume designers, editors, technicians, and others were constantly refining and improving upon their work. In addition, a promising two-strip Technicolor film process had been developed and, although quite costly, was being used in films to give them a more vibrant, true-to-life look. Seeing constant improvement in nearly every facet of the medium, audiences remained enthralled and box office receipts remained robust.

Another result was that, although the film industry was just a couple of decades old, it had become much more business-minded and, in many ways, more settled and risk-adverse. The emergence of radio in the 1920s, which provided news and entertainment for free (but with commercials, of course), cut into box-office revenues slightly during the decade. Overall, though, as long as the money kept pouring in to film company coffers, studio executives held to the philosophy "If it ain't broke, don't fix it."

Two exceptions were Fox Film Corporation and Warner Brothers. Both were small, struggling companies craving to compete on more equal footing with Hollywood's two reigning corporate powerhouses, Metro-Goldwyn-Mayer (MGM) and Paramount, and both saw sound as the way to do it.

Then the die was cast. In 1926, Warner Brothers started using a sound-on-disc system called Vitaphone, first producing shorts and then the 112-minute historical swashbuckler, *Don Juan*, starring John Barrymore. Although it had no spoken dialogue, it was the first feature-length film with recorded music and sound effects throughout. Fox followed in 1927 with a sound-on-film process called Movietone, using it both with novelty shorts and as music and sound-effects accompaniment for feature films.

When Warner Brothers released *The Jazz Singer* in October 1927, it was neither the first sound film nor the first film to synchronize moving pictures with speech and song. Instead, it was the first feature-length film to use synchronized sound as a way to tell a story.[7] Like *Don Juan* and several other films that had already been released, most of the film had been shot as a silent, and intertitles and a score were added in post-production. There were a couple of big differences, though. One is that five of the film's sequences employed synchronized speech. The other was that one of those sequences proved to be an absolute sensation with 1927 and 1928 audiences. In the scene, the title character, an aspiring entertainer played by Al Jolson, sings the song "Blue Skies" to his mother and then follows with exuberant, seemingly spontaneous patter about how his recent show business success will lead to a better life for their family. The patter is very brief, only about a minute and a half, but its naturalness, along with Jolson's undeniable warmth and charm, mesmerized viewers and transformed the way millions of people thought about motion pictures. It was 90 seconds that shook the world.

Although the debate about the future of sound in films continued for months after *The Jazz Singer's* release, a sense of urgency had now set in throughout much of the film industry. While some, including MGM's young production head, the 28-year-old Irving Thalberg, had dismissed sound as a "passing fancy" as late as December 1927,[8] the audience's love affair with the talkies showed no signs of fading. In fact, films with any sound element in them, no matter how good or bad they were in other respects, were quickly attracting legions of enthusiastic viewers. Soon the emphasis shifted from *if* studios should move to sound to *when* they should, *which* particular sound technology their studio should adopt, *how* their sound transition should take place, and *who*, especially actors, would be able to succeed in this strange, largely unchartered territory.

This new reality meant different things to different people, of course.

From one perspective, sound technology offered enormous new opportunities for both filmmakers and filmgoers. With this new sensory dimension, films could become less stylized and more realistic and lifelike; actors could speak directly to audiences, adding nuance to dialogue previously posted on the intertitle slides that appeared throughout films; songs could be sung by performers and enjoyed by listeners; audiences could hear the ambient sounds as well as see the sights in every scene; and studio orchestras could record soundtracks to fit a director's requirements to perfection. Potentially, a much richer entertainment experience was at hand. In addition, sound armed the film industry with a powerful new tool to bolster its competitive position against radio, which was quickly attracting audiences.

From another perspective (one shared by many silent film artists, film critics, and others), adding sound to the movies would lead to an artistic and cultural tragedy. In a mere 30 years, an entirely new art form had come into being, developed rapidly, and achieved a very high level of quality and sophistication. During this time, tens of thousands of films that exemplified this art had engaged and moved hundreds of millions of viewers throughout the world in ways no other art had ever done. Now, this art—just as it had blossomed into something magnificent—was about to be obliterated for all time.

Neither the destruction of the existing art nor a complete transition to the new one could occur, however, before the film industry had addressed a wide array of thorny issues. First, enormous investments had already been made in silent films that were currently in the production pipeline. Like it or not, it was simply good business to see these projects through, make whatever money could be made from audiences fast losing interest in silent films, and minimize losses. Second, the transition to sound, an alien world for most filmmakers, would be difficult, costly, time-consuming, and risky. The tasks of producing, directing, writing, filming, and acting in these movies would radically change. Which people now working in the industry would be able to adapt to this new world, and which people would not? Hordes of new people would also be needed. Who were they and where could they be found? Third, not only would every production studio need to be fitted for sound, but sound technology would also need to be installed in theaters all across the U.S. and around the world. Fourth, there was the problem of preparing U.S.-made films for world markets where people spoke languages other than English, markets that accounted for a substantial portion of the U.S. industry's revenues. With silent films supplying their universal language, the solution had been relatively easy: just edit out the English intertitles and replace them with ones written in French, German, Spanish, Japanese, or another language. Now, however, solutions became much more complicated. Would the U.S. studios need to make versions of the same film in languages other than English? If so, would they have to hire different actors who could perform credibly in these languages? If so, would the cost of doing all this simply become prohibitive?

There needed to be a period of transition to tackle these and other formidable challenges. But would it last for a few months, a year, several years? No one really knew.

Then, as studio heads and other film executives became increasingly preoccupied with, and mired in, this transition, a fascinating development occurred—the silent film artists were, relatively speaking, left alone. As a result, they received a level of freedom to work on their art in the ways they saw fit with minimal meddling and other interference from studio superiors, a level of freedom that most of them had rarely, if ever, enjoyed.

This, coupled with the realities that silent film was then at the height of its sophistication and that so many silent film artists (along with producers and executives) took such great pride in the art, led to what silent film historian William Everson has called "one of the most creative periods in all film history."[9]

Adding to the creative fervor of the moment was another factor, which Everson describes:

> There was a glorious kind of fatalism in the last days of the silents. The films were being produced purely for the moment; in a year or two, they would be dead for all time. Producers, directors, stars, and studio heads all seemed united in an unofficial and unspoken mass conspiracy to create one great Last Stand of the silent film, to show what it could do before the ultimate death at the coming of the microphones and soundtracks.[10]

This great outpouring of passion for the imperiled art had been building for a while, certainly since 1926 when Warner Brothers and Fox began making major investments in sound technology. Although Hollywood released excellent silent films all during the 1920s, audiences saw a sizeable jump in the quantity of high-quality work during the first nine months of 1927. Just a few of the excellent and, in some cases, great films released during this time included F.W. Murnau's *Sunrise*, William Wellman's *Wings*, Cecil B. DeMille's *The King of Kings*, Tod Browning's *The Unknown*, Clarence Brown's *Flesh and the Devil*, Josef von Sternberg's *Underworld*, Clarence Badger's *It*, and Frank Borzage's *Seventh Heaven*.

The release of *The Jazz Singer* further intensified this sense of fatalism. As Frances Goldwyn, the wife of Hollywood producer Sam Goldwyn, noted after watching film industry luminaries in the crowd at the end of *The Jazz Singer's* Hollywood premiere in late 1927, there was "terror in all their faces." They looked, she added, as if "the game they had been playing for years was finally over."[11]

The time for making silent films was running out. For anyone desirous of one last silent triumph, it was either now or never.

* * *

Of the more than 1000 U.S.-made feature-length and short films released during the Long 1928, the vast majority of these were filmed as silents. By late 1929, the situation had reversed: by far most U.S. films being produced and released were talkies. As the transition proceeded, audience demands for sound films increased, and a curious temporary solution emerged. Today, we call it the "hybrid." This is a film initially made as a conventional silent with a soundtrack added after the fact that included music, sound effects, and sometimes occasional dialogue. The hybrid wasn't really new: both *Don Juan* and *The Jazz Singer* more or less fit the definition. Now, however, it became a routine business strategy to market some silents as sound pictures in hopes that they would do better at the box office, even though these films were actually silents with some extras grafted on.

By today's standards, nearly all of the early talkies are crude, clunky, and sometimes just plain unwatchable. Sound recording quality was rough and inconsistent, even by the recording standards of the time. Overly dramatic film dialogue, which had worked when audiences read it from intertitle slides, often sounded ridiculous when coming directly from actors' mouths. Because the early sound technology put enormous restrictions on camera movement, most of these films were also visually static, simply uninteresting to watch. There were numerous other shortcomings as well. Still, audiences just couldn't get enough of films that supplied anything for their ears.

The amount of upheaval involved in making this transformation was immense. To accommodate the cumbersome new sound technology, production studios were refitted and often totally rebuilt. Sound recording advisors and technicians became integral parts of production teams and, much to the consternation of directors, cinematographers, and others, often had the final say over certain aspects of filming. Studios turned to New York's Broadway and other theater hubs to recruit playwrights, stage actors, and theatrical directors for films. Voice coaches were hired to teach silent film actors without stage experience how to talk like "real" actors.

As the old art form was phased out in the transition, so, too, were the careers of many who had been instrumental to its rapid rise and phenomenal success.

Perhaps the most notable casualty of all was D.W. Griffith, who, more than anyone else, had pioneered the art of putting specific film techniques together to create an impressive visual language. Along with many other silent film directors, he had difficulty integrating sound into what he always regarded as a distinctly visual form and seemed lost in the new medium.

By far the most visible casualties of the transition were actors, especially many of the great silent film stars. A popular assumption is that in most cases poor voice quality or a thick foreign accent was enough to keep them from moving to sound. The reality was more complicated. Sometimes voice quality or foreign accents were Hollywood career-killers. This was certainly true for Hungarian actress Vilma Banky and German actor Emil Jannings, whose thick accents quickly eliminated them from further work in Hollywood. Banky soon retired, and Jannings returned to Germany and continued his acting career there. Often a variety of other factors entered into the equation. Mary Pickford and Douglas Fairbanks, for example, both had acceptable voices. When the talkies arrived, however, audiences, who had associated both of them so strongly and for so long with silent films, simply couldn't accept them in talkies. Two other intriguing examples were Buster Keaton and Harold Lloyd, who, along with Chaplin, have been called "the three geniuses"[12] of silent film comedy. Initially, both Keaton and Lloyd were quite excited about moving to sound, believing that it would open up new comic possibilities for them. Unfortunately, though, their shared genius for highly inventive gags and other visual comedy bits quickly fell out of favor with the arrival of sound, and their verbal delivery, while satisfactory, was not especially distinctive or engaging. By the early 1930s, comedians such as W.C. Fields, Mae West, and Groucho Marx, who specialized in verbal humor and could deliver lines with a distinctive flair, had eclipsed them.

One of the towering figures of early film, D.W. (David Wark) Griffith was also one of the many industry luminaries whose career essentially ended soon after the arrival of the talkies (Photofest).

Although not as visible to the general public as the actors, other groups throughout the silent film ecosystem were also hurt by the change. Among those hit hardest, for example, were the theater musicians throughout the U.S. who performed the live musical accompaniment to silent films. In smaller theaters in smaller towns, this might simply consist of a single pianist or organist. In larger theaters in larger cities, this could be an entire orchestra. In 1926, an estimated 22,000 of these musicians depended on silent films for much or all of their livelihood. Within four years, it is estimated that more than two-thirds of these jobs had disappeared.

* * *

Despite the magnitude and profound nature of the changes that occurred during the Long 1928—and the disruption, dislocation, uncertainty, and downright fear that resulted from them—a remarkably large number of excellent-to-great U.S.-made silent and hybrid films were released. This in itself was a miracle: a rapturous swan song for a dying art, which, most people assumed, would soon be gone and forgotten forever. Complementing the miracle were also the talent, commitment, and sometimes courage of the filmmakers, many of whom would soon face harsh career reckonings of their own.

This book is about several of these films and the people instrumental in their making. The first 13 chapters include in-depth discussions of 14 of these films and the prime artistic movers behind them. To give readers a more complete sense of both the quantity and diversity of fine films released during this time, Chapter 14 provides brief snap shots of 28 other good-to-excellent and/or historically intriguing silent or hybrid releases.

Focusing on film releases during the Long (instead of the literal 12-month) 1928 also offers the opportunity to bookend the first 13 chapters with looks into the last silent film projects of each of two of the medium's greatest stars: Mary Pickford and Douglas Fairbanks. In addition to being their last silent films, Pickford's *My Best Girl* and Fairbanks's *The Iron Mask*, released at the beginning and at the end of the Long 1928, respectively, are excellent examples of the best work of these two legendary actors and impresarios. Although much of Pickford's earlier work is dated, *My Best Girl*, a romantic comedy with dramatic moments, holds up quite well with contemporary audiences largely because of its very skillful writing, acting, directing, cinematography, and editing. It's an opportunity to see that the silent medium's greatest female star was an exceptionally good actress who could also produce a very winning film that remains fresh and engaging today. In addition to being one of Fairbanks's finest achievements, *The Iron Mask*, his dramatization of the final chapter of the classic adventure saga of *The Three Musketeers*, was also, and quite consciously, his personal farewell to the art he loved. A performer who relished playing dashing swashbucklers, his main professional goal during 1928 was, like some of the flamboyant characters he brought to life on the screen, to go out with a grand flourish.

Three other chapters focus on the superb 1928-released efforts of three of the most acclaimed European-born directors working in Hollywood during the mid- to late 1920s. The oldest of this trio was Victor

Sjöström, who had established himself as a major filmmaker in Sweden before coming to Hollywood in 1923. In just a few years in Hollywood, he made several notable films, the most famous of which is *The Wind*. Released near the end of 1928, it is the result of an extremely fruitful partnership with actress Lillian Gish and is often ranked among the 10 best U.S. silent films ever made. The second of these directors was Erich von Stroheim, an Austrian who emigrated to the U.S., found work in films, and, despite his frequent clashes with producers, eventually directed several of the most artistically accomplished U.S.-made films of the 1920s. One of them was the sensitive and richly adorned romantic drama, *The Wedding March*, also released in late 1928. The third was Josef von Sternberg, another Austrian who came to the U.S., worked his way up in the film industry, and began directing in earnest in the 1920s. In 1928, his two dramas, *The Last Command* and *The Docks of New York*—both now widely praised for the sophistication of their visual storytelling, acting, and other elements—were released.

Complementing the work of these three extremely talented European-born silent film directors, three other chapters focus on the exceptional 1928-released efforts of three now-legendary U.S. directors, King Vidor, Raoul Walsh, and William Wellman. *The Crowd*, Vidor's drama about the false promises inherent in the American Dream, might be the director's best film ever in a Hollywood career that spanned more than 40 years. Walsh's *Sadie Thompson*, a drama that pits a plucky prostitute against a religious zealot determined to break her spirit, is a masterpiece of intensely spare, vividly visual storytelling. Finally, Wellman's *Beggars of Life*, is a poignant, beautifully rendered story of downtrodden souls determined to make better lives for themselves.

In addition, three chapters are devoted to the superb 1928-released films of the three great silent film comics, Charlie Chaplin, Buster Keaton, and Harold Lloyd. Chaplin's effort is the very under-appreciated *The Circus*. With a more cohesive storyline than many of the great comedian's other major feature films, and filled with ingenious gags, it more than holds its own when compared to other Chaplin masterpieces such as 1925's *The Gold Rush* and 1931's *City Lights*. Keaton's *Steamboat Bill, Jr.*, the last film the comic made as an independent producer, includes some of his very best film moments ever. One of these is the film's unforgettable cyclone finale, one of the most inventive and visually creative film sequences in all of Keaton's work. Lloyd's last silent film, *Speedy*—a delightful, highly original, thrill-packed gallop through late 1920s New York City—is also one of this comic master's very best.

Rounding out this book's first 13 chapters are two somewhat eccentric picks that wouldn't normally (if ever) be found on lists of the best 10 or 15 U.S. films of 1928. The first is director Tod Browning's *West of Zanzibar*, a very bleak, twisted melodrama starring the great silent film actor Lon Chaney. As well as looking at an excellent example of Chaney's "dark" work, his genius for finding the tortured humanity buried deep within the truly despicable characters he often played, this chapter discusses the highly productive but little-known artistic partnership the director and actor shared during the 1920s. The second film is one of 1928's big hits, Harry Beaumont's romantic drama *Our Dancing Daughters*. A look at flappers and the high-living 1920s party set, it is perhaps best known today as the film that made actress Joan Crawford a star. It was selected both to showcase her charismatic star turn in the film and to discuss how one facet of her own professional story markedly contrasts with the stories of the many other silent film stars who would soon fade from the scene. Unlike them, she was able to leverage much of the acting technique she'd learned from making silent films to enhance her sound film performances, helping to sustain a career that would continue for another 40 years.

Chapter 14 is essentially a list with brief write-ups of 28 additional noteworthy U.S. films released during the Long 1928. All are fascinating in different ways and, for people interested in learning more about this very rich period in film, worth seeing. Just a few examples include King Vidor's *Show People*, a comedy about 1928 Hollywood that stars the very talented and underappreciated Marion Davies; *The Cameraman*, Buster Keaton's first feature at MGM; and *Laugh, Clown, Laugh*, which features another bravura performance by the great Lon Chaney.

* * *

As the years pass by and the film conversation moves on to subjects from rapidly developing home entertainment delivery platforms to virtual reality festivals, it becomes easier and easier, just as U.S. film audiences did in 1928, to dismiss silent films as simply quaint vestiges of a bygone era. To a large extent, this is understandable. In the age of Lady Gaga, it may be increasingly difficult to relate to the work of Mary Pickford or Lillian Gish.

Yet, while many, if not most, silent films exist as little more than historical curiosities, a surprisingly large number are both vibrant today and are likely to remain so for centuries to come. Like all examples of great art, they transcend their place and time. And for those with only a relatively scant knowledge of this enormously creative, varied, and exciting period in film history, perhaps the best place to start learning more about it is at its end—by delving into the Long 1928, that remarkable 16½-month period when many of the brilliant practitioners of a sublime but dying art released some of their greatest films.

1

At the Precipice

Mary Pickford and My Best Girl

[Mary Pickford's] playing was completely naturalistic; neither her acting or her later silent films have dated in any way. She seems as fresh and vital now as when she was America's Sweetheart. She had legions of imitators but no rivals.—Kevin Brownlow[1]

At first, it seemed like a good idea.

On March 29, 1928, Dodge Motors hosted an hour-long radio broadcast featuring several of Hollywood's brightest screen luminaries, all of them stakeholders in United Artists, the powerful film studio and distribution company Mary Pickford, Douglas Fairbanks, Charlie Chaplin, and D.W. Griffith had launched to great fanfare nine years earlier. In addition to the four founders, the group included relative newcomers Gloria Swanson, Norma Talmadge, John Barrymore, and Dolores Del Rio. The broadcast's purpose was an intriguing one: in light of the growing acknowledgment that talking pictures were inevitable, it would connect Hollywood stars eager to prove that their voices were good enough for the new medium directly to audiences eager to hear them talk. The broadcast would be low-key and casual. Emanating from Pickford's private bungalow, it would consist of each celebrity talking for a few minutes about a subject that reflected him or her in some way. To make the event special, it would be transmitted into theaters around the U.S. rather than into homes.[2]

From Pickford's bungalow, all went as planned with each celebrity taking a turn at the microphone. Chaplin told jokes in a Cockney dialect. Barrymore recited lines from Shakespeare's *Hamlet*. Fairbanks, who reveled in his popular image of manly vigor and vitality, spoke about staying young at heart. And Pickford shared a "heart-to-heart" with the women of America.[3]

In movie theaters across the country, however, the response was nothing like the celebrities had assumed it would be. In New England, storms marred the quality of the broadcast, making audiences irritable and restless. In other parts of the country where weather wasn't a factor, the reaction of both critics and audiences was also, and surprisingly, belligerent. The show business publication *Variety* criticized "the dryness of the program and the length of the talks during which nothing much of anything was said that could be termed interesting." A reporter in Baltimore noted that it was a mistake to "take the public behind the Hollywood scenes and let them listen to entertainers whose talents were essentially visual." Newspaper headlines in major cities ranged from "Detroit Depressed" to "Frisco Not Interested." Also, in Memphis the audience in one theater grew so restless and vocally hostile that the management turned the broadcast off and simply went ahead with the scheduled feature, which, curiously, was Pickford's latest film, the silent romantic comedy *My Best Girl*.[4]

Along with her United Artists colleagues, Mary Pickford had miscalculated, and for this woman who had brilliantly cultivated legions of adoring fans worldwide, built a business empire, and now enjoyed a unique and seemingly omnipotent position in the motion picture industry, such a miscalculation seemed very much out of character. While not a major setback, the ill-fated radio broadcast certainly hinted that, for the world's first movie superstar, an ominous turning point might be at hand.

* * *

Born Gladys Louise Smith in Toronto, Ontario, on April 8, 1892, Mary Pickford acted on the stage as a child and teen and, at 17, made the transition to the movies, working first for D.W. Griffith beginning in 1909, launching her own production company in 1916, and co-founding United Artists in 1919, when she was 27. By then, she had become the best known and most beloved and popular movie star on the planet, and throughout the silent era her only serious rival for this title would be her good friend, Charlie Chaplin. Her nicknames ranged from "America's Sweetheart" (ironic, since she was a Canadian native) to "the girl with the curls" in honor of her long, curly blond locks that served as both a personal trademark and a symbol of the spunky virtue exemplified in many of her most popular roles. Throughout a career that, by 1928, included more than 150 shorts and nearly 50 features, she specialized in playing good, spirited girls, teens, and young women. During this time, she had also become one of Hollywood's most highly regarded film producers, widely respected for her mastery of virtually every facet of the industry from her superb eye for talent and production detail to her capabilities as a business woman, a trait that inspired Chaplin to sometimes call her the "Bank of America's

Sweetheart"[5] (one nickname she did not appreciate). Married to fellow movie superstar Douglas Fairbanks since 1920, the two were the acknowledged king and queen of Hollywood. Their movies always made money—lots of it. Also, throughout the 1920s, their grand Beverly Hills home, named "Pickfair" by the press, was the site of countless parties, receptions, and other gatherings that included, in addition to many others, such celebrated guests as George Bernard Shaw, Albert Einstein, H.G. Wells, Thomas Edison, and F. Scott Fitzgerald.

Along the way, Pickford had had her problems, of course. Her childhood was harsh, and from an early age she had been her family's main breadwinner. Her father, siblings, and first husband, actor Owen Moore, were all hopeless alcoholics. She was also the victim of Moore's periodic domestic violence. But, after her divorce from Moore in 1920 and her marriage to the dynamic, exuberant Fairbanks, life, in nearly all respects, could not have been better.

If anything, one of her main professional challenges in the mid–1920s was how to evolve from the spunky young girl and teen roles she had tired of playing and fashion a new screen image. This challenge had several key facets to it. First was her age. Now in her mid–30s, she was acutely aware that her days of playing young characters, no matter how much her fans loved seeing her in these roles, were numbered. Increasingly, too, she had tired of these roles and longed to play a range of characters, to stretch herself in her art. At one point, she even remarked that she craved a role where she could do "something wicked."[6] Second was changing tastes. The Victorian sensibility that had dominated films in the 1910s and early 1920s was quickly giving way to more irreverent and risqué 1920s attitudes and behaviors. How would she, who personified virtue and purity, remain relevant in the age of flappers, bobbed hair, slinky dresses, speakeasies, hooch, and jazz? Third was the looming prospect of sound. Was it really coming? If so, would it become a permanent thing? In that case, would it exist alongside silent films or squeeze them out altogether? Then, how would either of these scenarios affect the way movies were made and the people, such as herself, who had been making them?

* * *

All these subjects preoccupied Pickford in the spring of 1927 as she began work on her latest film, *My Best Girl*. Completed in good order and then released on October 31, 1927, just three-and-a-half weeks after *The Jazz Singer* first stunned and exhilarated audiences in New York, the film was rolled out slowly in theaters around the country during the first few months of 1928. As was almost always the case with Pickford's movies, it became one of the year's solid critical and box-office successes.

Joe (Buddy Rogers) and Maggie (Mary Pickford) have a cozy lunch together in an empty packing crate at work in an iconic scene from *My Best Girl*, Pickford's last silent film (United Artists/Photofest).

At its heart, *My Best Girl* is a Cinderella story. Maggie Johnson (Pickford), a bright, hard-working young woman from a dysfunctional family and very modest means, falls for young Joe Grant (Charles "Buddy" Rogers), a fellow employee at Merrill's Five-and-Dime stores, and he with her. She doesn't know, however, that he is really Joe Merrill, the son of the chain's owner, who has taken an assumed name to prove that he can be successful in the business without relying on his family name. Joe is already engaged to a young society woman named Millicent, but Maggie's down-to-earth charm and warmth almost instantly sweep him away. Eventually, Joe is ready to break up with Millicent and marry Maggie, but she is concerned that her family needs her more than he does. In fact, in front of her family and Joe's father, she tries to convince Joe that she's just a gold digger out for his money. Seeing that she really loves Joe, Maggie's father rises to the occasion, announcing that at long last he will be "the father to this family." The story ends with Maggie and Joe, among others, rushing to the ocean liner that will take them to Hawaii for their honeymoon. The boat's captain, of course, will marry them en route. In all respects (except perhaps Millicent's), the story ends happily.

While a familiar and ultimately predictable story, *My Best Girl* is wonderfully executed in nearly every respect. For this, Pickford's skills as producer must be credited. She had excellent instincts for picking the right behind-the-camera contributors as well as actors for her projects.

For *My Best Girl*, she brought in screenwriter Hope Loring, who had just completed work on Clarence Badger's hit comedy *It* with Clara Bow and William Wellman's World War I epic *Wings* with Bow and (coincidentally) Buddy Rogers, two films that became immediate classics. The similarities between this story and *It*, another department-store-based Cinderella tale, were certainly a factor in the decision to use Loring. In addition, Loring makes major contributions to two of *My Best Girl*'s great assets: the story's clever, ironic dialog and its constant juxtaposition of opposites to sharpen the contrasts between upper and lower classes, honest and dishonest behavior, strong and dashed hopes, and so on. One brilliant touch is the constant motion of a cash register recording sales—five cents, ten cents, five cents, ten cents, etc.—at the beginning of the story, then later on. The first time, the action immediately moves to the store floor where people are busily purchasing items and thus propelling the sales. The second time, the action dissolves to the mansion where the Merrill family lives, clearly showing who the main beneficiaries of all this commerce are.

To help with the film's many comic touches, Pickford brought in director Sam Taylor, a veteran of such Harold Lloyd comic masterpieces as 1923's *Safety Last!*, 1924's *Girl Shy*, and 1925's *The Freshman*. He delivers as well, providing many highly inventive and delightful visual bits that help to keep this film as fresh and entertaining today as Lloyd's best comedies. One bit that's particularly funny is a brief scene when we see an overbearing woman and her meek husband in the department store looking at rolling pins. She picks one up and looks it over. Reacting to it a little nervously, he suggests a much smaller alternative. She, however, immediately discounts this in favor of the largest rolling pin in the selection. This, of course, makes him more anxious than ever.

Rounding out Pickford's core behind-the-camera team was Charles Rosher, one of the silent era's most respected cameramen and a collaborator on every Pickford film since 1917. Sought after by other producers and directors as well, he had just finished shooting F.W. Murnau's *Sunrise*, which would soon net him and colleague Carl Struss the very first Academy Award for Cinematography. Among his contributions to *My Best Girl* are some exquisitely lit night scenes, often in the rain, that give certain moments an oddly beautiful, otherworldly look that mirrors the otherworldly feelings of Maggie and Joe, so smitten with each other that they seem totally in their own world and oblivious to everything else around them. In keeping with the main thrust of the film, some of these scenes also have a comic edge to them. A couple of times, for example, Maggie and Joe are so enraptured with each other that they have no idea they are actually walking through heavy, and potentially dangerous, city street traffic. On a more practical note, Rosher also created a special lens for the film, the "Rosher Kino Portrait Lens," for Pickford's close-ups. This enabled the 35-year-old actress to appear closer in age to, and more believable as, the much younger Maggie.

In addition to Pickford's ability to choose top behind-the-camera talent for her films, she chose her fellow actors with great care, creating fine ensembles, and in *My Best Girl*, there are no weak acting links. Even actors in very small roles, such as Hobart Boswell as Joe's father Robert Merrill, Sidney Bracey as the Merrill's butler, and William Courtright as the old man in the stock room at the Merrill store, bring unexpected levels of sensitivity and grace to their characters. Among the main supporting players, two performances are also particularly good. One is Rogers (just 22 during production) as Joe, who balances his character's youthful exuberance with levels of empathy, tenderness, and understanding that give his character a maturity beyond his years. Several film historians have speculated that Rogers and Pickford, who later married, actually did fall in love during the filming of *My Best Girl*. This may or may not be true, but the depth of feeling that Joe has for Maggie and the understanding he has for her conflicted feelings near the end of the story appear very real. It's a very compelling performance. The other especially notable supporting performance is character actor Lucien Littlefield's portrayal of Maggie's father, Pa Johnson. Littlefield, who was actually three years younger than Pickford, is absolutely convincing as a crusty old man and very funny in several scenes. In addition, he has the ability that relatively few comic actors have to turn dead serious instantly when the situation calls for it. He is quite good, for example, in the scene when, along with Mr. Merrill, he sees how much Maggie loves Joe and finally musters the courage to declare that he will step up to lead their family so Maggie can be freed of this responsibility.

Among the acting performances, however, no one outshines the film's star, Mary Pickford. "I lived my characters," she said in an interview in the 1960s. "That's the only way you can be. You have to live your parts."[7] And in *My Best Girl*, she *lives* the young, smart, sensible, good-hearted, assertive, vulnerable, slightly manipulative, and ultimately very noble Maggie Johnson throughout. She also does an excellent job of handling a variety of acting challenges that range from pulling off slapstick routines to playing tender romantic scenes, to communicating heartbreak when she learns Joe's real identity and that he's already engaged, to her final attempt to push Joe away by pretending to be a gold digger. We first see her, for example, at work as a Merrill's stock girl carrying too many pots and pans out to a store's main floor, dropping some, and putting one of her feet in one to drag it along. Here, she handles the slapstick quite confidently and naturally. Later, after she and Joe have fallen for each other, they have an eccentric picnic lunch in an open packing crate in the store's stock room, she gives him a modest watch for his birthday, and very tenderly they snuggle with each other and kiss. Often written about, this scene is an emotional and artistic high point of the film: an exquisite few minutes when Pickford shows that she can communicate both vulnerability and passionate feelings with the kind of honesty, naturalness, and depth few other actresses of her era could match. Her gold digger speech near the end of the film is another *tour de force*. Although Maggie tries valiantly to convince Joe and his father that she's a greedy opportunist, they both see through the act and are moved by her willingness to sacrifice her chance at love for the sake of her family. The excruciating irony is, of course, that the longer and more emphatically she argues that she is a "bad" girl, the nobler and more poignant she becomes to everyone watching her. This is a very difficult scene to pull off successfully, and Pickford manages to do it with great skill.

Several film historians have noted that a key reason why Pickford's performance in *My Best Girl* has such an authentic ring to it is that, unlike most of her other roles, this was very close, sometimes painfully so, to her own life. Like Maggie, Pickford was smart, practical, ambitious, hard-working, and fearless as well as quite sensitive and emotionally vulnerable. Like Maggie, she fell for an adoring young man who just happened to be Buddy Rogers. And like Maggie, she felt a mixture of embarrassment, impatience, and fierce loyalty toward her own often dysfunctional family members, who depended on her for just about everything. In many ways, one can make a strong case for her performance as Maggie as Pickford's most autobiographical, and most personally revealing, work.

* * *

When *The Jazz Singer* opened in Los Angeles in December of 1927, Pickford's reaction was mixed. From an aesthetic standpoint, she responded negatively to the integration of sound dialog and songs with the visual images, seeing it as an unnecessary frill and famously saying that adding sound to movies was "like putting lip rouge on the Venus de Milo."[8] She was also, however, a savvy businesswoman who sensed that talkies, even if they didn't eventually dominate the film business, would clearly be a force to be reckoned with. Unlike most other producers and stars, who continued their wait-and-see approach toward sound, she gamely decided to take the plunge.

During much of 1928, as *My Best Girl* delighted critics and audiences around the U.S., Pickford focused her energies on her next project, a "100% Talking Picture."[9] Based on a hit Broadway play called *Coquette*, this would feature her as a flirty Southern belle who loyally stands by her father after he kills her lover. While she was proud of her past stage experience and repeatedly said that her voice would not be a problem in the new medium, she was also concerned about how it came across on early recording technology. "Why, that sounds like a little pipsqueak voice!" she once commented.[10] So, as an insurance policy, she undertook a rigorous program of lessons both to prepare her voice for sound recording and to perfect the Southern accent required to play *Coquette's* heroine.

Feeling that this might also be a good time for additional changes, Pickford then made another fateful decision. On June 21, 1928, she went into Charles Bock's hair salon in New York City and asked that the long golden curls, which so emphatically represented her virtuous, "America's Sweetheart" image, be cut off in favor of a short 1920s bob. She had wanted to make this change earlier but had delayed in deference to her beloved mother, Charlotte, who had asked Mary not to cut her curls until after her death. When Charlotte passed away in March 1928, the timing, for Mary, finally seemed right.

As with the public's response to the Dodge Motors radio broadcast three months earlier, however, Pickford was in for a shock. The cutting of the curls was widely reported and public reaction overwhelmingly negative. Her fans, who for nearly two decades had loved "the girl with the curls," would have none of it. "You would have thought I had murdered someone," she said afterwards. "And perhaps I had, but only to give her a chance to live."[11]

Staying the course, Pickford moved forward shaping the new screen image she longed for. Assembling a top-notch team that that again included director Sam Taylor and cinematographer Charles Rosher, she continued her work on *Coquette*. The film opened in April 1929 to large audiences and polite reviews. Pickford even exerted some of her enormous political power in Hollywood to finagle the second-ever Academy Award for Best Actress for her work in it. While such details suggest a success, however, the ultimate result was quite the opposite. The film, although stylishly mounted, suffers from the staginess, excessive dialog, and static camera work that plagued most early talkies. Pickford seems ill suited for, and uncomfortable with, this very uncharacteristic role. Also, her contrived Southern drawl is particularly stilted and self-conscious. While the film did well at the box office, patrons came more out of curiosity than anything else. They wanted to hear what Pickford sounded like, and what they heard may well have sealed her doom as an actress in talkies. While many of the reviews were complimentary, they were so in deference to Pickford's unique position in the film industry. Although Pickford did nab an Academy Award for her portrayal, it was clear that the recognition was more for her entire career rather than for this performance. Considering the superb female performances in films released during that year's Academy eligibility period[12] (among them Louise Brooks in *Beggars of Life*, Betty Compson in *The Docks of New York*, Marion Davies in *Show People*, and Lillian Gish in *The Wind*), Pickford's Academy Award for *Coquette* seems all the more undeserved. Even at the time, many criticized the choice.

After *Coquette*, Pickford completed just three more feature films as an actress. The first was an awkward, stagy sound film adaptation of William Shakespeare's *The Taming of the Shrew* with Fairbanks, which premiered in late 1929. (This production is discussed in more detail in Chapter 13 of this book, which focuses on Fairbanks.) She has some fine moments in the last of these films, 1933's *Secrets*, an episodic love story with Leslie Howard, but all three were major critical and box-office disappointments.

Quietly, Pickford retired from acting, and, after divorcing Fairbanks in 1936 (the split largely resulting from the tensions that arose as both their careers disintegrated), she married her co-star in *My Best Girl*, actor Buddy Rogers. She did continue to produce films until 1950, along the way nurturing up-and-coming directors such as Douglas Sirk in 1948's well-received noir thriller *Sleep, My Love* and David Miller in 1950's Marx Brothers comedy *Love Happy*. She also maintained an interest in United Artists until selling her holdings in 1956.

Gradually, though, Pickford became more reclusive and dependent on alcohol, cloistering herself at Pickfair, the home where she and Fairbanks, had, in the 1920s, held court in the grand manner befitting Hollywood's king and queen. Her last public appearance of any consequence occurred in 1976, when she received an Academy Honorary Award. Speaking from Pickfair in a segment aired on that year's Academy Awards show, she looked painfully frail and seemed mentally diminished. She got through a brief prepared interchange that lasted just one minute, but for the hundreds of millions of people watching from all around the world, it was an odd, disturbing moment. Considering who she had been and the amazing things she had done, it was sad to see what had become of her.

Three years later, on May 29, 1979, Mary Pickford died of complications from a cerebral hemorrhage she had suffered the week before. She was 87 years old.

* * *

Unlike most of Pickford's films, *My Best Girl* has a very contemporary quality about it. Largely due to its timeless themes, its humanity and wit, its clever story construction, the freshness of the visual humor, and especially the authenticity of the performances by Pickford, Rogers, and other actors, it does not, in any important respect, seem dated. In recent years, appreciation for it seems to be growing as well. It has received screenings at, among other venues, The San Francisco Silent Film Festival, the Gene Siskel Film Center in Chicago, the New York Film Center, and the University of California at Los Angeles. At every showing, audiences have responded enthusiastically.

It is usually futile to ask "what if?" questions, but it is also irresistible. The growing acceptance of *My Best Girl* by contemporary audiences may lead us to imagine a different career arc for Pickford. Instead of taking on a radically different kind of character, early sound technology, and life without her trademark golden curls all at once as she did when she plunged into *Coquette*, what if Pickford had planned a more gradual transition? She could have been more cautious about primitive sound technology and delay her entrance into talkies for another year as MGM wisely did with Garbo. Also, in her efforts to evolve as an actress, she could have looked more closely at what she and her team had done in *My Best Girl*. In essence, this film is a deft blend of many traditional Pickford characteristics (such as her bright, spunky persona and her basic goodness) with many new elements (such as a contemporary urban setting and an easily identifiable modern "working girl" character who is closer to Pickford's actual age). *My Best Girl*'s success certainly shows that audiences could accept some variation from Pickford, and perhaps, if she had been more cautious in managing her acting evolution, she might have had a viable acting career for many more years than she did.

Then, perhaps no amount of caution and prudent decision making would have helped. As Pickford said later in her life, "I'd already been pigeonholed.... I was already typed."[13] With the possible exception of Chaplin's Tramp, no screen persona was as associated more with the silent era in the hearts and minds of movie audiences than Pickford's girl with the curls. For these fans, that silent image on the screen *was* Mary Pickford, and, perhaps for them as well, it was inconceivable that she could be anything else.

2

"The maddest idea in the world"

Gloria Swanson, Raoul Walsh, *and* Sadie Thompson

By mid–1927, both Gloria Swanson and Raoul Walsh had long been major Hollywood figures. Each had risen to prominence in the mid–1910s, Swanson first appearing in comedy shorts for Charlie Chaplin and Mack Sennett and then becoming a major star known for both her sophisticated roles and extravagant wardrobes, Walsh beginning as an actor and D.W. Griffith protégé and then becoming a director best known for male-oriented action pictures. Largely because they'd worked for different studios and on very different kinds of films, however, their professional paths had never crossed. In fact, their personal paths had only crossed once, when they'd met briefly at a party at the home of actress Pola Negri.[1]

Yet, both shared a special connection. Part of it was professional: they were great fans of each other's work. Swanson especially admired the creativity and exuberance behind Walsh's 1924 swashbuckler *The Thief of Bagdad* and the "frankness" and "naturalness"[2] of his 1926 World War I drama *What Price Glory?*. Walsh had always been impressed by the intelligence and vitality she brought to her roles. And part of it was personal. She was drawn to his robust good looks and masculine swagger, and, from the moment they were introduced at Negri's party, he had been captivated by her beauty and wit.

Then, in the early summer of 1927, Swanson went to see Joseph Schenck, the production head at United Artists. Now producing as well as starring in films, she had recently released her first independent venture, a drama called *The Love of Sunya*. To her dismay, it was underperforming at the box office and now she sorely needed a hit. Along with other confidants, Schenck advised her to choose something commercially safe for her next project. Repeatedly, he suggested adapting the hit 1925 stage comedy-romance *The Last of Mrs. Cheyney*. But she kept resisting, saying that "the gushy story sounded a bit too formula for me."[3] Then, in the middle of another of Schenck's speeches about the need to play it safe, she blurted out, "Tell me about Raoul Walsh. What's he like?"[4]

Taken aback, Schenck thought that hiring Walsh was a terrible idea, calling him "a crazy Irishman" and "a man's director"[5] and suggesting that, since he was currently under contract with Fox, he would probably not be available anyway.

But, the more Schenck talked, the more Swanson seemed fascinated with the prospect of working with Walsh. That night she phoned him, and he agreed to meet for breakfast at her home the following morning. Joining them would be her husband (her third out of would eventually be six), Henri de la Falaise, a French nobleman who dabbled in filmmaking.

Across the table in her garden the next morning, Swanson and Walsh instantly bonded, each amping up the energy and charm as they discussed the possibility of collaborating and story ideas they could develop. "The man was amazing," she later recalled.[6] At one point, Walsh suggested a film adapted from *Rain*, a recent stage hit based on W. Somerset Maugham's controversial (and to some, immoral) 1921 short story *Miss Thompson*. Swanson had read the story and loved it. She had also seen actress Jeanne Eagels in *Rain* on Broadway and felt that the main character, Sadie Thompson, would be a great role for her, too. "Every actress in America with a brain and a figure ... wanted to play Sadie," Swanson later noted, "and every producer had secretly dreamed of filming the work."[7]

There was also a big reason why producers were still dreaming about filming it, however: the tightening censorship rules now being imposed by the Hays Office, which enforced the U.S. film industry's Production Code.[8] The censors, Swanson and Walsh agreed, would never give their approval to such a project. First, the story involves a clergyman who rapes a prostitute. Second, the language, especially by 1927 film standards, was especially coarse.

After venting for a bit about the absurdity of Hollywood censorship, Swanson and Walsh moved on to discuss other properties that might work for their prospective project. But, all the while, according to Swanson, both were plotting in their heads how to get this story past the Hays Office. For 1927, it seemed like "the maddest idea in the world," she wrote decades later, "but every other idea suddenly seemed dull."[9]

Finally, Swanson asked Walsh, "Do you think I could play Sadie?"

"Sure, you'd be perfect," he said, "if anybody would let you."[10]

* * *

2. "The maddest idea in the world"

Gloria Swanson received the first of her three Academy Award nominations for Best Actress for her portrayal as the vulnerable but resilient title character in *Sadie Thompson* (United Artists/Photofest).

About six months later, on January 7, 1928, "the maddest idea in the world" had become *Sadie Thompson*, a major motion picture that was beginning to open in theaters around the U.S. to large, enthusiastic audiences and overwhelmingly positive critical reviews. The project had not been easy. The Hays Office had been frustrating to deal with. And the production phase had been beset with numerous problems and major cost overruns that led to Swanson's selling one of her homes, a farm in

Croton-On-Hudson in New York State, to pay the bills. This was, nevertheless, one of those happy (and not-all-that-common) cases in the film industry when a producer and her director followed their passion, threw caution to the wind, defied the odds, mounted a film that captivated audiences and critics at the time, and, in the process, also created a classic that remains fresh and vital nearly a century after its release. As an added bonus, the film picked up a couple of nominations for the very first Academy Awards, one for the film's cinematography and one for Swanson in the Best Actress category.

For both Swanson and Walsh, *Sadie Thompson* would be a final highpoint in their very productive and successful silent film careers. After a couple of routine silent projects, Walsh went on to pioneer outdoor talking pictures when he co-directed 1928's *In Old Arizona*, a film that eventually received five Academy Award nominations. And, after a bruising personal and disastrous financial experience with director Eric von Stroheim on the ill-fated *Queen Kelly* in 1928 (discussed in more detail in Chapter 10 of this book), Swanson both produced and starred in her first talkie, a lively domestic drama called *The Trespasser*, in 1929. A major hit with audiences that allowed her to recoup her financial losses from *Queen Kelly*, this film also netted Swanson her second Academy Award nomination for Best Actress in two years.

It's intriguing, too, that during this tumultuous period, as many of their industry colleagues fretted over the coming of the talkies, both Walsh and Swanson were quite calm and business-like about it.

Walsh, in particular, had little patience with fellow directors who complained about the constraints sound technology now imposed on production or bemoaned the death of the unique pantomime-like style of acting that had become a hallmark of silent film art. For him, sound was simply a new reality everybody had better get used to. As he noted in an interview in the 1970s:

> The transition from silent and to sound pictures didn't hit me in any way. I just kept the thing [a film] moving regardless of the sound.... Of course, there was a great upheaval amongst the directors when talking pictures came in. They called me a renegade because I was one of the first ones to do an outdoor talking picture. They said that they'd created a medium with pantomime, you know, and now this talking stuff was going to destroy it all. I said it was going to destroy us if we didn't get along and get in with it.[11]

Swanson's attitude was quite similar. When she began working on *The Trespasser*, for example, she fully embraced the new challenge and seemed irritated by actors who complained about the new demands being placed on them. As she later noted:

2. "The maddest idea in the world" 31

From the first moment I was on the set I was consumed with curiosity for the technical side of shooting a sound picture, but acting in one, as far as I was concerned, was no different from acting in any other picture. In quality films we had always had scripts, and we had memorized them, and we had said the lines as we played the scenes. We hadn't mouthed them or pronounced them in an exaggerated fashion. Therefore, the fuss that actors soon began making about the difficulty of "shifting" to sound struck me as perfectly foolish. The only adjustment was in knowing where the microphones were and playing to them as well as to the camera, and that was merely an exciting extension of regular acting in pictures.[12]

* * *

Walsh and Swanson may have shared similar attitudes about the inevitability of talking pictures, but the change affected each of them very differently.

Although talkies effectively ended the careers of several prominent silent film directors, Walsh adapted easily and forged ahead unfazed, directing more than 70 more films until 1964 when he retired at age 77. Along the way, he had his share of routine films and failures. For example, his very ambitious and costly 1930 sound effort, *The Big Trail*—a wide-screen western epic starring a young extra on the Fox lot named Marion Morrison who Walsh (according to some accounts) renamed John Wayne—flopped so badly that it took both A-list westerns and Wayne's acting career nearly a decade to recover. But Walsh had his share of critical and box-office successes, too. Perhaps the highpoint of his long career was a stint at Warner Brothers between 1939 and 1953,

Raoul Walsh began his film career as an actor and moved to directing for the rest of his half-century film career. *Sadie Thompson* was the last film in which he acted (Photofest).

when he had great success working with major male stars such as Errol Flynn, Humphrey Bogart, and James Cagney, often on westerns and crime films. Among his most notable films during this time are 1939's *The Roaring Twenties*; 1941's *High Sierra*, *They Died with Their Boots On*, and *The Strawberry Blonde*; 1942's *Gentleman Jim*; 1947's *Pursued*; and 1949's *Colorado Territory* and *White Heat*.

While he would eventually achieve "Hollywood legend" status among film historians as one of an incredible generation of directors that included, among others, Charlie Chaplin, John Ford, King Vidor, Alfred Hitchcock, William Wellman, Fritz Lang, Howard Hawks, and William Wyler, Walsh was, during his time, sadly underappreciated. Because he often worked on crime, western, and other genre films (often considered less "significant" than big-budget "prestige" pictures), he never received a Best Director Academy Award nomination or other major industry recognitions. Because he was so good at creating fast-paced, relentlessly active films, he was routinely dismissed as an intellectual "lightweight" whose films lacked emotional depth and didn't tackle weighty themes. And, because he was such a hearty man's man himself, he was often seen as a "man's director" who was not particularly interested in actresses or well-rounded women's roles.

In hindsight, however, there is much more to his work than many people have initially assumed. *High Sierra*, *Colorado Territory*, and *White Heat*, for example, are fast-paced genre films, but they are also fascinating character studies that probe deeply into the minds of figures in each story. In these and numerous other Walsh films there are also an incisive understanding of psychology and real emotional truth, characteristics many Hollywood films at the time clearly lacked. In addition, he could—and often did—treat the female characters in his films with great understanding and sympathy. During his Warner years alone, for example, he elicited excellent performances from, among other actresses, Ida Lupino (*High Sierra*), Olivia de Havilland (*The Strawberry Blonde*), and Virginia Mayo (*Colorado Territory*, *White Heat*).

Retiring after his poorly received 1964 western *A Distant Trumpet* starring Troy Donahue, Walsh and his third wife, Mary Simpson, lived quietly until he died of a heart attack in 1980 in Simi Valley, California. He was 93 years old.

Documentary filmmaker and film historian Michael Henry Wilson has called Walsh "probably the most underrated major American filmmaker."[13] Looking at his work closely, it's difficult to disagree. The sheer number of films he directed, more than 140 features over more than 50 years, is an immense achievement in itself. Far more impressive, however, is his authorial control. There's a distinctive outlook on life that's

2. "The maddest idea in the world"   33

prominent (and explored) in many of his films. His heroes and heroines are often dreamers and adventurers, people who live in the moment and want to experience life as fully as possible. We also see this preoccupation vividly reflected his style of filmmaking—immediate, vigorous, often quite sensual, and filled with urgency—a style that, after many decades, remains amazingly fresh and vital.

* * *

Although Swanson shared Walsh's fearless, "get-with-the-program" attitude toward the coming of sound, she did not share anything like a similar career trajectory. After her success with *The Trespasser*, she made five films over the next four years (starring in all five and producing two of them) that all fared poorly at the box office. Just 35 years old, but stoically accepting that her best days as a movie star were probably behind her, she took the setback in stride, retired from the screen, and focused instead on acting on the stage and for radio. In 1941, she was lured back to star in a lackluster comedy with Adolphe Menjou called *Father Takes a Wife*. Losing more than $100,000 at the box office, it did nothing to reignite her career, and again she withdrew from films.

Then, in 1950, Swanson had a resurrection of sorts. This was of course her legendary comeback playing the faded, entrenched-in-the-past, and mentally unbalanced silent film star Norma Desmond in Billy Wilder's *Sunset Boulevard*. The film, which received rave reviews and drew large, enthusiastic audiences, went on to receive 11 Academy Award nominations, including Swanson's third—and first in 21 years—for Best Actress. Although she did not win (losing to upset winner Judy Holliday for her performance in *Born Yesterday* that year), she did receive numerous other honors for her performance, including that year's Golden Globe for Best Actress in a Drama.

For a brief time, Swanson was again the toast of Hollywood. As before, however, she was unable to reignite her film career.

A great irony for Swanson in her later years was the association between her and Norma Desmond, the role for which she is best remembered. Partly because she had been a great silent star whose career had waned with the coming of sound, and partly because she had been so convincing portraying Norma, people assumed that she had pretty much been playing herself.

Yet, nothing could be further from the truth. While no longer a top-tier movie star, Swanson became a veritable Renaissance woman who, far from being obsessed with the past, was intensely engaged with the present on many fronts. She acted on the stage and made guest appearances on various television programs ranging from the popular situation comedy *My Three Sons* to the detective series *Burke's Law* (which netted her a second Golden Globe in 1964). In addition, she traveled extensively; was involved in several business ventures; wrote articles and columns for numerous periodicals; painted; sculpted; and, with her sixth husband, writer Michael Duffy, spoke extensively about macrobiotic diets and helped promote his book on the subject, *Sugar Blues*.

Then, in early 1980 when she was 81, Swanson was in the spotlight once again, this time with the publication of her 500+ page autobiography *Swanson on Swanson*. Called "The most significant book on Hollywood's heyday yet published" by *John Barkam Reviews*,[14] "vividly written" by the *Philadelphia Inquirer*,[15] and "phenomenal" by the *Los Angeles Times*,[16] it became a national bestseller.

Again, though, her notoriety would be fleeting. She died just three years later in New York City, which had been her primary home since leaving Hollywood in the late 1930s, of a heart ailment. She was 84.

Although they had discussed the possibility, Walsh and Swanson never worked together again after *Sadie Thompson*. But the special connection that first drew them together also grew into a warm friendship that lasted until Walsh's death. From time to time, delightful evidence of this pops up in memoirs and biographies. In 1974, for example, the two, who had not seen each other in a long while, made an appearance together at the Museum of Modern Art in New York. Afterwards, Walsh, then 87 and long happily married, wrote back to her:

My Dear Gloria,

My trip for the festival was worthwhile, just to see you again.

My quip I made at the luncheon about you finding the fountain of youth is all too true.

Your lips, your eyes, your hair have been with me for these many years. To me I can see my lovely Gloria. I will always remember her as a new phenomenon like some April evening, …

Good night my dear one,[17]

* * *

For years, *Sadie Thompson* had been considered a lost film. For much of that time, Swanson had searched far and wide in the hopes of finding a copy. She never did. After her death, however, her estate came across what still remains as the only surviving early print of the film. It had been stored years before in Mary Pickford's personal archive, and it was in less than mint condition. The most extensive damage was in the film's final reel (about 10 minutes), which was virtually unusable. Kino Video then bought the film and commissioned a team to reconstruct this portion using the

2. "The maddest idea in the world" 35

original inter-titles, still photographs, and footage from a 1932 MGM adaptation of the story shot by Oliver Marsh, one of cinematographers who'd also worked on Swanson and Walsh's 1928 adaptation. In addition, composer Joseph Turrin wrote a new musical score for the film.

This is the version that's available today. Although it is not pristine, it is an enormously valuable find that provides us with an excellent sense of what a superb film *Sadie Thompson* once was—and still is.

The story, which has been adapted numerous times, is about Sadie (Swanson), a San Francisco prostitute who comes to Pago Pago in hope of starting a new life. She meets jaunty U.S. Marine sergeant Tim O'Hara (Walsh), whom she nicknames "Handsome," and sparks immediately start flying. Also on the scene, however, is a religious reformer, Mr. Davidson (Lionel Barrymore), whose name was changed from the original "Reverend Davidson" to placate the censors. Not finding Sadie's past an issue, O'Hara suggests that they marry and move to Sydney in a month when his military hitch is up. Sadie is delighted. The relentless (and quite sadistic) Davidson, however, has plans to "save her" by forcing her to renounce her immoral ways and return to San Francisco to pay for her past sins. Eventually, he breaks her down. She repents, splits up with O'Hara, and agrees to go back and face punishment. In the meantime, though, the sexually repressed Davidson's interest in Sadie has turned to uncontrollable lust. At one point, as the rain pours down upon the hotel where Davidson and Sadie are staying, Davidson rapes her. Then, unable to live with his own sin, he kills himself. At first, Sadie is deeply disillusioned with all men. Ultimately, however, O'Hara wins her back, and again they plan to go to Sydney together.

* * *

On the surface, the story of *Sadie Thompson* seems to have the makings of a juicy melodrama and little more, but what makes this film version remarkable on many levels are the combined—and tightly integrated—artistic contributions of Walsh, Swanson, the other actors, the cinematographers (Marsh, George Barnes, and Robert Kurrle), the art director (William Cameron Menzies), and others. This is a film with many assets that show themselves in many ways.

First, there is the signature Walsh storytelling style with its economical, hard-driving narrative; in-your-face visual directness; and fast pacing. Although *Sadie Thompson* is not a traditional action picture, it often seems like one. Every bit of information that we get matters, characters are constantly on the move, and the cutting is often fast. Walsh also shows his skill at using visuals quite effectively to establish character and build dramatic tension in the film. One example of this is when Sadie plays her phonograph in one room as Davidson, in the next room, becomes increasingly agitated with it, enters her room, and furiously demands that she turn it off. In Turrin's 1987 score, the music being played is a visceral jazz piece, something that would obviously strike Davidson as indecent. It might also be triggering his own deeply repressed sexual urges. These scenes are so effectively shot and acted, however, that an actual piece of music isn't necessary to get the point across. Instead, the simple juxtaposition of the spinning phonograph record; Sadie's open, free-spirited reaction to it; and then Davidson's outraged reaction to it, is plenty. Through visual suggestion alone, the conflict is quickly established. Finally, Walsh also uses visuals quite effectively by telling much of the story in close-ups of characters' faces. Not only does this heighten the film's emotional intensity, but it also adds a special intimacy and simplicity to the proceedings. Film historian William K. Everson has even gone as far as to pay *Sadie Thompson* a great compliment, saying that this technique helps to give it an "austerity and pace" similar to director Carl Dreyer's 1928 masterpiece of French silent cinema, *The Passion of Joan of Arc*.[18]

Second, there is the acting. While it is consistently good throughout, the three performances that deserve the most attention are Swanson's Sadie, Barrymore's Davidson, and Walsh's "Handsome" O'Hara.

For 1928 audiences used to seeing Swanson in lavish clothes playing sophisticated roles, seeing her as Sadie must have been both a surprise and a revelation. Swanson's Sadie is utterly believable as a tough-talking but likable prostitute who still has hopes of starting a new life and perhaps finding a good man to love. Her walk, gestures, and facial expressions capture all of this superbly. Her walk especially is filled with the swaggering bravado that attempts to mask her own insecurity and vulnerability in a harsh world. Her scenes with Walsh are wonderful, too. We see the physical attraction between their two characters immediately. Almost as quickly, however, we also see that these two lonely people thoroughly enjoy being with, and learning about, each other as they talk, joke, and eventually make plans for a future in Sydney together. Unlike many other films of the period, the love story here unfolds quite naturally and credibly. In addition, Swanson is excellent at showing Sadie as simply not strong enough to withstand Davidson's efforts to "reform" her and, for a time, becoming a sad, fearful, broken spirit. Taken all together, it is little wonder that many film historians have ranked Swanson's Sadie as her best silent film performance.

Although most people today would look to Swanson's iconic performance in *Sunset Boulevard* as her best ever, a strong case can be made that her Sadie is even better. Swanson was undoubtedly very good at doing what director Billy Wilder wanted her to do in *Sunset Boulevard*: give an over-the-top portrayal of a hopelessly crazed faded silent movie queen. She certainly deserves the praise she received at the time for her effort. But, while *Sunset Boulevard* is very cleverly written, there is an emotional dishonesty at its core that's difficult to buy. Norma Desmond is a very theatrical creation that's fun to watch, but she is also a contrivance, more of a caricature than a truly disturbed human being. In stark contrast, Swanson's Sadie, while also beautifully realized, is a credible character who is also dynamic, undergoing several major personal changes during the story. It's a much more difficult role to pull off successfully, and Swanson does it with ease.

Barrymore's Davidson is another exceptionally well-conceived creation. The actor does an excellent job of emphasizing all the character's personal traits that make the clash with Sadie inevitable: his arrogance, his obsession to control, his repressed sexual urges, his intolerance, and even his sadism. As Davidson finally begins to break Sadie down, for example, Barrymore's eyes gleam with both pride and pleasure. Not only does he feel that he has the God-given right to put this woman through needless emotional torture, but he also gets a great thrill doing it. In his 1928 review of *Sadie Thompson*, *The New York Times* film critic Mordaunt Hall was quite enthusiastic about Barrymore's achievement, noting how he plays the "perfidious" character "in a singularly gifted fashion" and adding, "He creates an atmosphere of antagonism such as few villains are able to do."[19]

Walsh's "Handsome" O'Hara has several impressive moments, too. To focus on directing, Walsh had retired from acting several years before. But no doubt sensing that he was a natural to play this role and wanting to capitalize on the great rapport the two had off screen, Swanson urged him to step in front of the cameras once again. This turned out to be an inspired decision. Just as Swanson is warm, caring, charming, and playful in her scenes with Walsh, he is likewise with her. In addition, he excellently conveys Handsome's many qualities from his easy-going and tolerant nature to his resourcefulness when confronting various problems that arise.

Finally, *Sadie Thompson* has also been widely, and deservedly, praised for both its cinematography and its art direction, which superbly convey the steamy, exotic, and erotic atmosphere of the tropics. Most of the credit for cinematography goes to George Barnes and Oliver Marsh, who opted for a moody expressionistic look, which emphasized such elements as the otherworldly nature of the setting and the claustrophobic nature of the monsoon-like rain the characters experience. Art director William Cameron Menzies has often received praise for his designs of the run-down, ramshackle settings and other intriguing set additions (such as an out-of-place turnstile) that evoke a strange, far-away world. In fact, all these atmospheric touches were so effective with 1928 audiences that, in his review, Mordaunt Hall noted that, when patrons walked out of the New York theater in which he'd seen the film, they were genuinely startled to find that outside it was sunny and fair.[20]

Two other major adaptations of this story have been filmed. The first was Lewis Milestone's 1932 production, *Rain*, for United Artists, which starred Joan Crawford as Sadie and Walter Huston as Davidson. The second was Curtis Bernhardt's 1953 production, *Miss Sadie Thompson*, for Columbia, which starred Rita Hayworth and Jose Ferrer in the lead roles. While *Miss Sadie Thompson* received poor reviews when it was released and today only gets a 35 percent rating on Rotten Tomatoes, *Rain*, perhaps because Swanson and Walsh's 1928 version had been thought lost for so long, is often considered the best film version of the story. Looking closely at both the 1928 and 1932 films, however, the Swanson-Walsh effort towers over the other. The main reason is the acting. Crawford and Huston gave many wonderful performances during their careers, but their work in *Rain* is far from their best. Crawford's Sadie lacks the authenticity and much of the vulnerability and likeability that Swanson brought to the role, and Huston's Davidson comes across as wooden and mechanical as opposed to Barrymore's genuinely sinister and terrifying villain. In addition, the supporting roles, especially William Gargan's O'Hara, don't match up well, either. Walsh, in contrast, brought much more charm and panache to the role.

For film fans who have only seen *Rain*, a viewing of *Sadie Thompson* can be a fascinating discovery. Because Swanson, Walsh, and the others involved with the production handle the story with so much more insight, honesty, and depth of feeling than those involved with *Rain* did, there is—after we make all the important comparisons—really no comparison.

In addition to its many artistic strengths, *Sadie Thompson* is important for breaking new ground in subject matter. By maneuvering around the Hollywood censors, Swanson and Walsh managed to do what even they didn't think was possible when they'd had their fateful breakfast together. In the process, they helped pave the way for the relatively loose enforcement of the Production Code during the tremendously significant Pre-Code period of the late 1920s and early 1930s.

* * *

With *Sadie Thompson*, both Swanson and Walsh capped their silent film careers with a great critical and commercial triumph, but, at this turbulent and precarious time in the film industry, their professional destinies—like those of many of their colleagues—diverged. For Walsh, *Sadie* would only be the end of the beginning, an early chapter in an action-packed career story that would unfold over the next 36 years. But

2. "The maddest idea in the world" 39

for Swanson, 12 years younger and a true queen of 1920s cinema, this film would signal the beginning of the end of a film career that once seemed as if it would naturally go on for decades more.

It's intriguing to speculate why Swanson didn't make the transition to sound films as Garbo, Norma Shearer, and other top-tier silent film stars did. She was an excellent actress with a fine voice, and, as she proved in *The Trespasser* and other films, she had no problem adjusting to, and performing well in, talkies. Unlike Pickford, she could also play more contemporary characters more easily and tackle the kind of provocative storylines and themes early 1930s audiences would have responded to. One reason may have been the many years she had already been part of the silent era— about 15, a full decade longer than Garbo or Shearer. For late 1920s and early 1930s audiences infatuated with sound, everything that reminded them of silent films had suddenly become stale and old-fashioned. So, perhaps it was simply a matter of guilt by association—the hard fact that Swanson, so long and so closely associated with the vanishing medium, was expected to vanish along with it.

3

Tramp on a Tightrope
Charlie Chaplin and The Circus

For Charlie Chaplin in late 1925, life was a curious mixture of professional highs and personal lows. He had just released *The Gold Rush*, a film in which his alter ego, the Tramp, hopes to strike it rich in the Klondike in 1898, and audiences were enthralled. Theaters, especially in the major cities, were packed, and eventually *The Gold Rush* would become one of the highest grossing silent films of all time. Critics were unusually impressed, too. In his review of the film, Mordaunt Hall of *The New York Times* called it "the outstanding gem of all Chaplin's pictures."[1] Adding to the adulation, *Variety* proclaimed both that the film was "the greatest and most elaborate comedy ever filmed" and that it "will stand for years as the biggest hit in its field."[2] On the domestic front, however, Chaplin was entangled in a loveless marriage with Lita Grey, a 17-year-old actress he had reluctantly wed a year before after he learned she was pregnant by him. Now, she had given birth to a boy, Charles Chaplin III. Increasingly, Chaplin stayed away, preferring to work long hours and then, when not working, enjoy the company of friends and other women.

With *The Gold Rush* completed, Chaplin began to think about his next project. There were several possibilities. One was a film based on Robert Louis Stevenson's book of detective stories *The Suicide Club*. Another, an idea he had considered before, was a film about Napoleon. Then, according to his long-time colleague and confidante Henry Bergman, he and Chaplin had this exchange:

> [H]e said to me one night, "Henry, I have an idea I would like to do a gag placing me in a position I can't get away from for some reason. I'm in a high place troubled by something else, monkeys or things that come to me and I can't get away from them." He was mulling around in his head a vaudeville story. I said to him … "Why not develop your idea in a circus tent on a tightrope. I'll teach you to walk a rope."[3]

3. Tramp on a Tightrope

Chaplin responded positively, and bit by bit he fashioned a story about the Tramp joining a circus that would proceed to a climactic sequence in which he must cross a tightrope after his safety harness has broken off and, to make matters worse, as several monkeys are also climbing on his body and pulling off his pants. This is the stuff of nightmares, of course. But, as comedians have long understood, nightmares can often provide the inspiration for great comedy.

Many film writers have also asked if the idea of the Tramp on a tightrope being harassed by monkeys may, either consciously or subconsciously, have resonated with Chaplin because of his unhappy personal life at the time. This may well be true. Many of his films are deeply personal, and this was what he was experiencing as he began work in earnest on his next film, fittingly titled *The Circus*.

Premiering in January 1928, *The Circus* is one of Chaplin's most cohesive, inventive, and fully realized feature films. Comic bits, such as the scene when the Tramp masquerades as a mechanical mannequin in an amusement park, and thrill sequences, such as his scenes locked in a cage with a lion and walking the tightrope with the monkeys, show Chaplin

The Tramp (Charlie Chaplin) must endure harassment by monkeys in his harrowing journey along a tightrope in *The Circus* (Charles Chaplin/Photofest).

at the top of his game. There is also a touching but not overly sentimental romantic story. Nearly all of this is placed snugly into a circus setting, which helps to unify a succession of gags and give the story a more naturally flowing, less episodic quality than we see in many of Chaplin's other films. Easily one of the best, most widely praised, and most popular U.S. films of the late silent era, *The Circus* is also first-rate Chaplin, an effort that clearly holds its own when ranked against such other Chaplin silent masterworks as *The Gold Rush*, *City Lights*, and *Modern Times*.

As Chaplin biographer David Robinson observed, however, "The most surprising aspect about [*The Circus*] is not that it is as good as it is, but that it was ever completed at all."[4] The lead-up to the film's January 1928 release would be one of the most traumatic periods in Chaplin's long and sometimes turbulent life—a time when he would endure a series of personal and professional trials that dwarfed his late-1925 concerns. The Tramp's nightmarish tightrope walk took up only about two minutes of the finished film; Chaplin's real-life nightmares would take up more than two years.

* * *

Writing in the 1990s, film critic Andrew Sarris called Chaplin "arguably the single most important artist produced by the cinema, certainly its most extraordinary performer, and probably still its most universal icon."[5] Three decades later, all of these claims remain as legitimate as ever. Chaplin transformed crude, slapstick film comedy into a high art and served as an inspiration for countless entertainers ranging from Harold Lloyd, Red Skelton, Mel Brooks, Steve Martin, and Michael Jackson in the U.S. to France's Marcel Marceau and India's Raj Kapoor.

By the time Chaplin was 30, his unique talent and the universal appeal of silent film had enabled him to become both a wealthy man and one of the best-known celebrities in the world. But, although the journey to fame and fortune had been relatively rapid, it had also been filled with great hardship and emotional pain. Born in 1889 into grinding poverty, he grew up virtually without a father (who was absent most of the time) and a mother who struggled desperately both to make ends meet and with her own mental health. By the time he was nine years old, young Charlie had been sent twice to a workhouse, a government-run institution that provided food and shelter for impoverished children in return for menial work. When he was 14, his mother was committed to a mental asylum, and she would remain in similar institutions for most of the rest of her life.

Attracted to the stage about this time, Chaplin began working in music halls and later in stage productions as an actor and comedian, regularly impressing both audiences and critics with his ability to make small roles distinctive and memorable. This work led him, in his late teens, to the Fred Karno company, a British touring stage comedy troupe, and he quickly became one of its star performers.

In 1913, when Chaplin was 24 and touring the U.S. with Karno's company, he was recruited to make comic shorts for the fledgling movie industry. Soon afterwards, he created his Tramp character and started directing his own short films, becoming increasingly popular with each new release. After working briefly for several organizations, he launched his own company and, in 1919, partnered with silent screen giants Mary Pickford, Douglas Fairbanks, and D.W. Griffith to create the distribution company United Artists, a move that gave him complete control over his films. With the releases of his two feature-length comedies, 1921's *The Kid* and 1925's *The Gold Rush*, both stunning commercial and critical successes, he attained a considerable fortune to go with his worldwide fame. By late 1925, a classic rags-to-riches story seemed complete.

But there were other aspects to this story, too.

One was a deeply rooted apprehension about the coming of sound both for the film industry and for himself. Like many directors at the time, he adamantly opposed the new technology because he believed talkies would both detract from the essential nature of this visual medium and make the global distribution of films much more difficult. "Pictures are a pantomimic art," he declared when this subject came up in 1921.[6] But he also harbored fears about what sound would mean for him and the film pantomime he had spent his career perfecting, an art he believed to be totally incompatible with dialogue. As he said as late as 1931:

> For years I have specialized in one type of comedy—strictly pantomime. I have measured it, gauged it, studied. I have been able to establish exact principles to govern its reactions on audiences. It has a certain pace and tempo. Dialogue, to my way of thinking, always slows action, because action must wait upon words.[7]

Would the universal acceptance of dialogue films mean the end of his career? Especially as the prospect of the talkies became increasingly real, the world's preeminent film pantomimist must have frequently asked himself this question.

Another part of this story is Chaplin's personal life at the time, which film critic Roger Ebert once called "a calamity."[8] Six years before he married Lita Grey, he had (at age 29) married another 16-year-old named Mildred Harris, who claimed to be pregnant by him. This had been a false alarm, but Mildred quickly did become pregnant and their baby died three days after it had been born. Soon afterwards, the couple divorced. Then, after affairs with various women including actresses Pola Negri and

Marion Davies, Chaplin became interested in Grey, who may have been 15 when they first became involved. Soon after their marriage their relationship also deteriorated. He had as little to do with Grey as possible and probably assumed that their unhappy union would, at some point, be dissolved in a relatively low-key manner much as his marriage to Harris had been.

Unfortunately for Chaplin, though, new troubles emerged from all sides. The production of *The Circus* seemed jinxed almost from the start. In late 1925, a storm damaged the big top that had been built for the shoot, and filming was delayed. Soon afterwards, he learned that a bad job of film processing meant that he had to reshoot a significant amount of footage. Then, in late 1926, a fire swept through his studio destroying the circus set, which had to be rebuilt. Soon after the fire, Grey (taking their now two children) left their home and started divorce proceedings. Unlike Chaplin and Harris' divorce, though, this was much more acrimonious, public, and, for Chaplin, deeply humiliating. Grey's divorce application, which was 52 pages long (about 12 times the length of a typical claim), accused him of infidelity, abuse, and sexual perversion. Grey's lawyers then leaked the application to the press, the story became headline news, and groups formed across the U.S. calling for Chaplin's films to be banned. Reportedly on the verge of a nervous breakdown and eager to settle the divorce, Chaplin agreed to a cash payment to Grey of $600,000, at the time the largest divorce award by a U.S. court. Then, almost immediately, the Internal Revenue Service demanded that Chaplin pay another $1 million in back taxes. In the meantime, Chaplin had suspended production of *The Circus*, delaying its completion even more. Finally, in late 1927, after production had resumed and filming was almost complete, Chaplin learned about the frenzied public response to *The Jazz Singer*, immediately sensing that this could well be the death knell both for him and so many of his silent film colleagues.

Yet, despite all the setbacks, mercilessly negative press, and personal trauma, Chaplin persisted, *The Circus* premiered, and Chaplin even went on to receive a special honorary award for his contributions as the film's star, producer, director, and writer at the very first Academy Awards ceremonies in 1929.

It's easy to see this film's very existence and enormous success as a miracle. Perhaps it's more accurate, though, to see Chaplin's accomplishment more as a testament to his talent, mental discipline, and uncompromising artistic commitment. Like the Tramp, he had to find a way to walk his own tightrope, and, with the completion and success of *The Circus*, he had pulled off the feat.

Although he was finally free of Grey and *The Circus* had been a hit,

Chaplin carried emotional scars from these experiences for decades. In fact, in his 1964 autobiography, a work that covers more than 500 pages, he barely mentions the film, certainly one of his major artistic achievements, or the events taking place in his life at the time.

* * *

The story of *The Circus* has an elegance about it that stems from its tightly focused and relatively simple narrative.

The Tramp, suspected of theft and pursued by a policeman, runs into a circus tent as a clown act is in progress. The audience is bored with the clowns whose routines seem old and stale. But, when the Tramp and the policeman barge into the middle of their act and create chaos, the audience is thrilled and soon roars with laughter. This gives the circus's ringmaster and owner (Al Ernest Garcia) the idea to hire the Tramp to get audiences to laugh and, he hopes, boost sagging attendance. The trouble, as the ringmaster quickly learns, is that the Tramp is only funny when he doesn't try to be. When he tries, he's a washout.

The Tramp also meets, and becomes smitten with, Merna (Merna Kennedy), a circus rider and the stepdaughter of the ringmaster, who often slaps and berates her. The Tramp stands up for Merna and gets the ringmaster to treat her better. She becomes fond of him, but, when she meets Rex (Harry Crocker), the handsome tightrope walker who has just joined the company, she immediately falls for him instead. Later, when Rex misses a performance, the jealous Tramp attempts to strut his stuff for Merna by going on the tightrope in Rex's place. After a harrowing experience, which includes the broken safety harness and the monkeys, the Tramp—to everyone's amazement—manages to get to the other side of the rope, and the audience erupts in applause.

Afterwards, however, the Tramp, seeing the ringmaster again slapping Merna, hits him and is fired. He leaves, but Merna catches up with him and announces that she, too, is leaving the circus. Seeing that Merna really loves Rex and that he can also protect her from the ringmaster's abuse, the Tramp then finds Rex and helps the two get married. All three then return to the circus just as it is moving on to another town. The ringmaster allows all of them to remain with the show but, still irritated with the Tramp for hitting him, insists that he ride in the last wagon in the procession. As Merna and Rex head off in another wagon, the Tramp, realizing that it's probably best to let Merna, Rex, and the rest of the circus go on without him, decides against accompanying them. Instead, he wistfully watches the last wagon leave and starts walking—in his usual clunky, spunky way—in the opposite direction.

* * *

While much of Chaplin's work is personal, *The Circus* may be one of his most deeply personal feature films. Coming between two other very personal works, 1921's *The Kid*, which drew from Chaplin's impoverished childhood, and 1952's *Limelight*, which explores the life of a clown in old age, one can make a good case for calling it—as several writers have—his middle-age identity crisis film.⁹

The circus of course is a metaphor for Chaplin's world, the world of the comedian who makes people laugh in venues from circuses to music halls, to movie theaters. In this world, there's always an urgency to keep audiences amused because, when a comedian's audiences lose interest, unemployment and other crises may soon follow. So, in this world, the comedian must constantly be walking a tightrope to satisfy audiences, employers, and various dependents when there is never any security from falling flat on one's face. Chaplin was a comedian who also owned an entire film studio, was completely dependent on the success of his films, was responsible for the livelihoods of everyone who worked for him and their families, had now paid large divorce settlements to two wives, and (figuratively speaking) had just had his pants pulled off by the press for his personal transgressions. Clearly, he had a great deal riding on his ability to successfully walk his own real-world tightrope and gain control of his very complicated life at mid-life.

Silent film historian Jeffrey Vance has also extended the circus metaphor a little further, suggesting that the film not only works as a metaphor for Chaplin's current trials but also as one for his entire, and (with the arrival of sound) now very threatened, silent film career. As Vance once noted in an interview:

> He [the Tramp] joins the circus and revolutionizes the cheap little knockabout comedy among the circus clowns, and becomes an enormous star. But by the end of the movie, the circus is packing up and moving on without him. Chaplin's left alone in the empty circus ring.... It reminds me of Chaplin and his place in the world of the cinema. The show is moving on without him. He filmed that sequence four days after the release of *The Jazz Singer*.... When he put a score to *The Circus* in 1928, Chaplin scored that sequence with "Blue Skies," the song Jolson had made famous, only Chaplin played it slowly and sorrowfully, like a funeral dirge.¹⁰

* * *

In addition to having its interesting autobiographical layer, *The Circus* is a wonderful work of art.

One way Chaplin ably demonstrates his art is through his comic bits and thrill sequences, which in this film are often magnificent. In the amusement park arcade scenes just before a policeman chases the Tramp into the big top, for example, one sequence combines scenes in a fun house Mirror Maze and the fun house's exterior, which features mechanical mannequins going through repetitive robot-like motions, to great comic effect. Throughout, the Tramp's goal is to escape from both a policeman and a thief who are simultaneously pursuing him, and the magnificence lies in both how thoughtfully the sequence is developed and how ingenious the Tramp is in his attempts to confuse and elude his pursuers. First, the Tramp runs into the Mirror Maze and finds it very disorienting. Then, when the thief chases him again, he leads him into it and takes advantage of the thief's disorientation to again flee from him. Outside the fun house, the Tramp sees another policeman and, to blend in with his surroundings, he immediately takes the part of a decorative mechanical mannequin. The thief comes out and sees what the Tramp is doing, but, because he is also being pursued by the police, he must also pretend to be a mechanical mannequin. Now, the Tramp—who is not at all happy with the thief at this point—starts hitting him on the head and laughing all in a robotic motion, and the thief has no option but to play along. Soon, though, the thief collapses, the police figure out the ruse, and one policeman starts chasing the Tramp again. So, the Tramp leads him back to the Mirror Maze, where he now becomes disoriented, allowing the Tramp to escape and run into the big top.

Taking only about three minutes in the finished film, the sequence is a mini-masterpiece of Chaplinesque storytelling. And what makes *The Circus* all the more remarkable is that this sequence is then followed by so many other superb comic and thrill bits, including the chaos the Tramp and the pursuing policeman cause once inside the big top, the circus clowns' William Tell and barber shop skits, the Tramp's experience being locked in the cage with the lion, and of course the Tramp crossing on the tightrope.

Chaplin's artistry isn't only demonstrated through his gags and thrill sequences, however. He also brings additional depth and shadings to the story by giving many facets of it a point-counterpoint, or dual nature, to suggest a much more complex and nuanced world. The love story, for example, is both bitter and sweet, ultimately bringing out both the best (sensitivity, generosity) and the worst (jealousy, vindictiveness) sides of the Tramp. At one point, for example, we even see the Tramp split into two (courtesy of a clever double exposure) where, in his imagination, he sees himself hitting Rex, his rival for Merna's love. In the end, however, the Tramp graciously plays a crucial role in bringing Merna and Rex together. Another intriguing point-counterpoint concerns itself with the entertainer's identity. Chaplin, the renowned entertainer-celebrity, is playing the downtrodden Tramp (a character who by this time has become interchangeable in people's minds with his creator) who in turn performs as a circus clown who can only be funny when he doesn't try to be. It's fascinating to consider just who we are looking at as we watch certain scenes under the big top or especially in the film's finale as the Tramp remains behind as the circus moves on and he turns and walks in the opposite direction. Is it simply the Tramp realizing that he just doesn't belong in the circus anymore? Or is it Chaplin acknowledging that the circus of the film industry is moving in a different direction and that soon there may no longer be a place for either him or his Tramp in it? It's hard not to see both at the same time.

* * *

The Circus was the last film Chaplin made during the silent era, but it wasn't his last silent film. As so many of his silent film colleagues gamely worked to adapt to the new sound medium in 1928 and 1929, a defiant Chaplin resisted. He couldn't imagine his beloved Tramp talking and, if he did, what he would say or how audiences would react. So, he decided on a course of action unique within the Hollywood film industry: he continued to make his kind of films, and he did it in his studio and with his money. If he failed, then it would all be on him. The risk was immense, and he knew it.

The great irony is that, as Pickford, Swanson, and so many others who readily adapted to the new medium quickly found that audiences didn't accept them in it, Chaplin, to the amazement of nearly everyone including himself, achieved great success continuing to make silents—at least for a while. Both 1931's *City Lights* and 1936's *Modern Times* are, more accurately, hybrid films. And, although 1930s American audiences had almost entirely dismissed silent and hybrid films as quaint relics of the past, tens of millions of moviegoers made an exception when it came to Chaplin.

After *Modern Times*, Chaplin finally made his concession to sound with 1940's *The Great Dictator*, a full-fledged dialogue film in which he attacks Adolf Hitler and Nazism. In this film Chaplin also does something else different. He plays two roles, a buffoonish madman based on Hitler and a sympathetic Jewish barber. The Tramp, an essential element of his films over the previous quarter century, is gone. At long last it seems, Chaplin had come to terms with the fact that, while a continuing film career for him meant a transition to sound, the Tramp—a character created especially for, and only able to live in, the world of silent film—could not go with him.

Chaplin did allow the Tramp to speak on film once, though. Near the end of *Modern Times*, the Tramp must go on stage to sing a number but can't remember the lyrics. He enters with the lyrics written on his fasten-on shirt cuffs. When he grandly gestures at the beginning of the number, though, the cuffs fly off. Shouting from the wings, his companion (Paulette Goddard) says, "Sing!!! Never mind the words." So, he does a rousing number speaking in absolute gibberish, and the crowd loves it. The not-so-subtle message, of course, is that, even if you don't have the words, you can still succeed admirably as an entertainer.

* * *

Chaplin lived for nearly 50 years after *The Circus* premiered in 1928. Beginning in the 1940s, however, his work output slowed down considerably. Between the release of *The Great Dictator* and 1967, he only made four more films, the last one the poorly received *The Countess from Hong Kong* starring Marlon Brando and Sophia Loren. His personal life also continued to spark controversy. He married twice more, both times again to much younger women, actress Paulette Goddard and then Oona O'Neill, the just-turned-18-year-old daughter of playwright Eugene O'Neill (Chaplin was 54 at the time). The marriage to O'Neill again ignited public outrage about his moral behavior. In addition, Chaplin increasingly voiced left-wing political views, leading to further public disapproval. After leaving for London for the premiere of his film *Limelight* in 1952, he learned that the U.S. Attorney General had revoked his re-entry permit and declared that, to re-enter the U.S., Chaplin would have to submit to an interview concerning his political beliefs and moral behavior. Instead, Chaplin settled in Switzerland, where he and Oona lived quietly and happily with what would eventually be their eight children until his death on Christmas Day 1977. He was 88 years old.

While these were by no means his peak professional years, they did include some notable bright spots.

In 1972, nearly 20 years after his U.S. re-entry permit had been revoked, Chaplin returned in triumph to the U.S. to accept an honorary Oscar at the Academy Awards ceremonies. After receiving a glowing tribute, he then received a 12-minute standing ovation, the longest ever in the Academy's history. A new generation of Americans, it seemed, wanted to make amends with the great film artist whose work had continued to delight millions of them.

This wasn't the only attention he received from Hollywood. That same year, as part of a re-release, his 1952 film *Limelight* was shown in Los Angeles for the first time, finally making it eligible for Academy Award consideration. At the Academy's ceremony the following March, Chaplin and two co-composers received the Oscar for Best Original Dramatic Score for their work on the film. This was Chaplin's one and only competitive Academy Award.

In addition, Chaplin worked on numerous projects[11] from the late 1960s until in the mid–1970s when his declining health made future progress impossible. One of these efforts was to compose a new musical score and title song for *The Circus* as part of a major 1970 re-release, the first release of the film since its 1928 premiere. After 40 years, he was revisiting this film, which he had associated with so much personal and professional pain.

His new contributions to the film were quite good, too. The score—in Chaplin's trademark lush, sometimes wistful style of composition—is quite beautiful and excellently accents both the film's comic and bittersweet elements. And the song, "Swing Little Girl," which is sung over the opening credits and brief footage of a dejected Merna in the air in her circus rings, is a touching exhortation to keep pushing forward in the face of adversity, a theme that echoes back to what Chaplin must constantly have been telling himself when making *The Circus*. Originally, a professional vocalist was hired to sing the song, but Chaplin's musical director had also heard Chaplin sing it and preferred his version. Eventually, Chaplin, who was then 79, was persuaded to record it, and his very tender, heartfelt rendition gives the piece a special grace and poignancy.

It had taken Chaplin nearly half his long life, but he had finally faced his old nightmares and, by all accounts, made peace with them.

4

"A lyricist of light and shadow"

Josef von Sternberg, The Last Command, *and* The Docks of New York

Today, director Josef von Sternberg is best known for his artistic and romantic partnerships with actress Marlene Dietrich. The two made seven films together between 1930 and 1935,[1] after talkies were firmly established as the dominant motion picture form in the U.S. and elsewhere. Three of these—1930's *The Blue Angel* and *Morocco*, and 1932's *The Shanghai Express*—were major popular and critical successes. Largely due to his talents at capitalizing on the actress's charismatic screen presence to complement his own elegant, evocative, and sometimes controversial cinematic compositions, von Sternberg helped turn Dietrich into a cultural icon comparable in stature to her contemporary, actress Greta Garbo.

When their artistic and romantic partnerships had both run their course in 1935, the two went their separate ways. Dietrich, who remained popular with audiences, continued to act in films until the 1960s (occasionally working for top-tier directors such as Billy Wilder, Fritz Lang, Alfred Hitchcock, and Orson Welles) and perform in nightclubs and cabarets until the 1970s. She always seemed to be in the public eye. Von Sternberg, however, slowly faded into anonymity for just about everyone but a handful of classic film buffs and critics. He made a few more films, none of which achieved the popular or critical success of his earlier work; spent time painting and sculpting; taught courses on film aesthetics at the University of California at Los Angeles; and wrote a lively, often biting autobiography called *Fun in a Chinese Laundry*. For the most part, though, he lived in obscurity, largely ignored by the film community he had contributed so much to. In fact, when the BBC developed a short film biography of him to celebrate his centennial year in 1994, it was titled (most likely to attract more viewers) *Von Sternberg: The Man Who Made Dietrich*.[2] In the public's mind at least, the creation had clearly eclipsed the creator.

Even today, the assumption remains that Dietrich had also "made" von Sternberg, that she had helped "complete" him as an artist just as he had molded her into an icon. Yet, while Dietrich clearly inspired von Sternberg and was instrumental in helping him extend his art in new directions, she was by no means an equal partner in the process. In fact, even before he began to collaborate with her in late 1929, he had already worked in the film business for more than 20 years; directed eight silent films (including two that won Academy Awards) and one early talking picture; developed a rich, intensely personal visual style that would later prompt film critic Andrew Sarris to dub him "a lyricist of light and shadow"[3]; and received widespread critical praise for his work in both the U.S. and Europe. Well before Dietrich, von Sternberg had "arrived" as a major film artist.

* * *

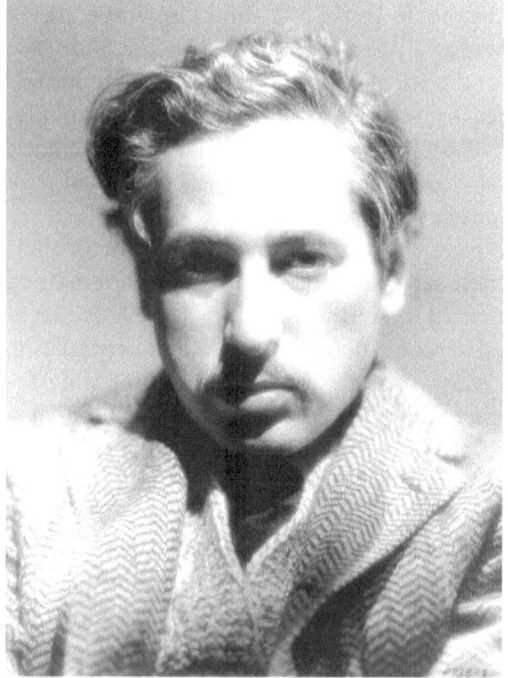

Although better known for the films he made in the 1930s with Marlene Dietrich, Josef von Sternberg made several superb films at the very end of the silent era, including 1927's *Underworld* and 1928's *The Last Command* and *The Docks of New York* (Photofest).

Born Jonas Sternberg in Vienna in 1894, the future Josef von Sternberg (who changed his first name during his teens and added the "von" when he was in his late 20s) moved to the U.S. with his mother when he was seven to join his father who had emigrated earlier. After a difficult childhood that included coping with his abusive father, dropping out of high school, and taking various jobs that included a stint as a door-to-door trinket salesman, he went to work at the World Film Company in Fort Lee, New Jersey, where his responsibilities ranged from running a film projector to writing intertitles. During World War I, he joined the U.S. Army Signal Corps and photographed training films for recruits. Then, between 1919 and 1923, he worked as an assistant director for several early silent film directors in both the U.S. and Europe.

In 1925, he made his directing debut in a film called *The Salvation Hunters*, which he produced himself on a shoestring budget. The film, while financially unsuccessful, was praised for its gritty realism and impressed filmmakers Mary Pickford and Charlie Chaplin enough for them to approach the 30-year-old director with projects. Pickford was first, engaging him to write and direct a film for her. After evaluating his screenplay, however, she considered the idea too experimental and the project was dropped. In 1926, von Sternberg also directed a film for Chaplin called *A Woman of the Sea*, which was planned as a comeback vehicle for former Chaplin leading lady Edna Purviance. Reportedly, it lacked the humanism that Chaplin had wanted, was never released, and, apparently for tax reasons, was eventually destroyed. Between these two projects, von Sternberg also worked for a brief time at MGM, where, after repeated art-versus-commerce clashes with studio executives, the director quit—turning the camera to the shooting stage ceiling in a gesture of defiance before walking off the set.

In 1927, Paramount producer B.P. Schulberg took a chance on the talented but temperamental filmmaker, offering him the more humbling position of technical advisor for lighting and photography. Von Sternberg accepted, and one of his first assignments was to try to salvage a failing Clara Bow film called *Children of Divorce*. He jumped into the project, reshooting nearly half the film in three days and presenting studio heads with a greatly changed, and far superior, finished product. As his reward, he was offered the chance to direct *Underworld*, a major production based on legendary writer Ben Hecht's original story for the screen about Chicago gangsters.

Then, in the 13 months between August 1927 and September 1928, von Sternberg delivered three outstanding late silent era films, which, fortunately, all survive. These include *Underworld*; *The Last Command*, the poignant story of a once-proud Russian general now forced to work as an extra in Hollywood movies; and *The Docks of New York*, a bittersweet tale of a rough and tumble ship's stoker and dockside prostitute who struggle at love. Soon afterwards, there may have been another fine von Sternberg silent film as well. In January 1929, *The Case of Lena Smith* premiered to widespread critical praise. After World War II, however, Paramount, for tax purposes, destroyed the only known prints of the film. Today, archivists, who sift through old film repositories in hopes of uncovering additional prints of films long thought lost, view it as one of the "Holy Grails" of their quests.

Of the three films available today, all remain, now more than 90 years after their release, visually and emotionally exhilarating. Among the three, *The Docks of New York* could very well be the best. While it may not have the elaborately designed sets of, say, von Sternberg's *Morocco*, and while some critics have had qualms about the ending, it is one of the director's most tightly integrated and aesthetically and emotionally satisfying films. Every essential element—writing, acting, cinematography, visual design, and editing—is extremely well rendered, and every element fits together extremely well to form a very satisfying whole. Many people have called it von Sternberg's finest silent film, but a strong argument can be made that it is also, with the possible exception of *The Blue Angel*, von Sternberg's finest film. Period.

Of these three silent films, both *The Last Command* and *The Docks of New York* premiered in 1928 and deserve to be singled out for close examination. Before delving into these, however, let's look briefly at *Underworld*, another remarkable achievement as well.

* * *

Although many consider *The Blue Angel* to be von Sternberg's breakthrough film, *Underworld* is actually the one that made people sit up and take notice. The story centers on three main characters: gangland boss Bull Weed (George Bancroft), his moll, "Feathers" McCoy (Evelyn Brent), and a curious former lawyer and rehabilitated alcoholic turned Bull's right-hand man, "Rolls Royce" Wensel (Clive Brook).

While robbing a bank, Bull notices that a drunk has witnessed the crime and takes him with him in his getaway car. Later, Bull says he is distrustful of this drunk keeping his mouth shut after seeing the crime because alcohol makes for "bums and squealers." But the man, who is surprisingly articulate, convinces Bull that, although he is a drunk, he is also a "Rolls Royce for silence." That's good enough for Bull, who first gives him menial work and eventually makes him his close advisor and confidant. On another front, tensions grow between Bull and Buck Mulligan, a rival gangster who is muscling in on his territory. On still another front, a serious romantic attraction develops between Rolls Royce and Feathers, one that creates conflicted feelings for them both. Eventually, Bull kills Mulligan, is sentenced to death, and goes to prison to await his fate. In response, Rolls Royce develops a clever escape plan, but this creates even more complications for him and Feathers because a "sprung" Bull would probably mean the end of their hopes to be together.

Released in August 1927, *Underworld* was, contrary to the studio's expectations, an immediate popular and critical success. In New York, for example, the film's popularity was so great that Paramount arranged for round-the-clock showings at its theater to accommodate the crowds eager

4. "A lyricist of light and shadow"

to see it. Overjoyed, Paramount's executives presented von Sternberg with both a $10,000 bonus and a gold medal. The critical response was positive as well. In Europe, French directors Julien Duvivier and Marcel Carne praised von Sternberg's tight, crisp film technique and Spanish surrealist filmmaker Luis Bunuel declared that *Underworld* was his all-time favorite film. In the U.S., Ben Hecht eventually picked up the very first Academy Award for Best Original Story.

Today, *Underworld* has lost little, if any, of the freshness and visceral impact that thrilled audiences in 1927. While it is often credited with sparking the growing demand for gangster films in the early 1930s, and although it has many of the standard features of other gangster films including a hoodlum hero, his moll, a gang war, and a climatic shoot-out with the police, it is in many ways quite different from, and more sophisticated than, most of them.

One intriguing element is the love triangle involving the three main characters, which is nuanced and deliciously complex in ways we rarely see in gangster films. Feathers and Rolls Royce feel considerable guilt and anxiety about being in love because they are both deeply indebted to Bull; fear the consequences if he finds out about them; and, despite this, can't bear to hurt him. Later, when Rolls Royce and Feathers both recognize that helping Bull escape from prison would probably mean the end of their hopes of being together, the two face a moral dilemma: go forward with the plan or abandon it—and Bull. Bull, too, shows unexpected depth and sensitivity when—at last—he sees how Feathers and Rolls Royce feel about each other. All three must make serious personal choices, which may also mean major personal sacrifices.

Another fascinating element of the film is a sequence featuring a "gangsters' ball" (held when the rival gangs declare an armistice for the night) that shows off von Sternberg's visual talents in breathtaking fashion. Beginning as an event filled with light-hearted exuberance amid sumptuous excess, the party room morphs into a place where, as one intertitle tells us, "The brutal din of cheap music—booze—hate—lust—made a devil's carnival." To mark the transition, von Sternberg's visuals become less upbeat and party-like and more delirious, disturbing, and grotesque. The attempt at a temporary truce among thieves becomes an inevitable descent into hell.

Although every von Sternberg film has his personal stamp on it, *Underworld* also benefits from a cooperative effort between the director and a group of talented artistic collaborators working at Paramount, many of whom would work with the director again in the future. They include Paramount's prolific and inventive art director Hans Dreier; Bert Glennon, for decades, one of the film industry's most respected cinematographers;

and his acting trio of Bancroft, Brent, and Brook, who would all become stars as a result of their performances in this film.

* * *

Immediately after *Underworld*, von Sternberg went to work on another silent effort, his first film to be released after the October 1927 premiere of *The Jazz Singer* had shaken the film world. Called *The Last Command*, it is loosely based on the true story of a Russian aristocrat and general in the Imperial Russian Army, who, after the Bolsheviks topple the Czarist regime, flees to the U.S. where, old and broken, he can only find work as a $7.50-a-day extra in Hollywood movies.

The story begins in 1928 Hollywood. The once-proud Russian general Grand Duke Sergius Alexander (Emil Jannings) is called for a day's work as an extra. The film director who has selected him is Leo Andreyev (William Powell), a former Russian revolutionary who had had a bitter

After once serving the czar as a general in the Imperial Russian Army, Sergius Alexander (Emil Jannings, right) is reduced to working as a Hollywood extra in *The Last Command*. Here he is thinking about the outfit he must wear for his upcoming scene, the uniform of a czarist general, and is overcome with traumatic memories. The actor on the left is unidentified (Paramount Pictures/Photofest).

encounter with Sergius Alexander during the war and who now finds the former general's current circumstances darkly humorous. Intending to humiliate the old man, he instructs an assistant to issue Sergius Alexander a Russian general's uniform for a battle scene for his film about the Russian Revolution.

As Sergius Alexander prepares to go before the camera, his mind flashes back a decade to when he, as a vigorous middle-aged man, also wore a Russian general's uniform. He meets a woman, a beautiful but potentially dangerous "revolutionist" named Natalie Dabrova (Evelyn Brent). She fascinates him, and, despite the danger she might pose, he takes her with him as oversees his army's efforts. Eventually, and despite their political differences, each realizes that the other also loves Russia and the two fall in love. Then, after the Bolsheviks have prevailed and a mob on a train wants Sergius Alexander hanged, she schemes so he can jump off the train and eventually leave the country. Moments after he jumps, however, he watches a bridge collapse just as the train is crossing it. Everyone on board, including Natalie, dies.

The story now flashes forward back to 1928 Hollywood. Sergius Alexander is called for his battle scene. There, Leo directs him to give a rousing speech to his downcast men. In the midst of this all-too-familiar scene from his past, Sergius Alexander begins to lose his grip on reality. Imagining himself on a real battlefield, he starts speaking, passionately urging the men before him to fight for Russia. Then, overtaxing himself emotionally, he collapses. Now weak and whispering, he asks if his side has won the battle. Greatly moved, Leo tells him it has. Pleased, Sergius Alexander dies. Leo's stunned assistant remarks, "That guy was a great actor." A much-changed Leo replies, "He was more than a great actor; he was a great man."

Released in January 1928, *The Last Command*, received enthusiastic critical reviews but made only a marginal profit, a disappointment for Paramount. In the decades since its release, though, the film has continued to receive interest and respect from various quarters. Filmmaker Preston Sturges once declared that it was perhaps the only perfect picture he had ever seen. In 2006, the United States Library of Congress selected it for the National Film Registry, an honor it bestows on only 25 films each year. Today, it remains a staple at silent film festivals around the world.

There are several reasons why, even after all these years, *The Last Command* continues to captivate audiences.

One is the relationship between Jannings' Sergius Alexander and Brent's Natalie, which is as layered and intriguingly ambiguous as some of the most complex relationships we see in contemporary cinema. As Andrew Sarris once noted about Natalie, "She seems fascinated by his power, and yet when he is completely helpless, she is not without pity or compassion. [She], like all Sternbergian women, remains enigmatic beyond the demands of the plot. Her perverse nature operates beyond good and evil, beyond the convenient categories of virgins and vamps."[4]

Another reason is the inventiveness that von Sternberg uses in employing visuals throughout to dramatically underscore events and reinforce the story's themes. An excellent example of this is an engrossing sequence that grew out of the director's own decision to organize the story in flashback form, beginning and ending with Sergius Alexander in Hollywood. Reporting to the studio for his one-day assignment, the former grand duke and general is, at first, caught in a large, rough crowd of extras as he waits to enter the studio gate and pick up his costume for the day's shoot. Then, in a long horizontal tracking shot, the camera follows him as he's herded in classic assembly-line fashion through a series of service windows to receive his uniform, boots, and sword: an experience the intertitle calls "the Bread Line of Hollywood." Here, von Sternberg skillfully sets up a relationship between the dehumanizing way that Hollywood treats movie extras and the similar way the Russian aristocracy treated its soldiers, who, in the flashback that follows, are frequently lined up and inspected in order to accommodate Sergius Alexander and other entitled authority figures. As well as making a statement about the way film studios, militaries, and, for that matter, many kinds of institutions treat their least valued and most vulnerable workers, could von Sternberg also be suggesting that Sergius Alexander is getting a comeuppance that he might to some degree deserve?

Still another reason is the well-aligned team effort by von Sternberg collaborators such as art director Dreier, cinematographer Glennon, Brent, and, working for the director for the first time, Jannings. Dreier and Glennon both do excellent jobs of differentiating the look and atmosphere of wartime Russia with that of late-1920s Hollywood. Finally, Jannings and Brent are quite good at integrating, respectively, their more traditional and contemporary styles of acting to assure that their many scenes together are sufficiently compelling. But then, von Sternberg's very precise, controlling directing style may have had a hand in this, too.

While some tensions apparently existed between the director and his male star during the film's shooting, everyone involved agreed that Jannings' excellent performance was worth the effort (and angst) it may have taken to get there. For his work on this film and on 1927's *The Way of All Flesh*, Jannings received the first Best Actor Academy Award at the Academy's first awards presentation in May 1929. Several months after that, von Sternberg also received an invitation from Germany's leading film

4. "A lyricist of light and shadow" 59

company, UFA (Universum-Film AG), to come to Europe to direct Jannings in his first talking picture, *The Blue Angel*.

* * *

After completing another gangster film called *The Drag Net*, a poorly reviewed and now-lost effort made to capitalize on the popular success of *Underworld*, von Sternberg began work on *The Docks of New York*.

In 2010, Charles Silver, the curator of the Department of Film at New York's Museum of Modern Art, called *Docks* "probably the last genuinely great silent film made in Hollywood, save for Chaplin's against-the-grain masterpieces [1931's *City Lights* and 1936's *Modern Times*] of the 1930s."[5] It is easy to understand why he and so many others regard this film so highly. In terms of craft, it is von Sternberg's most effective film, and, emotionally, it is his most affecting. The visual compositions, writing, acting, and other storytelling elements that integrated so well in *Underworld* and *The Last Command* come together here in near-perfect harmony to reinforce and strengthen each other in powerful, memorable ways. Many films aspire to be visual poetry; this is one of a very small percentage that succeeds.

Mae (Betty Compson) and Bill (George Bancroft) get acquainted after he has saved her life during a very eventful evening and following morning in *The Docks of New York* (Paramount Pictures/Photofest).

The story is set sometime around the turn of the 20th Century. Bill Roberts (George Bancroft), a rough, burly ship's stoker and his shipmates prepare for a single night of shore leave in New York. Dampening their spirits, their mean-spirited supervisor, Andy (Mitchell Lewis), threatens them with a double shift if they don't behave or return to the boat drunk the next morning.

When their ship lands, Andy heads for a waterfront dance-hall saloon known as The Sandbar. There he unexpectedly encounters his estranged wife Lou (Olga Bachonova), whom he hasn't seen in three years. She has come to The Sandbar for the same reason he has: to find companionship with the opposite sex. They talk, but the two clearly have a seething dislike for one another.

Meanwhile, as Bill disembarks from the ship and walks along the dock, he notices that a woman (Betty Compson) has intentionally jumped into the water. He jumps in, saves her, and carries her to a room above The Sandbar. Lou helps revive the woman, who we learn is a prostitute named Mae. Curiously, Bill becomes very proprietary toward Mae. He gets her a hot toddy from the saloon and even surprises her with a pretty dress he steals from a pawn shop next door. He then asks her to join him for the evening, and later they meet downstairs in The Sandbar and chat. Andy, also attracted to Mae, tries to cut in, but the intimidating Bill gets him to back off. After more conversation, Bill—in a bit of bravado to show Mae that he considers her special—impulsively offers to enter into a "marriage" with her right then and there. Knowing that this is probably just for show but inwardly longing for the respect she associates with marriage, she agrees. The other revelers at the tavern love the idea, so a local missionary named "Hymn Book" Harry (Gustav von Seyffertitz) is called to perform the ceremony.

Although everyone at the tavern considers this whole business a lark, Harry approaches his task with great seriousness. As he, Bill, and Mae go through the ceremony, the whole room becomes still, quiet, and acutely aware that marriage is a serious matter and that solemn vows are being exchanged.

The next morning as Mae sleeps, however, Bill slips quietly from their room to return to his ship. Andy, observing that the stoker is abandoning his "wife," goes to Mae's room just after she has discovered that Bill has left her and attempts to rape her. But Lou arrives and shoots him. Hearing the gunshots, Bill returns to the room. At first, the police suspect Mae of the shooting, but Lou confesses and is arrested. Then, after things appear to have calmed down, Mae surprisingly explodes with anger at Bill for leaving her and kicks him out of the room.

Back on his ship stoking the furnaces, Bill realizes he has made a

4. "A lyricist of light and shadow" 61

mistake. He leaps off the ship and swims to shore. There he learns that Mae is in custody at night court, charged with stealing the clothing he had taken for her. He goes to the court, confesses to the crime, and promises to return to Mae after he completes the 60-day sentence the judge has just given him. Hopeful, she agrees to wait.

As this summary suggests, the story itself is largely the stuff of melodrama, complete with sordid characters, a suicide attempt, a rape attempt, a murder, heartbreak, and even a major (and, to some, implausible) twist at the end. What makes *The Docks of New York* so compelling, however, is the way virtually all the film's visual and dramatic elements fuse together so tightly, yet naturally, both to provide considerable aesthetic pleasure and to give the narrative greater credibility and depth.

There are, for example, the beautifully lit but startlingly hellish scenes of the ship's furnace room near both the beginning and end of the film that excellently communicate the grueling, dirty, and oppressively hot work world of Bill and other ship's stokers.

There are the raucous, frenzied shots of The Sandbar, the place where a ship's stoker and his like can drink, carouse, and maybe find comfort with a woman. As film writer Ed Howard has observed, "One of the remarkable things about von Sternberg's bar scenes is … that it's easy to forget that there's no sound, that one can't actually hear the clamor that's so vividly conveyed through the silent images. There are few silent films that seem so noisy."[6]

There is the lovely scene on the fogbound dock outside The Sandbar just after Bill and Mae's marriage ceremony. As Bill gently puts his coat over Mae, she says, "You don't know what this means to me." and "I'll be a good wife to you, Bill." And all the while the thick fog drifting about them suggests a future, which, like their relationship, is shrouded in haze and uncertainty.

There is also the stunning moment in the scene the next morning when Bill's shirt pocket is ripped as he is about to leave Mae. Emotionally devastated but also poised and resigned to the reality of the situation, she offers to sew the pocket up. As she holds the needle and thread in front of her, we see the two items in a point-of-view shot: as her eyes would see them. At first, the needle and thread are clear. Then, quite unexpectedly, they blur so much that it's impossible for Mae to put the thread through the eye of the needle. We don't even have to look into her eyes to know that they have welled up with tears of grief. The blurred image of the needle and thread, of course, heightens the emotional impact of an especially painful, bittersweet moment. As we instinctively link the blurred image to Mae's tears, we feel her heartbreak all the more viscerally and acutely.

All of these moments in *Docks* are examples of the use of *expressionism*, the distortion of the image of reality in order to convey an interior feeling or idea. These expressionistic touches are used throughout the film with great success, greater than in perhaps any of von Sternberg's other films. Again, von Sternberg and his visual collaborators teamed with great effectiveness to envision moving and dramatically meaningful compositions and then bring them to cinematic life. In addition to art director Dreier, the director worked this time with Harold Rosson, a widely respected cinematographer who had been in films since 1915 and who, as film writer Eddie Muller once put it, "reveled in the challenges presented by [von Sternberg's] fresh, innovative ideas."[7] After *Docks*, Rosson would work on dozens of films into the 1960s, including such classics as 1939's *The Wizard of Oz*, 1950's *The Asphalt Jungle*, and 1952's *Singin' in the Rain*.

Two other von Sternberg collaborators who also warrant special notice are his two leading actors George Bancroft and Betty Compson.

Bancroft, who plays Bull Weed in *Underworld* so effectively, plays another rough, physically intimidating character in *Docks* and does so in a very restrained, precise way. Every facial or other physical gesture he makes is clear, on point, and totally in sync with what his character is thinking or feeling at a particular moment. Although Bancroft often played coarse characters, he could do it with great discipline, subtlety, and, as odd as it may sound, refinement. He has been called a poor man's Wallace Beery, a reference to a much more prominent star of that period who played similar roles. But this comparison is unfair because Bancroft's focus, unlike Berry's, was always on the character and not on trying to ingratiate himself with audiences. In other words, he wasn't the "ham" that Beery could often be.

Compson is a revelation in *Docks*. Largely forgotten today, the actress is dazzling as her Mae moves from the profoundly depressed person who has just attempted suicide to someone willing, just maybe, to give life another chance; to a woman deeply touched by Bill's interest in, and tenderness toward, her; to a rejected lover crushed by heartbreak; to ultimately a somewhat stronger person willing to keep going and wait for Bill. All along this roller-coaster emotional journey, she conveys every step with great conviction and authority, becoming ever more intriguing and entrancing along the way. She has been called "the spiritual and sensual soul"[8] of the film, and she certainly is.

One part of *Docks* that has drawn criticism ever since its release has been its conclusion. The day after it premiered in New York, for example, one reviewer called the ending "preposterous," adding that the film would "take a higher rank" if Bill had simply left Mae in the morning.[9] But, it might be shortsighted to view what happens here as simply a typical Hollywood happy ending contrived to please audiences.

4. "A lyricist of light and shadow" 63

Upon closer inspection, the ending appears more ambiguous—and much closer to von Sternberg's storytelling preferences. A typical Hollywood ending would have consisted of a close-up of Bill winking at Mae as he swaggers off to serve his 60-day jail sentence followed by a close-up of Mae beaming back with joy and then a fade-out. That is not what occurs here. Bill goes off and Mae remains, but then a new group of defendants is brought in to the courtroom, the camera pulls back to show the courtroom almost in its entirety, and now Mae is more anonymous, just another face in the crowd.

As we see her standing alone while the world about her moves on, it's almost impossible not to wonder: Will Bill, always full of bravado, actually make good on his promise? Is Mae also willing to wait for the full 60 days? If so, what will she do to support herself during this time? Will she simply lose heart and attempt suicide again? It's clear that, at this moment, Bill and Mae are both willing to wait, but will they both feel the same way in two months, one month, or even a week? If the two finally do get together, what will their chances be of living happily ever after? It's impossible to predict the future, which is true for every couple just starting out. In this couple's case, though, we see that lasting happiness together is a real longshot.

When released in September 1928, *Docks* was, unfortunately, overlooked by the public in all the anticipation that was building over *The Singing Fool*, Al Jolson's part-talkie musical follow-on to *The Jazz Singer* which premiered the same week. While *The Singing Fool* became Warner Brothers' most commercially successful film ever (a distinction it would hold for more than a decade), *Docks* quickly sank into obscurity, and it wasn't until decades later that it found audiences in revival theaters and began to receive the critical acclaim it so richly deserves. It's an irony among ironies that, while *The Singing Fool* is painfully dated and almost unwatchable today, *The Docks of New York* continues to delight film audiences around the world.

* * *

After making *The Case of Lena Smith*, von Sternberg moved—by various accounts, quite naturally and enthusiastically—from silent to sound films. Although many other leading film directors of the time fretted about how sound would negatively affect their ability to tell a story visually, he welcomed the new technology, seeing it as another tool at the director's disposal to enhance the medium's storytelling capability and rouse the audience's imagination. As he wrote many years later, "To be correctly and effectively used, sound had to bring to the image a quality other than what the lens included, a quality out of the range of the image. Sound had to counterpoint or compensate the image, add to it—not subtract from it."[10] In his early sound films such as *Thunderbolt*, *The Blue Angel*, and *Morocco*, we see, and hear, that he practiced what he preached in the inventive ways he incorporated both dialogue and music into his stories in order to "add to" his visuals and the overall story experience.

On a less abstract level, it's also been noted that one other reason the director welcomed sound was to control the music on a film's soundtrack, and not leave the important work of musical accompaniment to local movie theater organists or piano players: silent film fixtures the control-obsessed director couldn't abide.

* * *

Perhaps Josef von Sternberg will always be best remembered as "the man who made Dietrich," but, if this is the case, it would be a shame. While not nearly as well known or widely seen as his films with Dietrich, his three surviving late silent films, *Underworld*, *The Last Command*, and *The Docks of New York*, are all first-rate achievements that absolutely deserve the attention they continue to receive at silent film festivals and other venues today. Of these, *Docks* especially stands out, showing in scene after scene the director's mastery of composition to complement and enrich a deeply affecting human story.

During the waning days of silent films, von Sternberg more than proved that he was a true visual poet and a worthy peer of such poet-director contemporaries as F.W. Murnau and John Ford. Yes, he was, in the early and mid-1930s, the man who made Dietrich. But he was also, by the late 1920s, the man who had made *Underworld*, *The Last Command*, *The Docks of New York*, and a place for himself in the top tier of Hollywood directors.

5

"The highest reaches of the form"

King Vidor and The Crowd

> Bernard Shaw said *The Docks of New York* was the only perfect film he'd ever seen. For my money, Vidor's *The Crowd* is even a couple of notches better, but we are speaking here only in the highest reaches of the form. Virtually every frame of *The Crowd* tells its own story; with utter simplicity Vidor conveys a great complexity. Angles, size of image, cutting, continuous shots—in Vidor's work, as with all the first great filmmakers—these are profoundly well chosen to portray meanings beyond words.—Peter Bogdanovich[1]

"Now this is the way I believe a film should begin," director King Vidor wrote many years after the fact. "A director has a simple theme or idea upon which to base his whole story. The producer approves the premise, and the project is begun."[2]

Vidor was recounting with some fondness a very brief, warm conversation he had had on the MGM lot in 1926 with the studio's production head, Irving Thalberg. The director's latest film, a World War I epic called *The Big Parade*, had received unusually positive critical praise, become an enormous commercial hit, and was on its way to become one of the highest grossing silent films of all time.

"Well, what are you going to try next?" asked Thalberg. "It's going to be hard to top *The Big Parade*."

Unprepared for this particular conversation, Vidor began to improvise. And, as his thoughts took shape, he told Thalberg about the story of an average young man who simply goes through life doing what other people did but still "sees a lot of drama taking place around him." Then he added, "Objectively, life is like a battle, isn't it?"

Intrigued, Thalberg asked if Vidor had a title, and Vidor, still improvising, suggested *One of the Mob*. "How long will it take you to write it?" Thalberg asked enthusiastically.³

With that exchange, a new film project, with one of Hollywood's leading producers and one of its leading directors already on board, was born. Very quickly the title was changed to *One of the Crowd* and then *The Crowd*, and pre-production was underway. What began as a spur-of-the-moment idea soon became a director's labor of love and ultimately one of the undisputed masterpieces of the silent film era.

The story of John and Mary Sims, an ordinary young couple who dream and struggle amid the everyday challenges of New York City, *The Crowd* is remarkable in a number of respects. Not only does it break new ground in the treatment of its subject by digging deep into the painful realities that often live alongside the American Dream,⁴ but it does so in an uncompromising, non-judgmental, humane, and sometimes gently humorous manner. In addition, it is an unusually well-orchestrated production filled with impressive elements from the sensitive and convincing portrayals of John and Mary by little-known actors James Murray and Eleanor Boardman to an array of dramatic expressionistic visuals that reinforce meaning in highly creative and effective ways. It is little wonder then that, in the 1960s, when the French film director and critic Jean-Luc Godard was asked why more films weren't made about ordinary people, he responded by saying, "Why remake *The Crowd*? It has already been done."⁵

One of Hollywood's top directors during the late silent era, King Vidor continued to helm major studio films for the next 30 years, along the way picking up five Academy Award nominations for Best Director (Photofest).

* * *

Born into a well-to-do Galveston, Texas, family on February 8, 1894, King Vidor had the makings of a filmmaker even before he knew much, if anything, about movies. Later in his life, he recalled an experience that had taken place at the end of a pier in Galveston in 1904 when he was a boy of 10 waiting for his first swimming lesson. Many other boys of various ages and sizes were also on the pier, diving into the water from different platforms, hurriedly swimming back, and scrambling to get in line again to make another dive. Thrilled by the energy and exuberance he saw, he closely studied everything before him. "I saw in the scene music reduced to movement," he wrote. "I felt its rhythm, tempo, beauty, humor; I was aware of form and composition, of line and action. I wanted to record it, to show others what had been shown to me; there must be some way of capturing and preserving what I saw and heard. I would think about it. I had not yet seen, or even heard of, the motion-picture camera."[6]

Soon, however, the young Vidor's fascination with recording people and experiences on film began to manifest itself in different ways. Before he was a teenager, he began to take and develop still pictures of his relatives with a Brownie box camera. At 16, he dropped out of high school and began to work as a ticket taker and projectionist in a Galveston nickelodeon, one of the thousands of small, crude movie theaters that flourished in the U.S. between 1905 and 1915. At 18, he was working as an amateur newsreel cameraman. At 19, he made his first fictional movie, a story titled *In Tow* about a local automobile race. At 20, he and a vaudevillian named Edward Sedgwick formed a company to produce one- and two-reel short films. Soon, however, they went out of business when they couldn't collect royalties from the theaters that screened them. At 21, he married Florence Arlo, an ambitious young actress. Now penniless from their business failure, but still filled with ideas, energy, and hope, Vidor, Florence, and Sedgwick all left Texas for Hollywood, the fast emerging "film capital" of the world.

Between 1915 and the early 1920s, Vidor worked on dozens of short and then feature-length films for a couple of companies and then embarked, in partnership with the New York–based film exhibitor First National Pictures, on another entrepreneurial venture to make films to compete with the major Hollywood studios. Whimsically named Vidor Village, the small studio folded after a few years. About this time, Vidor's marriage to Florence also ended (most likely a result of an affair he was having with rising silent film star, actress Colleen Moore), and the two officially divorced in 1924.

Then came the opportunity that dramatically changed Vidor's career trajectory. In 1922, Louis B. Mayer, then an independent producer, asked Vidor to direct a film version of the Broadway hit *Peg 'o My Heart* starring legendary Broadway actress Laurette Taylor. The production was difficult, and, although the finished product was not especially engaging, the film made money. Pleased with the professionalism Vidor showed through the trying experience, Mayer gave the director additional work and also introduced him to fellow producer Samuel Goldwyn. The timing was propitious, because Mayer and several business partners were on the verge of establishing a major new filmmaking and distribution enterprise, Metro-Goldwyn-Mayer. Vidor came aboard and quickly formed a very strong, close working relationship with Mayer's brilliant young protégé, Irving Thalberg.

Initially, Vidor's work for the new studio consisted of unexceptional "bread and butter" movies, but, in 1924, he made *Wild Oranges*, one of his most interesting earlier efforts. A drama about a widower who comes to a remote island off the Georgia coast and befriends a young woman who is being terrorized by an escaped prisoner, *Wild Oranges* conveys much of the humanism and distinctive visual style that would mark his best future work.

Yearning to take on something far more ambitious than the films he had been working on, Vidor convinced Thalberg about this time to support a much grander project that would allow him, in his words, to "put much more effort, and love, into its creation."[7] Eventually, the two agreed on a story about World War I. A young writer named Laurence Stallings—who, with the veteran playwright Maxwell Anderson, had just co-authored the highly praised Broadway play about World War I *What Price Glory?*—was brought in to help with the script. Actor John Gilbert, then MGM's top male box office draw, was cast in the lead role of an American doughboy. And production began.

Premiering on November 5, 1925, *The Big Parade* (the title referring to the seemingly endless line of troops that marched up to the war's battle front) was a critical and popular sensation that eventually played in some big city theaters for more than a year. Immediately hailed as the best film ever made about World War I, it heavily influenced major films that soon followed, including G. W Pabst's *Westfront 1918* and Lewis Milestone's *All Quiet on the Western Front* (both released in 1930).

Today, roughly a century after its initial release, *The Big Parade* remains as moving and vital as ever. One key reason for both its immediate success and its continuing popularity with audiences is Vidor's great ability to weave a deeply affecting personal story—a romance between Gilbert's doughboy and a young French woman played by actress Renee Adoree—so seamlessly into the grim larger canvas of a horrible and pointless war. As is often the case in Vidor's best films, certain sequences leave indelible marks on the minds of viewers. One such sequence in *The Big Parade* is the film's very tightly choreographed, visually gripping, and emotionally wrenching march through France's Belleau Wood, which Vidor later dubbed "a ballet of death."[8] As Charles Silver of New York's Museum of Modern Art has noted about the sequence, "The result is like nothing else in American silent film, save perhaps the rhythmic climaxes of *The Birth of a Nation* and *Intolerance*."[9]

After making two more films, a very moving version of *La Boheme* with Lillian Gish and John Gilbert and a swashbuckler called *Bardelys the Magnificent*, again with John Gilbert (both released in 1926), Vidor turned his professional energies almost exclusively to *The Crowd*.

Like other Hollywood directors such as Josef von Sternberg and John Ford, Vidor was greatly impressed by the work of F.W. Murnau, Fritz Lang, and other German directors who relied on the use of *expressionism*, the distortion of the image of reality in order to convey an interior feeling or idea. Wherever possible in the film, he wanted to use expressionistic visuals to show the relationship between the individual and the crowd and to highlight the tensions that inevitably exist between them. Throughout the production process, he worked closely and very productively with MGM's technical teams to create the visual effects that he wanted.

Having made four out his last five films with MGM's biggest male star John Gilbert, Vidor also took an entirely different casting approach for this effort: the lead would not be a well-known, charismatic star but someone who appeared very average and ordinary, someone who could easily be just one of the crowd. He eventually found the actor he was looking for in James Murray, an extra who had also played a few bit roles in films. He made a screen test of Murray, showed it to Thalberg, and the two agreed that Murray, as Vidor, recounted, "was one of the best natural actors we had ever had the good luck to encounter."[10] As the female lead, Vidor cast his new wife, MGM contract player Eleanor Boardman, a fine actress who had played significant roles in several films but had not quite achieved stardom.

* * *

It's curious that, when *The Crowd* premiered on February 28, 1928, the trade publication *Variety* described it as "a drab actionless story of ungodly length and apparently telling nothing."[11] In fairness to the film, this was not a typical review. Mordaunt Hall of *The New York Times* was much more in the critical mainstream at the time, calling it "substantial and worthy" and "a powerful analysis of a young couple's struggle for existence" while also praising the film's "inspired" camerawork and "masterly" depiction of certain scenes.[12] But the reviewer for *Variety* does make an interesting reveal: if you want to see a glamorous, tightly plotted Hollywood film that doesn't have much of a relationship to everyday life, *The Crowd* will probably *not* be your cup of tea.

After meeting on a blind date and then having the time of their lives at Coney Island, John (James Murray) and Mary (Eleanor Boardman) realize that they have fallen in love in *The Crowd* (MGM/Photofest).

The Crowd begins with John Sims's birth in 1900 on July 4, the most American day of the year. Thrilled and overwhelmed, John's father tells the doctor who's just helped with the delivery, "There's a little man the world is going to hear from all right, Doctor. I'm going to give him every opportunity."

At age 12, however, John's father dies unexpectedly, and John is told, "be brave now, little man."

Nine years later, a 21-year-old John, who has now braved tragedy and struggle without a father, arrives in New York filled with hope.

"You've got to be good in that town if you want to beat the crowd," another man tells him as the two survey the city.

"Maybe," John replies, "but all I want is an opportunity."

John finds a clerical job where he spends spare moments thinking of ad slogans and is studying at nights to improve his professional prospects, when he meets Mary, another clerical worker, on a blind date. Along with another couple, they are heading to Brooklyn's Coney Island amusement park. He and Mary are immediately attracted to each other and on the subway ride back from Coney Island, John sees a magazine ad for a model home and tells Mary, "That's the home we're going to have, Honey, when my ship comes in."

Soon, John and Mary are married, go to Niagara Falls for their honeymoon, return to New York, and set up housekeeping in a small, very modest flat. Inevitably, however, there is real life to deal with. At Christmas, Mary's mother and two brothers show their displeasure with John, leading to a disastrous evening in which John and Mary fight but soon make up. The following April, after numerous frustrations associated with financial struggle and other issues mount up, the two fight again. After John leaves for work, Mary calls him back to say to him what she wanted to say before their fight: that she is having a baby. Again, the tone changes. John, overwhelmed by the news, promises, "From now on I'm going to treat you different, dearest."

In October, the baby, John Sims, Jr., is born. As John and Mary absorb the magnitude of the event, John says, "This is all I've needed to make me try harder, dear. I'll be somebody now. I promise."

The next visual we see is an intertitle that reads, "During the next five years, two eventful things happened to the Simses. A baby sister was born … and John received an $8 raise."

Soon, however, more things do happen. First, John receives news that he has won a $500 prize for an advertising slogan. He buys presents for Mary and their two children, and Mary looks at all the bills this prize money will pay. Both are ecstatic. But, as they call their two children in so they can share the news with them, an oncoming truck hits their excited daughter. Soon, she is dead, and John and Mary are devastated. Sinking into a deep depression, John suddenly quits his job. Eventually, he realizes that he must find a new one and starts several, only to quit each very quickly. Nothing, apparently, is good enough for him. His frustrated brothers-in-law even offer him a position for the sake of Mary and their son, but again John's pride keeps him from accepting what he considers a "charity" job. Finally, Mary has had enough and makes plans to leave. John, spiraling down even farther, considers suicide, but, in one of the film's most moving scenes, changes his mind when his young son assures him that he still believes in him.

That's enough to get John to change. He gets a job as juggler who wears a clown outfit and walks up and down the street with a sandwich board advertising a bar and grill: a job he would have never considered before. As Mary is leaving, he tells her his news—and that he will not be leaving this job—and asks her and their son to go to a vaudeville show with him that evening. Still in love with him despite his flaws, she agrees, and we see the three in the theater enjoying the entertaining respite from life's many struggles.

Then, as film historian Tim Dirks eloquently writes, "In an audacious, pull-back overhead trolley shot, the camera pulls away from their row in the center, further and further until they are lost and disappear in the midst of a sea of laughing faces in the audience's crowd—indistinguishable from everyone else. They cannot escape the crowd, but now, they are protected by their love for each other and the anonymity of the surrounding masses. There's still hope that they can adjust to the painful experiences they have had and enjoy a life together."[13]

* * *

The Crowd would be a daring film for a major Hollywood studio to make at any time, but it was especially daring for the late 1920s. In an era when glamor and escapism were fashionable and very few Hollywood films depicted the daily trials and tribulations of ordinary people with such unflinching realism, *The Crowd* must have been difficult for many people (in addition to that reviewer from *Variety* mentioned earlier) to absorb, much less appreciate.

The film also probes into one subject many viewers must have found deeply disturbing: the dark side of the American Dream, the stark realities that often get in the way of fulfilling the dream's implicit promise. In the 1920s, this subject was just beginning to be explored in the literary world in the work of Sinclair Lewis, F. Scott Fitzgerald, Edward Arlington Robinson, and other writers. Soon, during the brutal economic times of the 1930s, more films such as William Wellman's moving 1933 drama *Wild Boys of the Road* would start exploring the subject. In recent years, of course, this subject remains a film staple in offerings as diverse as 1999's *American Beauty,* 2006's *The Pursuit of Happyness* and *Little Miss Sunshine,* 2013's *The Wolf of Wall Street,* and 2020's *Minari*. But, for 1928 film audiences with little to no experience seeing the American Dream questioned and challenged in such a way, *The Crowd* must have seemed like something akin to an attack on their religion.

Today, of course, audiences may be more skeptical about the American Dream's promise of opportunity for all than audiences were in 1928. But the steady flow of dream-themed films that continues to this day also suggests that this subject still resonates deeply with us—that, to varying degrees, many of us see some of John, Mary, and their struggles in our own lives. In turn, this continued relevance, along with Vidor's fresh, probing, clear-eyed treatment, enables *The Crowd* to speak across the decades with a forcefulness and urgency relatively few other silent films can still manage.

In addition to telling its story in such an honest, uncompromising way, *The Crowd* reinforces its thematic points with expressionistic visuals that are often startlingly compelling. One example is the scene when the 12-year-old John enters his home, learns that his father has died, and, as a crowd of people watch from below, climbs up what appears of be an unusually long, formidable flight of stairs. Visually, the enormity of the situation is underscored. A 12-year-old boy must face the reality that his loving father, the person who had promised to give him "every opportunity," has suddenly died and will no longer be able to give him anything. Another example—and perhaps one of the most famous film sequences of the silent era—is the montage of New York that occurs immediately after John first takes in the city, is warned that he will have to be good to "beat the crowd," and says that all he wants is "an opportunity." First, we see a barrage of street shots showing huge numbers of people, automobiles, and buses bustling here and there. Repeatedly, the shots of crowds of people dissolve into different, then more different people. We also see long shots of the city, emphasizing its enormity. Then, the camera begins to pan up an immense office building. Up it goes, floor after floor. Finally, it turns and moves into one window on one floor far from the ground. Once inside, we see a huge open office filled with clerks at their desks. There seem to be scores of these people, all sitting at the exact same kind of desk, all desks evenly spaced from one other, all clerks appearing to be doing the same or similar kinds of work. The camera keeps moving in across this sea of desks, and at last it comes to one where John Sims (now also known as number 137) sits. The impact is devastating. This young man, so filled with hopes and dreams, now appears to be little more a just another ant in an ant colony of seven million inhabitants, just another non-descript face in a colossal crowd.[14]

The film's visuals are excellent at conveying the brighter sides of life as well. When John and Mary enjoy their date at Coney Island, for example, the non-stop action and almost delirious pacing of some scenes are very effective at underscoring the joyous, giddy energy John and Mary feel as both realize that they are falling in love.

Another highlight of *The Crowd* is the acting, especially the outstanding performances of James Murray and Eleanor Boardman as John and Mary. At a time when over-acting often passed for intense or passionate acting, both brought exceptional craftsmanship and emotional integrity to their roles. Boardman is wonderful at underplaying a woman who feels both deep love for her husband along with gnawing frustration with his inability to make good on his many promises. There are moments when she shows great subtlety and sophistication in silent screen pantomime. One excellent example is the scene in which she indicates to the audience that she is pregnant simply by moving her hand close to her stomach and indicating her awareness of this with her face. Murray clearly turned out to be the great "natural" actor that both Vidor and Irving Thalberg saw in their initial screen test. Only in his mid-twenties and with no prior experience playing a role this large or demanding, he conveys the many sides of John—from the fun-loving, good-natured family man to the despairing, broken survivor of a profound personal tragedy—with exceptional skill, honesty, and clarity of purpose. A fine example of his work is the scene late in the film when John considers suicide and then changes his mind when his young son tells him he still believes in him. In lesser hands, this could have turned into absolute hokum. But Murray gives the scene an authenticity that still rings true nearly a century after it was filmed. There are no histrionics or affectations here; there is only pure acting.

For each of these fine actors, however, *The Crowd* would be the highpoint in an abbreviated film career. Boardman made several more films and, after divorcing Vidor in 1931, retired from acting altogether in 1935. In 1940, she remarried and lived a very private life until her death at 93 in 1991. In great demand after *The Crowd*, Murray's film career quickly fell apart because of alcoholism, and, by the mid-1930s, he was back working as an extra and playing bit parts. Vidor often told the story of approaching Murray in 1934 as the actor was panhandling on the street with an offer to play the lead in his upcoming film *Our Daily Bread*. After Vidor diplomatically advised Murray that, if he wanted the role, he would have to stop drinking and lose weight, Murray angrily rejected the offer. Two years later, Murray drowned in New York's Hudson River. It was never determined whether his death was an accident or a suicide. He was 35 years old.

As *The Crowd* was in production, Vidor mentioned to Thalberg that, while he thought the critics would look favorably on the film, he also thought that, because of its subject matter and approach, it would not be popular with audiences and lose money at the box office. Thalberg assured him not to worry because MGM could certainly afford "a few experimental projects."[15] While these words offered some comfort to the director, Vidor undoubtedly felt much greater relief when the film eventually grossed well over $1 million at the box office, about twice the cost of production. *The Crowd* was by no means a commercial hit on the scale that *The Big Parade* had been, but it wasn't a commercial flop, either.

* * *

After making *The Crowd*, Vidor made two more silent films, comedies called *The Patsy* and *Show People*, both starring the very talented Marion Davies, with whom Vidor had often socialized at newspaper publisher William Randolph Hearst's celebrated "castle" in San Simeon, California.[16] (Both films were also released in 1928 and are discussed briefly in Chapter 14 of this book.) Then he and Boardman took an extended vacation in France.

One day in Paris, he noticed headline in a copy of *Variety* that read: "Pix Industry Goes 100 Percent for Sound."[17] Treating the news as if it were a summons to take up a formidable new challenge, he and Boardman headed back to Hollywood and the strange new world of talking pictures. "I was excited, but greatly saddened," he later recalled. "I realized that so much magic would disappear from the screen. I also realized that new techniques would have to be discovered, invented, and established.... The dragon of sound must be met head-on and conquered."[18]

Vidor adapted to talking pictures with the same kind of energetic, innovative spirit with which he approached so many other challenges in his life. Over the next 30 years, he directed 29 feature films for MGM, Warner Brothers, Paramount, independent producers Samuel Goldwyn and David O. Selznick, and other organizations. Just a few of his notable sound film efforts include 1929's *Hallelujah*, 1931's *Street Scene* and *The Champ*, 1932's *Bird of Paradise* (when he became involved with Elizabeth Hill, a scriptwriter who eventually became his third wife), 1934's *Our Daily Bread* (which Vidor envisioned as a sequel to *The Crowd*), 1937's *Stella Dallas* (featuring a memorable Oscar-nominated performance by Barbara Stanwyck), 1938's *The Citadel*, 1946's *Duel in the Sun* (with Gregory Peck, Jennifer Jones, and a cast of thousands), 1949's *The Fountainhead* (with Gary Cooper and Patricia Neal), and 1956's *War and Peace* (with Audrey Hepburn and Henry Fonda). Before leaving MGM in 1944, he was also given occasional uncredited directing assignments. Perhaps the most noteworthy of these was directing the Kansas scenes in the 1939 classic *The Wizard of Oz*, in which Judy Garland sings *Over the Rainbow*. Beginning with *The Crowd*, Vidor was also nominated for the Best Director Academy Award five times but never won.[19] He did, however, receive an Academy Honorary Award in 1979 for his many achievements and contributions to the film industry.

In 1959, after making the critically panned but financially successful Biblical epic *Solomon and Sheba*, Vidor retired from commercial filmmaking. He was still receiving offers to direct films, but he cited his age (65 at the time) and a growing desire to concentrate on smaller, more personal projects as his main reasons for stepping aside. One of Vidor's later personal projects was developing a biographical film called *The Actor* about James Murray, who had been so brilliant in *The Crowd* but whose troubled life and early death had long haunted him. In the 1970s, Vidor wrote a script and then sought financing for the film, but his efforts ultimately proved unsuccessful.

Always a thoughtful and articulate speaker and conversationalist, Vidor was occasionally interviewed later in his life for television documentaries about Hollywood, especially as it was during the late silent and early sound eras. One excellent example is the 13-part 1980 British documentary called *Hollywood: A Celebration of the American Silent Film* produced by Kevin Brownlow and David Gill. Featured in several episodes of the series, Vidor describes his silent film experiences with great fondness and some sadness as he recalls the end of an art form that brought the world together through the interplay of the universal languages of pantomime and music—an art form he had grown up with and then taken to new heights.

On November 1, 1982, Vidor died of a heart attack at his ranch in Paso Robles, California. He was 88 years old. The previous weekend, he and his long-ago lover and longtime friend actress Colleen Moore had driven to the Hearst Castle to watch home movies made when they had been guests there 60 years earlier.

* * *

Although King Vidor made many fine films between 1929 and his retirement from commercial filmmaking in 1959, he made his most impressive mark during the silent era. With the decline in quality of D.W. Griffiths' films in the late 1920s, one can even make a credible case that, during the final four or five years of silent films, Vidor was Hollywood's best director. Two of the best proof points for this assertion are *The Big Parade* and *The Crowd*. Both are undeniable masterpieces, brilliantly conceived and executed, brimming with integrity and humanity, and delving deeply into themes that resonate with audiences today. Of the two, *The Crowd*—because of its stunning visual innovation, uncompromising emotional honesty, and exceptional lead turns by Murray and Boardman—probably deserves the edge. Not only is it one of the two or three best American films released in 1928, but it is also one of the best silent films ever made—American or otherwise.

6

The End of an Amazing Run
Harold Lloyd and Speedy

One day in early 1929, Harold Lloyd, whose immensely popular silent comedy features had made him the most commercially successful film producer/star of the 1920s, was passing a movie theater in downtown Los Angeles when he heard raucous laughter coming from inside. Always fascinated by what struck people as funny, he went in. To his surprise, the reasons for the laughter had nothing to do with the sight gags he'd long used to delight film audiences. Instead, people were laughing at the most mundane of sounds—from eggs cooking on a griddle to ice clinking in a glass—coming from a short-subject comic talkie. "[I]t was a different medium now," he recalled years later. "Gags and comedy 'business' we wouldn't think of using were getting laughs...."[1]

Now deep into the editing phase of his latest silent feature, a comedy called *Welcome Danger*, Lloyd had a "Eureka!" moment. Seeing sound as a gift that could just possibly make his films even funnier, he confided to his associates, "I think we've missed the boat on this."[2] Telling them to stop everything, he announced that they would turn *Welcome Danger* into a talkie. Then, for the next several months, that's exactly what they did: cutting some existing scenes from *Welcome Danger*, dubbing others, and shooting new scenes intended to delight audiences with witty dialogue as well as sight gags. The exercise was costly. Originally budgeted at slightly less than $600,000, the finished picture cost Lloyd nearly $1 million. At the box office, the gamble paid off. Audiences came in droves, and the movie racked up more than $3 million in receipts. Breathing a sigh of relief, Lloyd couldn't have been happier.

Lloyd had no idea of course, but his days as one of the reigning kings of film comedy were already behind him. A hit mostly because audiences were curious to hear Lloyd talk, *Welcome Danger* would eventually be regarded as one of his weakest efforts. Between 1930 and 1938, he would

Jane (Ann Christy, center left) and Harold (Harold Lloyd, center right) find a New York subway ride a little too crammed for comfort in one of many captivating scenes in Lloyd's last silent film, *Speedy* (cineclassico/Alamy Stock Photo).

produce and star in five more features, all of them major box-office disappointments. Then, at age 45, he would retire.

As the years passed, it became clear that the film Lloyd had made and starred in immediately before *Welcome Danger*, his comedy *Speedy* (which opened in theaters on April 7, 1928), would not only be his last silent, but also the last great Harold Lloyd film. Coming at the end of an amazing run of silent classics—which also include 1922's *Grandma's Boy*, 1923's *Safety Last!*, 1924's *Girl Shy*, and 1925's *The Freshman*—*Speedy* is in many ways the best of the batch. Filmed on location in New York, it brilliantly uses the city as a backdrop for story in ways that might make even Woody Allen envious. In terms of both the quality and quantity of his signature visual gags, it is probably his most inventive film (which is saying quite a lot). Like the iconic skyscraper climb in *Safety Last!*, which features Lloyd hanging from clock hands high above the city streets, or the spectacular chase near the end of *Girl Shy*, it has a breathtaking final sequence with hired thugs chasing a horse-drawn trolley through the city's crowded streets. Adding to all of this, baseball great Babe Ruth makes a delightful supporting appearance as an anxious fare on one of Harold's wild taxi rides. From beginning to end, *Speedy* is Lloyd in top form.

Over the years, people have offered numerous explanations for Lloyd's inability to remain a popular movie star. Of these, two seem the most plausible.

One was his highly visual comic style. He and the people he worked with were brilliant at developing and extending visual gags with, as film writer Peter Kobel has noted, "the clockwork precision of a Swiss watch,"[3] and engineering daring, seemingly perilous action sequences. In the unreal world of a silent film, these could be extremely effective, both delighting audiences and ratcheting up suspense to almost unbearable levels. Beginning with *Welcome Danger*, however, Lloyd focused on finding what he liked to think of as the right balance of visual and verbal humor in his films. Instead of complementing his visual gags, the addition of sound often proved a distraction that lessened their impact. While Lloyd's voice was perfectly fine, he also lacked the flair for verbal comedy of other contemporary comedians such as W.C. Fields or Groucho Marx.

The other reason had less to do with talkies than with Lloyd himself. As much as Chaplin or Keaton, he was (from the early 1920s on) a true auteur. While he generously gave others credit for writing and directing his films, everyone involved knew that these were first, last, and always Harold Lloyd projects. The stories and particularly the iconic "glasses" character he played (often named "Harold") were all extensions of his sensibility, preoccupations, and worldview. For the 1920s, this was a perfect fit. Lloyd, who saw himself as the embodiment of the American Dream, played characters like himself: optimistic, resourceful everymen who were determined to succeed and, with success, get the girl. They were, if you will, Horatio Alger heroes with charm as well as grit. Lloyd was proud of this, too. He felt that, unlike Chaplin's Tramp or Keaton's "Great Stone Face" persona, his characters were more real and easier for audiences to relate to. As film historian David Thomson has noted, this made him "the least deviant of comedians, a man who never dreamed of being out of the ordinary."[4] By the 1930s, however, the Great Depression had changed much about America. People found it far more difficult to relate to the Lloyd character's unflagging belief that, if you were smart enough and worked hard enough, success was right around the corner. Unsurprisingly, it was Chaplin's plucky but hard-luck Tramp who seemed to resonate better with audiences during this time.

* * *

In addition to being the title of his last silent film, "Speedy" was also Lloyd's lifelong nickname. Born in Burchard, Nebraska, on April 20, 1893, he gained a reputation as a boy for being lightning fast at just about everything from figuring out complex problems to mastering, and consistently winning, games. From a young age, he was also drawn to amateur theater. His desire to act, he once recalled, "goes back to the first time I can remember knowing what an actor was."[5]

In 1910, after Lloyd's father had failed at several business ventures, he and Lloyd's mother divorced, and father and son moved to San Diego, then to Los Angeles, where young Harold tried breaking into the movies. These, as Lloyd recalled in the 1960s, were very hard times. "It was during those days ... that I hit rock bottom," he recounted. "I was literally down to one nickel. I bought six doughnuts with it, and they were the finest doughnuts I ever ate in my life. I went 24 hours on them, and then I bobbed up again with some salary that somebody owed me."[6]

Soon, though, he began getting more extra work and small parts in movie shorts. He also met Hal Roach, another movie extra with high aspirations, and the two started working together on comic one-reelers (usually about 10 minutes in length) with Lloyd starring and Roach producing and often directing. Since most of the other movie comics at the time were imitating Charlie Chaplin's tramp, Lloyd and Roach decided to follow suit. What followed over the next couple of years were scores of one- and two-reel comedies with characters such as Willie Work and, most notably, Lonesome Luke.

But one day Lloyd, who made a lifetime habit of listening to and studying audiences, overheard a boy in a theater as his Lonesome Luke appeared on screen. "Oh, here's that fellow who tries to do like Chaplin," the boy said.[7]

The experience shook Lloyd to the core. "[T]hat settled it for me," he recalled. "I went back and told Roach I was going to quit. I wasn't going on forever being a third-rate imitator of anybody, even a genius like Chaplin."[8]

Soon he and Roach began to develop a new comic persona, one that would catapult Lloyd from Chaplin imitator to great comedian. Taking a different approach from other comedians, Lloyd wanted to develop a more natural character, one people could more easily relate to. And, when he put on his signature glasses for the first time, things quickly fell into place. His character was more like the boy next door: an average fellow determined to overcome various obstacles, succeed in the world, and, yes, find love. To make these characters more appealing to audiences, he often gave them certain vulnerabilities they had to struggle with throughout each story, such as a fear of bullies, a stutter, or extreme shyness with women. The glasses subtly reinforced these vulnerabilities, endearing his characters to audiences even more.

6. The End of an Amazing Run

In 1917, Lloyd introduced his "glasses" character in a short called *Over the Fence*, and he and Roach were off and running. Now they were churning out scores of short films each year, nearly all of them successful with audiences.

Then, in August 1919, Lloyd's promising career nearly ended just as it seemed to be taking off. A mock bomb he was holding for a publicity photo shoot turned out to be real, and it exploded in his right hand. The hand was severely injured (he lost both his thumb and forefinger), his face was badly cut and burned, and for a while it seemed that he would be blind for life. "The months that followed were so tough that I can't speak about them without turning cold," he said. "Up to that time, I'd led a normal, carefree, happy life. I'd known discouragement, poverty, worry, [and] hard work. But nothing mattered because the future was rosy, I was young and strong, and everything was fun. With that explosion I knew real suffering for the first time."[9]

After recovering for nine months, however, Lloyd's sight returned, the wounds on his face healed, and a special glove was fitted to his right hand to mask the loss of his thumb and forefinger. He was ready to work again.

He and Roach collaborated on scores more shorts until 1922, when, working on a short called *Grandma's Boy*, Lloyd and director Fred Newmeyer couldn't stop shooting. The story about a boy who must overcome cowardice was far more character-driven than any of their previous films and, clocking at roughly an hour, much longer. When Roach objected to an early cut, saying that it just wasn't funny, Lloyd countered, saying, "Hal, this has got heart. It's different from what we've ever done. It's much finer." After arguing for an hour, the two agreed to put some laughs into the picture but not compromise the story's basic premise. "I wouldn't let go of one inch of it," Lloyd noted emphatically.[10]

The result was an enormous hit. Produced for less than $95,000, *Grandma's Boy* made $1.1 million at the box office. From this point on, Lloyd would focus almost exclusively on making feature-length films.

Lloyd often divided his best films into two categories: character-driven such as *Grandma's Boy* and thrill-driven such as his next breakthrough film, 1923's *Safety Last!*.

Featuring a rich mix of gags that remain wonderfully fresh today and edge-of-your-seat thrills, *Safety Last!* is one of the great silent film comedies. The highlight, one of the iconic sequences in all of film, follows the Lloyd character as he scales a tall city building and, at one point in the effort, dangles high over the streets from the hands of a huge clock near the top of the building as the clock is coming apart. This sequence is a vivid testament to the great creativity and wit that went into the best silent film comedy, and seeing it for the first time on the big screen as part of a large theatrical audience is an unforgettable filmgoing experience.

After *Safety Last!*, Lloyd and Roach amicably parted ways, Lloyd founding his own production company and Roach enjoying a long and successful career producing a wide variety of films and television shows. Roach's films ranged from Laurel and Hardy and Our Gang comedy shorts to major features such as 1937's *Topper* with Cary Grant and the acclaimed 1939 production of John Steinbeck's *Of Mice and Men* with Burgess Meredith and Lon Chaney, Jr. In all, he also produced thousands of hours of television shows including the entire runs of actress Gale Storm's two popular situation comedy series, *My Little Margie* (1952–5) and *The Gale Storm Show* (1956–60).

Although Roach was enormously influential in Lloyd's development, Lloyd, now the sole producer of his films, pushed ahead without missing a beat. In the next two years, he made four more extremely successful features. Two of them, 1924's *Girl Shy* and 1925's *The Freshman*, are especially well regarded both for their many clever and well developed gags and for how well they integrate many of the character-driven elements of *Grandma's Boy* with the brilliantly rendered thrills of *Safety Last!*. Both, for example, have fairly complex versions of the "glasses" character along with very elaborate, visually thrilling finishes. The Harold character's frantic quest to stop an ill-conceived wedding before it's too late in *Girl Shy* is especially noteworthy. A chase sequence involving various vehicles from a trolley car to a police motorcycle, it is filled with invention and excitement.

* * *

After two more hits, 1926's *For Heaven's Sake* and 1927's *The Kid Brother*, Lloyd made *Speedy*, which film historian Jeffrey Vance and Lloyd's granddaughter Suzanne have called "a superb valedictory to the silent era."[11]

Speedy is the story of Harold "Speedy" Swift, a cocky young New Yorker who is constantly losing jobs yet always confident that he can quickly get a new one. Speedy also loves the Yankees baseball team, his girlfriend Jane (Ann Christy), and her kindly grandfather "Pop" Dillon (Bert Woodruff), who drives the last horse-drawn trolley in the bustling city.

The plot—involving a greedy corporation's efforts to close down Pop's trolley line and Speedy's resourceful efforts to save the business—is little more than a framework for Lloyd to hang the scores of gags he throws at us during the film. But this is fine, because this film is much more about fast action and Lloyd's often ingenious and constantly developing sight gags than it is about intricate plotting or penetrating character development.

One curious characteristic about *Speedy* is its structure. Unlike other Lloyd films such as *Safety Last!* or *Girl Shy*, which begin slowly and build to thrilling final sequences, *Speedy* is more episodic, with thrilling sequences sprinkled throughout. While many of these are highly engaging and entertaining, three in particular stand out.

The first is Speedy and Jane's date at Coney Island, which is filled with Lloyd's clever gags and brimming with an unabashed exuberance for life. One early highlight is the couple's trip on the subway to the fabled amusement park. With all the nearby seats filled, Speedy, ever the gentleman, devises a clever way to secure a seat for Jane. He attaches a string to a dollar bill, drops the bill on the floor in front of a seated passenger, and, when the passenger gets up to grab the dollar, Speedy, in one fluid motion, gently pushes Jane into the seat and retrieves the dollar by pulling back on the string. Next, he tries the same trick to get a seat for himself, but this time, in typical Lloyd fashion, it backfires and he must continue to stand. Once at Coney Island, Lloyd begins with establishing shots that show off some of the fascinating and beautifully shot location footage captured by his cinematographer, Walter Lundin. Then, he follows with scenes of Speedy and Jane in the midst of all this, the pair enjoying several of Coney Island's thrill rides and side show attractions. Later, we see Coney Island after dark, with all its exciting amusement park lights, in some spectacular night shots. Along the way, we are also treated to a seemingly endless supply of Lloyd sight gags, all growing naturally out of the situation and many of them building and building in ingenious ways. One of the best is when Speedy, who sees himself as absolutely upright and normal, passes a fish stand, and, without his knowledge, a live crab falls into his coat pocket. As Speedy and Jane continue to walk through the crowd, the crab is incorrigible, pinching people on their backsides and at one point even snatching a woman's nightgown from her purse. Speedy, of course, is blamed for all of this bad behavior without understanding why so many people are angry with him, and the humor builds as he encounters person after person who reacts to him as if he were a pervert. As critic James Agee once noted, "Lloyd was outstanding even among the master craftsmen at setting up a gag clearly, culminating and getting out of it deftly, and linking it smoothly to the next."[12] This cleverly conceived and brilliantly developed gag is an excellent example of this key facet of Lloyd's talent.

A second standout sequence is when Speedy, now working as a cab driver, picks up baseball great Babe Ruth as a fare. The Babe needs to get to Yankee Stadium for a game and asks Speedy to get him there quickly. Speedy complies, but he is also so mesmerized by the Babe that he keeps looking back starry-eyed at his famous fare and chatting rather than paying attention to traffic. At first, Ruth is flattered, but he quickly realizes the danger he is in and begs Speedy to pay more attention to the traffic than to him. The tension builds until Speedy finally gets Ruth to the ballpark—to the Babe's amazement—all in one piece. Ruth, who was a good actor and appeared in several other films (most notably 1942's *Pride of the Yankees*) plays off Lloyd quite well here, his fear steadily building as his clueless driver repeatedly just misses crashing the cab. For fans of old-time baseball, these scenes also provide an added treat. Just as Speedy drops Ruth off at Yankee Stadium, a tall man walks behind the cab, smiles toward the camera, and then, in just a second or two, is gone. The man, making a cameo appearance within Ruth's cameo, is Ruth's famous teammate, Lou Gehrig.

The third standout sequence is the film's final chase. In it, thugs working for the corporation pursue Speedy as he drives Pop's horse-drawn trolley across town to preserve Pop's right to his trolley route. As with other fine moments in Lloyd films, the combination of thrills and cleverly developed gags keeps viewers on the edge of their seats. Here, one unexpected thrill, when the trolley crashes against a steel beam, was also unexpected for the filmmakers. During shooting, the trolley, quite by accident, crashed. Rather than reshooting the scene, however, Lloyd chose to keep the crash in the film and, with his writers, rewrote the scene on the spot to show Speedy's resourcefulness as he replaces the trolley's broken wheel with a nearby manhole cover. The decision helped to make the chase even more engaging and suspenseful.

While gags are what people most often talk about when discussing Harold Lloyd films, Lloyd's acting is definitely worth noting as well. Although not as balletic as Chaplin in his physical movements, he is exceptionally agile and acrobatic (perhaps a bit like a comic Gene Kelly as opposed to Chaplin's comic Fred Astaire). He is also quite good at communicating with facial expressions and other physical gestures precisely what is happening inside his characters' heads at the moment. His reactions to many of the confounding and sometimes bizarre situations he finds himself in are always very real, too. This ability—to respond to the extraordinary in an honest, grounded, and relatable way—is part of Lloyd's lasting appeal. Although silent films are often disparaged for their "hammy" overacting, Lloyd rarely over-did and could often convey subtle and conflicting emotions with great skill. As an actor in *Speedy*, Lloyd is consistently excellent.

In addition to Speedy, Jane, and Pop, another of the main characters in *Speedy* is the city of New York in 1927. At the time, nearly all films used stock footage for establishing shots if the location was any place other than the greater Los Angeles area or one of the nearby deserts. But Lloyd, who believed that realism was always better (and could afford large-scale location shooting), took his crew and several of his cast members to New York for much of the filming. Originally scheduled at four weeks, the location work lasted 12 weeks. The result, while costly, was clearly worth it. In fact, the extra shooting helps to make *Speedy*, in addition to its other assets, a fascinating visual record of the New York of the time, capturing numerous sights from the Brooklyn Bridge and Times Square to Central Park and Greenwich Village. More than merely serving as interesting travelogue, however, many of these shots also reinforce meaning in the story in striking ways. The shots of Coney Island at night, for example, are beautiful and enchanting, reflecting the romantic feelings of Speedy and Jane on their date. The long shot of Speedy driving the horse-drawn trolley at full speed through New York's iconic Washington Square Arch and adjoining area is dramatic and dazzling, enhancing the intensity of the chase. As Speedy drops Babe Ruth off at the ballpark, we are looking at the real Yankee Stadium in the background, underscoring that, yes, this is the real Babe Ruth at his real place of work. For decades now, Woody Allen, Martin Scorsese, and other directors have captured the many facets and moods of New York City in very creative and exciting ways. Decades before they were even making films, however, Lloyd and cinematographer Walter Lundin had already beaten them to it.

* * *

Unlike many of his silent film colleagues whose careers essentially ended with the coming of sound, Lloyd's life never took a tragic turn. An excellent businessman, he invested well and lived on a magnificent 15-acre estate in the Benedict Canyon section of Beverly Hills that he affectionately named Greenacres. Impressive even among movie stars' homes, it included such features as a 44-room mansion; a small golf course; several outbuildings; spacious, immaculately kept walking gardens; and a 900-foot canoe run. Lloyd was also happily married to actress Mildred Davis, his co-star in the late 1910s and early 1920s, and loved being a doting father to their three children. Their 46-year marriage lasted until her death in 1969. After an ill-fated return to films in 1947 to star in the Preston Sturges comedy *The Sin of Harold Diddlebock*, Lloyd more or less accepted the role of a grand old man of the industry. In his later years, he received numerous film recognitions, including an Academy Honorary Award in 1953 for his work and a standing ovation at the 1962 Cannes Film Festival for a feature-length compilation of scenes from his films called *Harold Lloyd's World of Comedy*. In addition, he became quite involved in other activities ranging from the Shriners, for whom he worked to raise money for 22 hospitals, to both color and 3-D photography, at which he became quite accomplished. Long after Lloyd's death, his granddaughter,

Suzanne Lloyd, supervised the publication of two books featuring his photography.

Harold "Speedy" Lloyd died of prostate cancer on March 8, 1971, less than two years after Mildred passed away. He was 77.

* * *

When evaluating Lloyd's films today, two seemingly contradictory realities stand out.

One is the incredible freshness and vitality of his gags and thrill sequences. They hold up so well, quite simply, because they are so good: cleverly conceived, arising naturally from the situation, brilliantly extended and developed, precisely timed, and often also serving to provide insightful glimpses into character. When seen on a big screen with a large, engaged audience, *Speedy* and Lloyd's other top-tier films can be among the most exhilarating silent comedy viewing experiences a person can have. As actor Jack Lemmon, who became friends with Lloyd in the 1950s, once wrote, "Harold Lloyd was one of the most charismatic innovators of film comedy, an excellent actor, and a consummate filmmaker. His films should be seen, not just for their historical value, but for their sheer pleasure."[13]

The other is Lloyd's continued obscurity relative to the two people he is most often compared to, Charlie Chaplin and Buster Keaton. If his films remain so fresh and vital, we ask, why isn't he—and why aren't his films—better known?

A key reason may be Lloyd's long-time reluctance to make his films available for television and then his estate's reluctance to make them available for home viewing on video. He felt strongly that this compromised the viewing experience. That may be true, but the result was that, for decades, very few people actually saw his films. Later, in the early 1980s, silent film historians Kevin Brownlow and David Gill produced an excellent television documentary on Lloyd and his work called, *Harold Lloyd: The Third Genius*. While this aroused great interest in Lloyd's films among viewers, very few of these films were actually available for home use at the time.

Another key reason may be critical neglect. Why, we ask, have critics, who routinely gush over Chaplin and Keaton's comedies, remained more aloof toward Lloyd's work? Film historian Richard Griffith has proposed one theory. As he has written, "It's the optimism which chiefly sticks in the highbrow craw and accounts for the continued fundamental lack of interest in him and the continued rating of him below Chaplin, Keaton, and even [fellow silent film comedian Harry] Langdon."[14]

In an age when film critics and audiences tend to prefer darker fare and Lloyd's optimism may seem naïve, Griffith makes an interesting point.

6. The End of an Amazing Run

As Peter Kobel has noted, however, while Lloyd's "optimism and aggressive pursuit of success epitomize the [1920s], they are really timeless American values."[15] We may live in an era when pessimistic sensibilities and stories resonate with film critics and audiences more deeply than Lloyd's happy, bustling comedies. But we may also concede that, even today, there is a bit of Harold Lloyd in every young person who aspires to become a sports star, launch a Silicon Valley start-up, or even find love. Lloyd's brand of optimism may be out of fashion, but it is always alive and kicking. In film comedy, Lloyd may still be its foremost proponent and practitioner. As he said late in his life, "It has been amazing to me that these comedies can still strike a responsive note of laughter with audiences of all ages and in all parts of the world. Laughter is the universal language. It establishes a common identity among people—regardless of other differences. It is the sweetest sound in the whole world."[16]

7

In a Blaze of Windswept Glory

Buster Keaton and Steamboat Bill, Jr.

As one of Buster Keaton's biographers, Edward McPherson, astutely put it, it was "an offer he couldn't refuse."[1]

The silent film comic first heard that changes were afoot that would dramatically affect his professional life in late 1927 as he was wrapping up principal photography on his latest feature, *Steamboat Bill, Jr.* Joseph Schenck, who had produced Keaton's films since 1920, announced that he was getting out of independent production to work in an executive role at United Artists. Schenck also wanted to take care of his star and had arranged a deal for Keaton to join MGM, where he was assured that the comedian would be well paid and have ample access to the abundant resources the studio had to offer.

After some negotiating, the "offer," a two-year contract with MGM, emerged. For his services, Keaton would receive $3000 a week, making him the studio's third highest paid star. In addition, MGM would put one-fourth of each of his film's profits into the comedian's company, Buster Keaton Productions. Finally, he would receive consultation rights on scripts, directorial choices, and other key facets of his films. In many ways, the terms seemed quite generous.

In return, however, there was one big consideration. Although Keaton could consult on his films, the all-important "final say," a power he had pretty much had during his years working with Schenck, would now reside with an MGM-appointed producer.

In hopes of retaining some independence and creative control over his films, Keaton explored other options. But he made no headway. Films were becoming more expensive to make, and, if talking pictures eventually prevailed (as growing numbers of people expected they would), costs would go up even more. The big film conglomerates such as Paramount

7. In a Blaze of Windswept Glory

and MGM clearly had the upper hand. The number of independent producers such as Schenck was dwindling. For the independent, freewheeling Keaton, desirable options were dwindling as well. On January 26, 1928, he agreed to the offer he felt he couldn't refuse.

The change was enormous for Keaton. Since 1920, he had enjoyed unusual freedom creating films that featured his iconic "Great Stone Face" character: a sensible everyman who comes up with ingenious responses to the many challenges presented him in an absurd, chaotic, and sometimes hostile world. Soon, however, he found himself in a production role subordinate to people with far less imagination than he had and often little understanding of the value he could bring to a film. An artistic adventurer who reveled in stumbling onto nuggets of comic gold that frequently offered intriguing insights into human behavior and societal relationships, he now saw himself as a film industry equivalent to an assembly line worker. He became difficult to work with and started to drink heavily. Both his personal and professional lives fell apart, and it would take him years to return to at least some level of personal and professional stability and peace of mind. As he remarked in his later years, his decision to move to MGM was the worst mistake of his life.

As had been true for so many of Keaton's silent film colleagues, 1928 marked the end of his most productive and artistically successful years. Professionally, he would never again have the freedom or the resources at his disposal to make a true, top-to-bottom Buster Keaton film. He was only 32 years old when he signed the MGM contract, and, although he couldn't, even remotely, conceive of the thought at the time, nearly all the work he is remembered for today had already been done.

Yet, what a body of work it is! Between 1920's two-reel short *One Week* and 1928's feature-length *Steamboat Bill, Jr.*, Keaton starred in, directed or co-directed, and came up with most of the good ideas for 19 shorts and 10 feature films: efforts, as film critic Roger Ebert once boldly declared, "that make him, arguably, the greatest actor-director in the history of the movies."[2]

A crucial word here, as Ebert would have doubtlessly agreed, is "arguably." Many other film scholars would likely grant this title to Chaplin or Orson Welles over Keaton. But the fact remains that Keaton *is* held in exceptionally high regard today and that his standing is based almost entirely on his output during eight years beginning in 1920: an extraordinarily creative period when he and his team conceived of and orchestrated hundreds of inspired, often outlandish film moments from an underwater diver's surreal swordfight with a swordfish in 1924's *The Navigator* to the dazzling cyclone sequence in *Steamboat Bill, Jr.*

All this is certainly impressive. Yet, as writer Nicholas Barber has

Steamboat Bill, Sr. (Ernest Torrence) and his son Bill Jr. (Buster Keaton) have great trouble agreeing on a hat suitable for the younger Bill to wear as he takes on his new role on a Mississippi River paddle steamer in *Steamboat Bill, Jr.* (United Artists/Photofest).

noted, "[I]t's hard not to wince at the thought of what else this astonishing innovator might have achieved had he been permitted."[3]

* * *

Joseph Frank "Buster" Keaton, the vaudeville, film, and later television comic whose inventive physical stunts and deadpan facial expressions delighted audiences for more than 60 years, was born in tiny Piqua, Kansas, on October 4, 1895. His parents, Joe and Myra, were passing through town with their vaudeville act, a traveling show they owned and which for a time also featured the legendary escape artist and illusionist Harry Houdini. Young Joseph reportedly received the nickname Buster when, at the age of 18 months, he toppled down a flight of stairs, landed unscathed, and immediately shook off the fall. A family friend who saw this remarked in amazement, "He's a regular Buster!"[4] And the name stuck.

In 1899, when he was just three years old, young Buster joined his parents in the act. Largely knockabout comedy, much of the family's routine consisted of Buster's provoking his father to toss him into the scenery, the orchestra pit, and sometimes even the audience. From time to time, the

7. In a Blaze of Windswept Glory 91

family had to deal with charges of child abuse. Buster insisted throughout his life, however, that his father never hurt him and that the falls were safe because they were always executed with the proper stage techniques.

Buster quickly became the act's main attraction and stayed with it throughout his teens. After serving with the U.S. Army's 40th Infantry Division during World War I, he shifted his professional focus to films, initially working for comedian Roscoe "Fatty" Arbuckle as a co-star, assistant director, and gagman on 14 Arbuckle shorts from 1917 to 1920. Arbuckle, the most popular silent film comic during the 1910s and a mentor to Chaplin and Lloyd as well as Keaton, had an enormous impact on the young Buster. Rather than simply performing, Keaton threw himself into the entire filmmaking process, soaking up everything he could from Arbuckle and others about film comedy as well as other key aspects of filmmaking such as cinematography and editing. Through Arbuckle, he also met Schenck, who produced Arbuckle's films, suitably impressed him, and persuaded him to bankroll a new production unit, Buster Keaton Productions. By early 1920, with less than three years of filmmaking experience, Keaton was making his own movies.

After a false start, a short called *The High Sign* that Keaton filmed but did not release right away because he was dissatisfied with it, he saw a Ford Motor Company documentary about the modern wonders of pre-fabricated housing. Fascinated by the comic possibilities of spoofing the do-it-yourself housebuilding process, he went to work on a two-reel short called *One Week*. The film is the story of a just-married couple who receive a new house as a wedding present, are duly thrilled, go to the house's address, and to their surprise find an undeveloped lot cluttered with boxes filled with all the materials they need to build their house in just one week. The two gamely accept the challenge, often devising inspired solutions to problems that pop up, but, as we might also expect, numerous mishaps occur along the way and very little actually goes as planned.

Widely praised by critics and a hit with audiences when it was released in September 1920, *One Week* represented a major career turning point for Keaton. First, it put him on the map as an independent filmmaker with a distinctive sensibility and point of view. Second, it established the basic format he would develop and refine for the films he made over the next eight years. Following this format, each story begins slowly, introducing a love interest and a major challenge that the Buster character must tackle. Then, a series of related minor challenges, each of which the Buster character must also deal with, comes his way. After this, there is a big climatic sequence usually involving lots of action and great danger. These sequences could vary wildly, ranging from an on-foot, automobile, or railroad chase to an attack by fierce man-eating cannibals (as he stages in *The*

Navigator). Finally, the major challenge is resolved and Buster and his love can get on with their lives.

Another key aspect of Keaton's work is the unpredictability of his gags, which often delight audiences all the more by misleading them. An excellent early example comes from *One Week*. After building their house, the couple learn that they have built it on the wrong lot and must move it to the correct one, which is on the other side of nearby railroad tracks. They make the structure portable, and, as they are pulling the house across the railroad tracks with their car, their effort is stalled—they can't move the house any farther. Suddenly, they hear and then see an oncoming train. Terrified, they move out of the way, dreading the crash they envision coming. Then the train comes and passes right by because it is traveling on another set of tracks that lie just beyond the house. Seeing this, they both breathe a huge sigh of relief. A moment later, however, a train coming in the opposite direction roars right through the house, smashing it to smithereens.

After a series of mostly successful two-reel shorts, which also include the very clever 1922 release *Cops*, Keaton plunged into feature-length films in 1923 with the release of *Three Ages*, a send-up of D.W. Griffith's 1916 epic *Intolerance*, and *Our Hospitality*, a riff on the legendary feud between the Hatfields and the McCoys. Then, in 1924, he made two films that showed that he was quickly becoming a master of the longer, more complex storytelling form: *Sherlock, Jr.*, and *The Navigator*.

The first of these, *Sherlock, Jr.*, involves a lowly movie theater projectionist studying to become a detective who, in one sequence, falls asleep in the projection room and dreams that he actually steps from the theater into the film that is being shown. In the film, he assumes the role of Sherlock Jr., the world's greatest detective, solves a mystery involving the theft of a pearl necklace, saves the abducted heroine, and, after a hair-raising car chase, defeats the evildoers. The entire sequence, along with being brilliantly imagined, is excellently developed and executed. Over the years, it has received much praise, even provoking film historians Gerald Mast and Bruce F. Kawin to call *Sherlock, Jr.*, "one of the greatest movies about the movies themselves."[5]

As film enthusiasts may have also figured out, other filmmakers have occasionally appropriated this idea. A well-known example is the very direct "homage" to this sequence in Woody Allen's 1985 film *The Purple Rose of Cairo*. One wonders, too, if the *Sherlock, Jr.* sequence also played a role in inspiring James Thurber's classic 1939 short story about an ordinary man who constantly dreams of extraordinary exploits, *The Secret Life of Walter Mitty*.

Released six months after *Sherlock, Jr.*, *The Navigator* is another fresh and highly inventive effort. This time the story focuses on a wealthy, pampered young man and woman who find themselves alone on a ship set adrift in the Pacific Ocean. After struggling to learn how to take care of themselves (after relying on servants all of their lives), they find that the ship has grounded itself near a tropical island and is taking in water. So, to patch the hole, the man must put on a diver's suit and submerge himself in the water where he faces many challenges, including a combative swordfish. Once out of the water, he and the woman must then defend the ship against a tribe of attacking cannibals. Eventually overpowered, they flee to an empty native canoe. This soon capsizes and all they can do is cling to each other and a single life preserver as cannibals in other canoes come after them. Slowly, their heads sink into the ocean. But a few moments later, they reappear finding to their great good fortune that a surfacing submarine just beneath them is pushing them back up. They enter the submarine and escape the cannibals. Essentially two separate sequences, the underwater scenes and the scenes with the attacking cannibals, this final section of the film is yet another fine example of Keaton at his best: novel in both concept and execution, consistently inventive, unpredictable, and outlandish while also appearing to be marginally credible.

In 1926, Keaton made *The General*, the film he considered to be his masterpiece. Released in the U.S. in early 1927, it is based on an event that occurred during the U.S. Civil War when several pro–Union men hijacked a train named *The General* in Northern Georgia and headed for Chattanooga, Tennessee, on a mission to thwart Southern war efforts by doing as much damage as possible to the railroad line and the telegraph wires. Fearing that audiences would not accept Confederates as villains, Keaton changed the story to give it a Southern point of view. And he played a plucky young Georgian who, after being rejected to serve in the Confederacy, becomes involved in the proceedings in part to prove his courage to the Southern belle he loves.

There's no doubt that *The General* is Keaton's most ambitious film. In terms of its scope and all the resources put into its making, it verges on being truly epic in scale.

In many respects, it is also a major achievement in direction and production management. Its many large and complicated scenes are handled with great skill and authority. The various stunts (as was usually the case for Keaton) are cleverly conceived and—considering the difficulty of, and danger involved in, many of them—expertly and sometimes courageously executed. The story is less episodic and more unified than any of Keaton's previous films. Great effort was also put into giving the film as authentic a Civil War era look about it as possible.

With all of this in the film's favor, it must have been enormously disappointing to Keaton and Schenck when the film proved to be both a commercial and critical failure. Costing about $750,000 to make, its U.S. box-office receipts came to less than $500,000, a major financial setback. The initial reviews were also overwhelmingly negative. *Variety* bluntly stated "The result is a flop."[6] Mordaunt Hall of *The New York Times* wrote, "This is by no means [as] good as Mr. Keaton's previous efforts."[7] The *New York Herald Tribune* called it "long and tedious—the least-funny thing Buster Keaton has ever done."[8]

Since then, however, *The General* has been extensively reevaluated and has now become a darling of film critics and scholars worldwide. In fact, none other than Orson Welles once called it "the greatest comedy ever made ... and perhaps the greatest film ever made."[9] Today it is constantly ranked at or near the top of most of best films lists from the British Film Institute's *Sight and Sound Magazine*, the American Film Institute, and other organizations. In the prestigious *Sight and Sound* once-a-decade poll of international film critics, for example, it has been named one of the 10 greatest films of all time twice.

It's not uncommon for certain films to be panned upon initial release and then, over time, acknowledged as masterpieces (as *The Wind* has been), but it is difficult to see *The General* as simply another example of contemporary reviewers not getting it right. Although it is an impressively directed film with some good Keaton gags, *The General* is not especially funny or even engaging. It lacks the whimsy, charm, imaginative flights, and overall comic flair of *Sherlock, Jr.*, and other previous Keaton efforts. It drags during the railroad chase scenes, which are often tedious and repetitive. And, while dark comedies can be extremely funny, the scenes of young men dying in this film, especially during its climatic battle scenes, are not. Far from being the greatest comedy ever made, it isn't even the best example of Keaton's work.

(This is, of course, a minority opinion at odds, it seems, with just about everyone else who has written or spoken about the film except its 1927 reviewers. Those unfamiliar with *The General* who wish to learn more about Keaton and his work are encouraged to see the film and evaluate it for themselves.)

* * *

After starring in and co-directing 1927's lackluster *College*, the story of an academic type who tries to excel at college sports to impress a young co-ed who prefers athletes to bookworms, Keaton turned his sights on *Steamboat Bill, Jr.* Released on May 12, 1928, this film would be the last effort for Buster Keaton Productions and mark the end of the comic's successful eight-year partnership with producer Joseph Schenck.

7. In a Blaze of Windswept Glory

The story idea came from Charles Reisner, an actor/director who had worked with Chaplin and was signed to co-direct the film with Keaton. The screenplay was then developed by Carl Harbaugh, a veteran screenwriter and actor whose Hollywood career extended from the 1910s to the late 1950s.

As the film opens, William "Steamboat Bill" Canfield (Ernest Torrence), the strapping owner and captain of the rundown Mississippi River paddle steamer *Stonewall Jackson*, watches the local business leader J.J. King (Tom McGuire) show off his shining new paddle steamer to a cheering crowd. Bill worries that he will be up against some serious competition for customers. He also learns that his college student son, William Jr., whom he has not seen since the lad was a baby, will soon arrive.

Expecting a big, strong man like himself—or maybe someone even bigger and stronger—he is startled to learn that his son (Keaton) is short, slight, fumbling, and somewhat affected (he wears a thin moustache and a beret and carries a ukulele). Insisting that this must change, Bill Sr. takes his son to the barber to have the moustache shaved off and then to the hat shop to find headgear more suitable for his new life.

At the barber shop, Bill Jr. runs into King's daughter Kitty (Marion Byron) also home from school, and they immediately take a fancy to each other. The more the two meet and talk, however, the more both fathers, who already dislike each other, are adamant that this relationship needs to stop.

Meanwhile, Bill Sr. also tries to make a riverboat man out of his son, but the more he works at it, the more he sees that the task may just be hopeless. Finally, realizing that things just aren't working out for Bill Jr. on any front, Bill Sr. buys his son a ticket to go back east.

Bill Sr.'s troubles mount even more when the *Stonewall Jackson* is condemned as unsafe. He blames King for being behind it. Then, after assaulting King in a rage, he is put into jail.

Learning about this just as he is about to leave town, Bill Jr. vows to stay and help his father. His first attempt is to bring a loaf of bread with tools baked inside to Bill Sr.'s jail cell. The plan backfires when the sheriff figures out what's happening, however, and, in the resulting scuffle with Bill Jr., the sheriff hits him on the head and he is sent to the hospital.

As Bill Jr. recuperates in the hospital, a cyclone hits the town, destroying buildings, and threatening the steamboats. Rising to the challenge, he jumps up from his bed; makes his way through town as one building after another collapses; goes to his father's ship; sees Kitty, his father, and King all in danger of drowning in the river; and—staying poised throughout—rescues each of them one by one. His brave, resourceful actions earn Kitty's abiding love, his father's respect and admiration, and even King's appreciation and acceptance. When Kitty goes to embrace Bill Jr., however, he jumps in the water. She is puzzled at first, but we understand when we see that he has gone to save a clergyman also struggling to stay afloat in the river—just the person who can marry Kitty and Bill Jr. right then and there.

* * *

Like most previous Keaton films, *Steamboat Bill, Jr.,* is designed to start modestly and then build to a rousing climax. In this case, the climax is the film's cyclone sequence, one of the most spectacular finishes in all of silent film comedy.

Before this sequence, the film also offers many fine moments. One is a clever comic bit when Bill Jr. arrives by train. Writing to his father, who hasn't seen him in years, he says that he will wear a white carnation so his father will recognize him. When the train arrives, however, nearly all the men on it are wearing white carnations, and Bill Sr. and his first mate must struggle mightily to find the right person. Another is the scene in the hat shop when Bill Sr. insists on buying his son a more practical and "manly" hat to replace his beret. The selections of hats and reactions of both Bill Sr. and Jr. to each hat as it's put onto Bill Jr.'s head are often very funny.

Another major asset of *Steamboat Bill, Jr.,* that critics have often overlooked is the fine performance of Ernest Torrence as Bill Sr. A tall, intimidating looking Scottish actor who often played villains, Torrence, in this rare comic role, brings great life and humanity to the elder Canfield, a rough man of the river who strains to accept a son who is so unlike him and, it appears, so unfit for riverboat life.

Still another major asset, of course, is Keaton himself, who repeatedly proves the adage that only a person with great physical talents and agility can effectively play an often bumbling, physically awkward person. We see this, for example, in his various falls and other mishaps on board Bill Sr.'s steamboat. He is especially funny in scenes when he tries to posture and comes across as, shall we say, less than impressive.

Then comes the film's rousing climax. As both the father-son relationship and Bill Jr. and Kitty's hopes for romance reach pivotal turning points, the cyclone strikes and events go into high gear. The bad weather, which has already started, gets much worse, with the pouring rain now accompanied by gale-force winds. An automobile is blown down the street. King's new steamboat breaks free from its dock. Papers, boxes, and even barrels are blown high into the air and swirl about. The fronts of buildings are blown off. Patients flee the hospital. The frame of the hospital building separates from its foundation and flies into the air. The public library collapses. Still in his hospital bed recovering from the jail scuffle, Bill Jr. finds himself and his bed being transported by the wind through a horse stable and then into the street. Dazed, he stands up in front of a house to get his bearings. An instant later the entire front of the house crashes down all around him. Had he not been standing in the exact spot where the house's small, open attic window was, he would have been crushed like an eggshell. Miraculously, he walks away unscathed. As the wind picks up even more, he makes his way through town, encountering dangers from collapsing houses to a live, dangling electrical wire. He jumps on to and hugs a tree trunk he thinks might be rooted firmly enough in the ground to withstand the storm. But the tree is immediately uprooted by the wind and flies through the air and into the river with Bill Jr. holding on for dear life. Meanwhile, the jail that holds Bill Sr. is loosened from its foundation, slips into the river, and starts floating down steam, gradually sinking as it goes. Bill Jr. swims to his father's steamboat. Once on board, he sees Kitty in distress, holding on to the side of a floating house. Rising heroically to the occasion, Bill Jr. saves Kitty. Then, seeing the sinking jail floating by, he ingeniously rigs the steamboat to ram the jail and free his father, who climbs aboard the steamboat. Immediately, they see J.J. King himself, holding on to his sinking steamboat, and Bill Jr. saves him as well. Finally, he rescues the cleric who happens to be floating by just in time to perform a wedding.

Lasting only about 14 minutes, this final section of *Steamboat Bill, Jr.*, is an amazing sit-on-the-edge-of-your-seat experience and might be the most riveting sustained sequence in all of Keaton's films. Brilliantly conceived and staged, it also showcases Keaton—as Bill Jr. proves his mettle and wins everyone's respect—at his most athletic and daring. If riding aboard the trunk of a flying tree and jumping up multiple levels of the steamboat "Douglas Fairbanks style" isn't thrilling enough, Keaton also—in perhaps the most famous and dangerous stunt in all of his work—stands perfectly still as two tons of housing façade fall all around him leaving him standing (deadpan as always) within the small frame of the open attic window. "The episode is breathtaking in its audacity and poetry," film writer Adam Gopnik once noted, "an unexampled work of pure special-effects ballet."[10]

If Keaton's career as an auteur filmmaker had to end with this sequence, it ended in a blaze of windswept glory.

* * *

After finishing *Steamboat Bill, Jr.*, Keaton dutifully headed to MGM where, initially, he enjoyed some creative freedom. His first film at the studio was 1928's *The Cameraman*, a story about a young man who aspires to become a newsreel cameraman to impress a young woman who works as a receptionist for MGM Newsreels. Although the film's sole director was studio contractor Edward Sedgwick, Keaton offered many ideas that were incorporated into the story and greatly enhanced the film. The result is not pure Keaton, but his comic signature is clearly on it. (A brief entry on *The Cameraman* is included in Chapter 14 of his book.)

After *The Cameraman*, however, life became grim for Keaton. Increasingly, he was forced to work within the very rigid MGM production structure, the quality of his films suffered, and his unhappiness grew. Soon, the visually minded, understated Keaton was paired (quite awkwardly) with the loquacious, broadly comic Jimmy Durante in a series of unfunny comedies, tensions increased, and Keaton's lucrative arrangement with MGM was terminated. On the personal front, there were other setbacks. Keaton's wife, Natalie Talmadge, left him, taking their two sons with her, and (most likely out of spite) legally changing their surnames from Keaton to Talmadge. Keaton went into an alcoholic spiral. Then, after being admitted to an alcohol recovery program, he married his nurse, Mae Scriven, who soon divorced him when she learned he was having an affair.

Eventually, though, Keaton's life turned around. In the mid-1930s, he managed to stop drinking. In 1937, he returned to MGM, not as a star but as a gagwriter making only about one-tenth his previous studio salary. Then, in 1940, he married Eleanor Norris, a dancer who was 23 years his junior. Despite the long odds many people initially gave the union, their marriage proved to be strong and durable, lasting until his death and providing him with the emotional support that enabled him to stay sober and work regularly.

Although Keaton never again enjoyed the level of creative freedom or professional stature that he had had during the 1920s, he continued to keep a busy work schedule for the rest his life. In the 1940s, he continued his gag writing at MGM, helping rising stars such as Red Skelton and Lucille Ball. In the 1950s and early 1960s, he made cameo appearances in films ranging from 1950's *Sunset Boulevard* and 1952's *Limelight* with Chaplin to 1963's *It's a Mad, Mad, Mad, Mad World* and 1965's *How to Stuff a Wild Bikini*. With the proliferation of television in the 1950s, he also became a familiar face on the small screen, appearing in numerous commercials and making about 70 guest appearances on weekly shows such as *The Ed Sullivan Show*, *Route 66*, and *The Twilight Zone*.

In the 1950s, he and Eleanor also went into a business partnership with film collector and programmer Raymond Rohauer to re-release his silent films to a new generation of viewers. Since then, these films have become regular features at revival theaters and film festivals around the world.

7. In a Blaze of Windswept Glory

With greater exposure from his television and film appearances as well as the re-releases of his silent films, Keaton finally began to receive the rightful recognition that had eluded him for so long. One of these was an Academy Honorary Award presented to him in 1960 "for his unique talents which brought immortal comedies to the screen."[11] Since then, seven of his films—*One Week, Cops, Sherlock, Jr., The Navigator, The General, Steamboat Bill, Jr.,* and *The Cameraman*—have been added to the Library of Congress's National Film Registry, tying him with Chaplin for number of films on this distinguished list. In addition, numerous books and documentaries have focused on him and his work. (Two very good documentaries are Kevin Brownlow and David Gill's 1987 three-part effort, *Buster Keaton: A Hard Act to Follow,* and Peter Bogdanovich's 2018 feature-length piece, *The Great Buster: A Celebration.*)

Keaton continued to work steadily through 1965, but by then his health was clearly deteriorating. On February 1, 1966, he died at age 70, a victim of lung cancer. Eleanor lived for another 33 years and spent much of that time appearing at Keaton film revivals, participating in interviews about Keaton and his work, and otherwise helping to promote his legacy.

* * *

Like many of his silent film contemporaries, Buster Keaton faced a reckoning in 1928. In his case, however, it wasn't sound technology he had to confront as much as it was the film industry's deepening commitment to the strict assembly-line-style business model we know today as the "studio system." The small, free-wheeling, rough-and-tumble operations such as Buster Keaton Productions were being squeezed out, and, without the financial reserves of other stars such as Chaplin and Lloyd, Keaton was faced with the inevitable change-or-die choice. For him, however, this particular change also meant a kind of death at his personal core: the loss of the freedom he had had to create at the very high level he was capable of and happiest working at. It is little wonder that his life fell apart in the 1930s.

It is also to his great personal credit that—with Eleanor's help—he was able to build both his life and, to some degree, his career back up again. This personal and professional resurrection took great courage and resilience. But then why should this be any surprise? Courage and resilience were, after all, the same qualities that had enabled Keaton, while making *Steamboat Bill, Jr.,* to stand completely still as two tons of building façade fell on him and, as a toddler 30 years earlier, to get up unruffled after he had fallen down an entire flight of stairs. Yes, he *was* a regular Buster!

8

A Star Is Born

Joan Crawford and
Our Dancing Daughters

While so much, if not most, of the literature about the end of the silent era focuses on actors whose careers came to abrupt and sometimes tragic ends, this was by no means always the case. Sound films ended or greatly diminished the careers of many silent film stars, of course, but the arrival of sound also meant immense opportunity for those actors who could adapt to the new, untried, and in many ways very different art form of the talkies. Just a few examples of this latter group include Ronald Colman, Greta Garbo, Norma Shearer, John and Lionel Barrymore, Mary Astor, Gary Cooper, William Powell, and an emerging MGM contract player named Joan Crawford, whose careers all gathered momentum with sound and, in some cases, remained vital for decades.

Of all the major silent film stars to successfully move to sound, perhaps the one with the longest and (with the possible exception of Garbo) most iconic sound film career was Crawford, who appeared in more than 60 sound films between 1929 and 1970 and about 20 television shows between 1953 and 1972. Crawford was sometimes called "the ultimate movie star," and she certainly lived up to the title. She played the role of star to the hilt, dressing glamorously every time she made a public appearance, responding to letters and requests from fans with great diligence, arranging regular appearances at the Academy Awards and other awards shows to stay in the public eye, and much more. But she was also a much more accomplished and versatile actress than many modern film viewers realize, and, during a run of brilliant performances in films from 1945's *Mildred Pierce* to 1952's *Sudden Fear*, she was as consistently good as any actress in Hollywood.

Film historians have often, and correctly, credited Crawford's longevity to an uncanny ability to reinvent herself, adapting her screen image and selection of roles to stay relevant as the world and audience tastes changed.

She moved from playing ingenues and flappers in the high-living 1920s to independent working women in the economically depressed 1930s, to complex noir heroines in the dark post-war 1940s and 1950s, to horror film leads in the 1960s, when the horror genre was in vogue. She played a wide variety of other roles during these periods, too, but her knack for sensing changes in the market and adapting herself to new realities was remarkable.

What is equally remarkable but not discussed nearly as often is Crawford's ability to apply so much of what she learned about silent film acting during her first four years at MGM to the 40-year sound film career that followed. In a very short time, she had learned how to excel at silent film acting. When she moved to the talkies, she immediately began to apply methods she'd learned for the old medium to the new. The result was a fascinating, if not unique, melding of the best technique of silent film acting with the best technique of sound film acting that often gave her performances great authenticity, depth, and emotional resonance. Just as she could excel at delivering a critical line of dialog such as Mildred's "Get out before I kill you." to her daughter Veda in *Mildred Pierce*, she could communicate complex and often conflicting feelings in split-seconds with extremely precise and very credible facial expressions and other body language.

In a very insightful essay discussing Crawford's performance in *Sudden Fear*, film historian Sheila O'Malley writes: "In her half-century career, Joan Crawford was a master of so many elements of her craft: gesture and silhouette (a lost art), using the shape of her body to tell the story (another lost art), stepping into key lights with emotions at full-throttle (lost art, etc.), as well as the eternal arts of great actresses through time: belief in the reality of the story, understanding her role on an intimate level, and a fearlessness in showing qualities considered unladylike or unattractive (rage, ambition, envy). She had enormous range.... She had great affection and empathy for the characters she played.... She understood her own persona intimately...."[1]

What's especially intriguing about this quote for this discussion's purposes is its emphasis on the visual methods Crawford used to communicate: "gesture and silhouette," "using the shape of her body to tell the story," and "stepping into key lights with emotions at full-throttle." These are lost arts, of course, because they were some of the communication techniques that actors relied on much more heavily during the silent era when they couldn't also rely on the spoken word. By continuing to use and refine these visual techniques throughout her long career in what has always been a mainly visual medium, Crawford gave her best performances a highly distinctive and emotionally rich quality.

Diana Medford (Joan Crawford) cuts loose in *Our Dancing Daughters*, a box-office hit for MGM and the film that made Crawford a star (MGM/Photofest).

* * *

September 1928 was the month and year that Joan Crawford became a major star. The occasion was the release of a new MGM film, a romantic drama called *Our Dancing Daughters* directed by journeyman Harry Beaumont. The film, which focuses on the lives of "Dangerous" Diana Medford (Crawford) and her two socialite girlfriends, all of whom are very much a part of the "roaring twenties" party set, was an immediate and enormous hit, eventually making more than six times its production budget at the box office.

Audiences responded enthusiastically to many facets of the film. One was the immediacy of the subject matter. At the height of a decade known for its excesses and devil-may-care attitudes, here was a story depicting lavish parties with young people wildly dancing the Charleston, coyly consuming alcohol, and eagerly looking for even more pleasure anywhere else they could find it. Another was the superb art direction from MGM production designer Cedric Gibbons and his colleague Richard Day, which included lavish art deco sets occasionally featuring nude female figurines not-too-subtly reinforcing that, yes, we were indeed in an extravagant, racy world. But by far the most fuss was made over Crawford, whose vibrant, expressive performance as the fun-loving and adventurous but also honest, kind-hearted, loyal, and emotionally grounded Diana, captivated audiences.

The literati took notice as well. After seeing *Our Dancing Daughters*, the novelist and astute chronicler of 1920s manners and mores F. Scott Fitzgerald famously wrote about the film's lead actress in quite glowing terms. "Joan Crawford," he said, "is doubtless the best example of the flapper, the girl you see in smart night clubs, gowned to the apex of sophistication, toying iced glasses with a remote, faintly bitter expression, dancing deliciously, laughing a great deal, with wide, hurt eyes. Young things with a talent for living."[2]

Within a week of the film's release, theater managers across the country had Crawford's name put up in big letters *above* the film's title on their marquees, an honor she had never previously received. Soon, the number of her fan letters increased to thousands each week, and magazines and newspapers were pestering MGM for interviews with her. Quite taken with all of this, Crawford, as she admitted later in life, drove around the Los Angeles area with a small box camera and took pictures of theater marquees with her name in lights.[3] After three and a half years of toiling at MGM as an unbilled extra, bit player, and supporting player in 25 films, Joan Crawford had become Hollywood's newest star.

* * *

Although Crawford's rise to the top in Hollywood had been relatively fast, it had not been easy. Born Lucille Fay LeSueur, probably in 1904 or 1905,[4] into an impoverished, seriously dysfunctional Oklahoma family, she received little formal education and spent most of her youth working in hard, menial jobs. Determined to improve her lot, she began dancing in the choruses of traveling reviews in the early 1920s, eventually arranging for a screen test in 1924 that was sent to MGM producer Harry Rapf and led to a modest contract. Beginning work at the studio in January 1925, her first assignment was as the body-double for the studio's reigning star, Norma Shearer, in a film called *Lady of the Night*. Small roles followed, and, later that year, as people began to take notice, studio executives, feeling that her last name sounded too much like "sewer," arranged for a "name the star" contest in a film magazine. The name eventually selected was "Joan Crawford."

The films that Crawford appeared in before *Our Dancing Daughters* proved to be an invaluable apprenticeship for her. Unlike most of her fellow studio starlets, she wanted to learn about *every* aspect of the profession, and, in addition to studying the work of other actors, she constantly studied the work of directors, cameramen, lighting technicians, set and wardrobe designers, and virtually everyone else connected with the filmmaking process. She also read script after script, and, when she found a role that she felt was right for her, she would tirelessly fight to get it. As MGM screenwriter Frederica Sagor Maas once noted, "No one decided to make Joan Crawford a star. Joan Crawford became a star because Joan Crawford decided to become a star."[5]

Among the highlights of this apprenticeship period for Crawford was the experience of working with the great silent film character actor Lon Chaney (who is covered in Chapter 12 of this book). The film was 1927's *The Unknown*, a very strange, disturbing love story set in the circus world. During the filming, she watched his work closely and quickly developed an intense admiration for his approach to his work. "[With him] I became aware for the first time of the difference between standing in front of a camera and acting," she later said. "Until then I had been conscious only of myself. Lon Chaney was my introduction to acting. The concentration, the complete absorption he gave to his characterization, filled me with such awe that I could scarcely speak to him."[6] Describing the dramatic conclusion of *The Unknown*, she also recalled how Chaney "was able to convey not just realism but such emotional agony that it was both shocking and fascinating."[7]

The experience made an enormous impact on the young actress. "He demanded a lot of me," she said. "Watching him gave me the desire to be a real actress."[8] She worked hard to deliver an excellent performance, very effectively portraying a character who was repelled by certain aspects of the Chaney character while also being quite sympathetic toward him. The critics also took note. As one reviewer at the time, Langdon W. Post of the *New York Evening World*, wrote, "Joan Crawford is one of the screen's acknowledged artists. Certainly, her performance in this picture is a most impressive one."[9]

This role led to other important parts in films starring other top MGM leading men at the time. Two were comedies with the popular William Haines, 1927's *Spring Fever* and 1928's *West Point*. Three others were dramas with two of the studio's biggest male romantic leads, 1927's *Twelve Miles Out* and 1928's *Four Walls* with John Gilbert and 1928's *Across to Singapore* with Ramon Novarro. While the roles were generally more interesting than the small parts she had played during her first couple of years at MGM, Crawford was still slotted in secondary roles as the love interest.

As ambitious as ever, she longed for a good leading role, and, after reading the script for a film eventually titled *Our Dancing Daughters*, she fought hard for the role of "Dangerous" Diana Medford, the role that would catapult her to top-tier stardom.

* * *

Although 1928 audiences flocked to *Our Dancing Daughters* for its energy, risqué qualities, and "timeliness" in depicting the no-holds-barred 1920s, the film presents some challenges for viewers today. One shortcoming is the writing. The story—which focuses mostly on two young women, the vivacious, kind-hearted Diana (Crawford) and the scheming Ann (Anita Page), as they compete for the love of a very eligible suitor, Ben Blaine (Johnny Mack Brown)—is clunky and often very contrived. A major plot complication near the film's end is resolved, for example, with an extremely convenient fatal accident. With the exception of Diana, the characters are stereotypical and one-dimensional. The film's dated aspects are apparent, too. For example, the moral issues the characters grapple with, such as the importance for women to preserve their virginity until marriage, seem old-fashioned even by the standards of films that soon followed in the much more candid Pre-Code[10] period of the early 1930s.

With the possible exceptions of a historian's desire to see a contemporary depiction of the high-living 1920s or an art lover's interest in the fascinating art deco sets by Cedric Gibbons and Richard Day, perhaps the most compelling reason to see this film today is Crawford's commanding performance, especially during the first two-thirds of the story. The culmination of her silent film apprenticeship, this work also provides many glimpses into the distinctive Crawford acting style that would evolve for decades in sound films while always remaining heavily dependent on its silent film roots.

From the film's first moments, we are intrigued by Crawford's Diana. As she dances exuberantly, she finishes dressing to go out to a party. Then she chats playfully with her parents. After this, she dances up a storm at the party—a lavish, glittering event—as spectators cheer her on. As she dances, she catches the eye of one spectator looking into the party from outside, the handsome Ben Blaine. She makes eye contact with him, too. Both feel the first tingles of romance.

In just a few minutes of film time, and almost entirely through only her facial expressions and body language, Crawford conveys so much about Diana: her energy, zest for living, caring nature, playfulness, love and respect for her parents, curiosity about this handsome young man who stares at her from afar, and growing attraction to him after they meet.

Later, as she sees more of Ben, we see that Diana is also capable of intense romantic feelings and has fallen deeply in love. She also shares a wonderful scene with her friend Bea (Dorothy Sebastian) as she shares her feelings and expresses confidence that Ben will soon ask her to marry him.

In these scenes, we see that, although Diana can be fun-loving and even wild at times, she is also a person of who can be quite sensitive and vulnerable. One element of many of these scenes that helps to make Crawford's visual communication appear so authentic is the dramatic contrast in acting capability between her and co-star Johnny Mack Brown. His Ben has been swept away by her Diana as well, but Brown's acting is wooden and his responses come across as staged. While almost everything we see from Crawford appears to be coming from deep within Diana's core, most of what we see from Brown betrays an uncertain actor who appears to be simply responding to direction.

Perhaps Crawford's best acting in the film comes in the next phase of the story when Ben is lured away from Diana by the lying, manipulative Ann.

As time passes and Ben doesn't appear, Diana becomes more anxious but tries to hide her anxiety when she is with her friends. In one brief lovely scene, she leaves a party in a boat cabin to walk out to the side of the deck to be by herself. There are no inter-titles or elaborate visual business, just a single shot of a confused, uncertain women sensing that something is wrong and feeling quite vulnerable. It is a simple, quiet, poignant moment.

Soon afterwards, Ben finally reappears, this time with Ann, and the two announce that they will be married. Diana, of course, is stunned and crestfallen. We see her, first in long shot behind several other people receiving the news, and then in close-up where we can see more of what she's feeling. Her uncertainty has now turned to profound disappointment, sadness, and anger at what she perceives as betrayals by both Ben and Ann. She knows exactly what has happened: this man has quickly discarded her to be with a woman who, unknown to him, is only interested in his money. Finding the situation unbearable, she retreats to another room to process her grief.

Again, Crawford's expressive face and body convey all the intense emotions surging through Diana at this moment in a very clear, honest, and understated way. It is almost impossible not to feel that we are in the presence of a woman who, while normally strong, fun-loving, and resilient, has truly had her heart broken.

These, along with other especially effective scenes throughout the film, made a big impression on the critics of the time, many of whom singled out Crawford's work for high praise. "Joan Crawford, as the girl who was free and wild but maintained her ideals, does the greatest work of her career," declared the *New York Mirror*.[11] *Motion Picture Magazine* added, "Joan Crawford ... acts better than she ever has."[12] And the *New York World* predicted that Crawford was indeed ready to "get going as a star in her own right."[13]

The success of *Our Dancing Daughters*, would immediately lead to two popular follow-up films, 1929's *Our Modern Maidens* (Crawford's last silent), and 1930's *Our Blushing Brides* (Crawford's fourth sound film). In quite a departure from the roll-out of *Our Dancing Daughters*, the promotional materials for both these films would feature Crawford's name all by itself, and in suitably large letters, above the title. A true Hollywood star had been born, one whose relentless drive, dedication to craft, resilience, and talent would keep her in the film world's top tier for four more decades.

* * *

It's intriguing to ask why Crawford was able to move so easily and successfully to the sound medium when stars as popular as Mary Pickford, Gloria Swanson, and Clara Bow weren't.

One reason may be that Crawford's physical tools were especially well suited for sound. Unlike Bow, for example, whose rough Brooklyn accent clashed badly with the vision of loveliness she projected on the silent screen, Crawford's voice was pleasant and distinctive, and she quickly learned to use it as an instrument, maximizing its value in the new medium and, in the process, enhancing her own screen persona. In some of her early sound films such as 1931's *Possessed* with Clark Gable, for example, she sings briefly and quite well. She also had an instinctive sense of using words for dramatic impact and delivered dialogue with great authority and effectiveness, providing pauses and emphasis in exactly the right places to emphasize emotion and reinforce meaning. In addition, she could dance, which, with the coming of spoken dialogue, music soundtracks, songs, and full-scale film musicals, became a far more common and valued element in film. While not quite Ginger Rogers, she could more than hold her own as a hoofer, even, as in 1933's *Dancing Lady*, when her dance partner in several numbers was none other than Fred Astaire.

Another reason for Crawford's success in the new sound medium may be that audiences saw her as thoroughly modern. By the late 1920s, audiences were in a very different world from where they had been just a few years before when actresses such as Pickford and Lillian Gish routinely played more quaint, old-fashioned characters, often from bygone eras. These audiences, and especially their younger members, wanted to see less of what Pickford and Gish had long provided and more of *their* own world reflected back at them from the big screen. Crawford, who represented a new face and a new sensibility for a new time, excellently fulfilled this need.

Still another reason may be a dimension to Crawford's acting mentioned earlier: how well she fused her amazing ability to convey her character's inner emotional state through facial expressions and other body language with an ability to deliver the spoken word effectively. From the start, this gave her sound film acting a more authentic, more well-rounded quality than most actors attempting to make the transition could muster. While they often appeared forced or exaggerated, she appeared much more real and credible.

* * *

After *Our Dancing Daughters* and three more silent films, Crawford began a storied sound film career that lasted for four decades. During this time, she achieved great fame and many honors, including an Academy Award for her performance in *Mildred Pierce* and two additional Academy Award nominations for her performances in 1947's *Possessed* with Van Heflin[14] and 1952's *Sudden Fear* with Jack Palance. In an industry that routinely discarded aging actresses, she also developed a well-deserved reputation for repeatedly finding ways to come back from what seemed to be certain professional oblivion. After being labeled, along with several other prominent stars, as "poison at the box office"[15] in an ad in the *Hollywood Reporter* in 1938, for example, she took a supporting role playing against type as a "bad girl" in the 1939 film version of Clare Boothe Luce's play *The Women* and stole the movie, winning rave reviews for her daring turn. After being nudged out of MGM in 1943 reportedly so the studio could concentrate more on its younger female stars such as Ava Gardner and Lana Turner, she signed with Warner Brothers for less money but more production leverage and went on to make a stunning comeback with film noir hits such as *Mildred Pierce*, 1946's *Humoresque*, 1947's *Possessed*, 1949's *Flamingo Road*, and 1950's *The Damned Don't Cry*. When interest in her at Warner Brothers waned in the early 1950s, she engineered another comeback with another major noir hit, the independently produced thriller *Sudden Fear*. Then in the early 1960s, when she was considered well over the hill for an actress, she cajoled her fellow acting diva and long-time nemesis Bette Davis into co-starring with her in still another major hit, the 1962 horror thriller *Whatever Happened to Baby Jane?*.

Unfortunately for Crawford, however, this film proved to be her last comeback. During the 1960s, she often took poorly written roles in badly produced low-budget films and eventually finished her film career with the embarrassingly bad science fiction horror film *Trog* in 1970.

One footnote to that episode is a *New York Times* review, which, while roundly panning the film, gives Crawford the backhanded compliment of being a "determined lady" who is "working grimly at her craft."[16] Although this clearly indicates a sad end to a long and distinguished career, it also shows a sincere respect for a professional who, no matter how bad a film's story or its production values were, never gave anything less than her best to a project. Even in the most absurd and pathetic of situations, she was—to the end—committed to summoning the best within herself for her role.

During her final years, Crawford lived in New York, where she died in her sleep on May 10, 1977.

For those who enjoy reading about the personal lives of celebrities, Crawford's life, amply documented in several biographies, is jam-packed with fascinating information. On one hand, there are the gossipy items such as the tempestuous romances; many sexual escapades; explosive outbursts of temper; heavy alcohol consumption; and troubled relationship with her oldest adopted child, Christina, whose damning and still-controversial 1978 "tell-all" memoir *Mommie Dearest* and the 1981 film based on the book did irreparable damage to Crawford's personal and professional legacy. On the other hand, however, there are Crawford's many kindnesses to the behind-the-scenes studio staff who worked on her films and their families, her loyalty and devotion to long-time friends that extended even to ex-husbands Douglas Fairbanks, Jr., and Franchot Tone, her lifetime support of charities, and even her decade-long stint as a member of the Board of Directors for the Pepsi-Cola Company. She was a person, it sometimes seems, of as many parts as all the roles she played in all her films combined.

* * *

Because Joan Crawford's silent film career was fairly brief and her sound film career so long, most students of classic film, even some die-hard Crawford fans, tend to forget that she was both a silent film actress and, for a brief time, a silent film star. During this apprenticeship, she both learned a great deal about her craft and many other facets of filmmaking and delivered fine performances in *Our Dancing Daughters*, *The Unknown*, *Across to Singapore*, and other films: work that would serve as the foundation for a very personal and distinctive acting style that would develop and grow richer over the next several decades. In four short years, she had mastered one film medium and, in the process, had excellently positioned herself to master another.

9

"Astonishing elegance"

William Wellman, Louise Brooks, Wallace Beery, and Beggars of Life

As Warner Brothers and Fox pushed ahead with sound technology in 1926 and 1927, Hollywood's two largest and most profitable studios, MGM and Paramount, were much more cautious. Unlike their two upstart competitors, they figured, they could afford to wait and let the others take the risks. If, as many people were predicting, sound was just a passing fad, then they would be fine. If there really were something to sound, they would simply hop aboard the bandwagon a little later—after many of the problems that invariably come with innovation had been worked out. Either way, they felt, it was better to sit tight.

After the enormous success of *The Jazz Singer*, however, both MGM and Paramount understood that, whether they liked the idea of sound films or not, the time for them to hop aboard that bandwagon had come. One of Paramount's first steps was to call its contract directors together for a meeting with its two top executives, Jesse Lasky and Adolph Zukor. To give the event added gravitas, Zukor also invited many of the studio's New York–based bankers.

Lasky was first to speak, informing the directors that Paramount was moving to sound. Then, he made an announcement that sent a bracing chill through his audience. "We have hired the best stage directors in New York," he said. "John Cromwell, George Cukor, George Abbott—these are the first that are coming. They will work with you and share credits."[1]

As the other directors sat dejectedly in their seats, one of them—a 32-year-old named William Wellman who had only been directing for five years—got up and looked Lasky straight in the eye. "I have bad news for you," he snarled. "Have you forgotten that I have a seven-year contract with you gentlemen of Paramount? It has nothing to say … about any lousy stage director coming in and making half of my picture. Furthermore, I

9. "Astonishing elegance"

won't accept one of them on my set...."[2] At this, Wellman, or "Wild Bill" as he was often called, emphatically stomped out of the room.

Soon, the New York stage directors did come. Although several of them, including Cromwell and Cukor, had long, successful film careers, none of them ever worked with, let alone shared directorial credit with, William Wellman.

Although young and fairly inexperienced, Wellman (1896–1975) was perhaps the one director at Paramount with both the brass and the clout to get away with this kind of outburst—especially in the presence of two industry figures as powerful as Lasky and Zukor. The brass was all his. A natural born rebel, he had once been expelled from high school for dropping a stink bomb on the principal's head. Now, still a relative newcomer to the industry, he had already gained a reputation for being both fearless in the face of authority and an incorrigible prankster on film sets. His clout, at least for the moment, was due to the resounding financial and critical success of *Wings*, his breathtaking World War I aviation film, which had been released a few months earlier. Still playing in theaters nationwide, *Wings* was also on its way to becoming one of the biggest box

After directing silent film masterpieces *Wings* and *Beggars of Life*, William "Wild Bill" Wellman remained a major Hollywood figure for the first 30 years of the sound era (Photofest).

office hits of the 1920s and the recipient of the very first Best Picture Academy Award.

At this meeting, Wellman's main issue wasn't, of course, the coming of sound. He didn't have the emotional attachment to the silent medium that others such as Griffith, Pickford, or Chaplin had. For him, the issue was, as it would be throughout his 35-year directing career, control. Whether silent or sound, he wanted to make films that meant something to him, and he wanted to make them his way. During the studio era when contract directors were expected to take assigned scripts, salute, and compliantly do the work, he was constantly battling with production heads, producers, stars, and anyone else who had different ideas about what was best for projects. Today, decades after his death, his battles with studio heads and producers not only at Paramount but also at Warner Brothers, MGM, 20th Century–Fox, and elsewhere remain the stuff of Hollywood legend. It's no mystery that the nickname "Wild Bill" has stuck to him like glue.

* * *

Around the time of this meeting, Wellman was also using his recently earned clout to do something that was then new for him: secure a studio's commitment to produce a so-called "personal project." Titled *Beggars of Life*, this film would be based on the autobiographical story of the same name of life on the road by Jim Tully, a one-time hobo turned boxer, tree surgeon, and finally writer. The story is quite simple and straightforward. A young man on the road meets a young woman who has just killed her foster father after he's repeatedly abused her. The two run away, sneak aboard trains, spend nights in hobo camps, and dream of reaching Canada where they believe she will be safe from the law. Finally, with the unexpected help of a hard-edged but sympathetic hobo named Oklahoma Red, they finally get their chance. While others at Paramount found the story too gritty and grim, Wellman, always sensitive to underdogs and people on the fringes of life, loved it, pushed for the project, and got it.

Opening on September 22, 1928, the film starred up-and-coming Paramount ingénue Louise Brooks as the young woman, handsome leading man Richard Arlen (who had just co-starred in Wellman's *Wings*) as the young man, and veteran character actor Wallace Beery as Oklahoma Red. In addition to several more actors in supporting roles, the cast included a generous sprinkling of real-life hoboes that Wellman had rounded up to give the story greater authenticity.

Unlike *Wings*, however, *Beggars of Life* did not receive a groundswell of critical and fan support. The initial reviews were quite mixed. The *Chicago Tribune* named it one of the six best films for October.[3] In a poll conducted by *The Film Daily*, it was named one of the best films of the year.[4] Several critics singled out Louise Brooks for her work, Mordaunt Hall of *The New York Times* declaring "Miss Brooks really acts well...."[5] and Quinn Martin of the *New York World* asserting "This is the best acting this remarkable young woman has done."[6] Others, however, weren't nearly as supportive. Claiming that the film's grim subject matter would translate into limited audience appeal, one Baltimore newspaper blithely dismissed it as "not a flapper fetcher for the daytime trade."[7] Writing in the *Los Angeles Examiner*, long-time Hollywood reporter Louella Parsons, who preferred Brooks in her lighter flapper roles, was "a little disappointed" in her work in *Beggars*.[8] As the Baltimore newspaper had predicted, audiences, too, were less than enthusiastic. Box office was lackluster, and *Beggars* soon stopped playing in theaters and was largely forgotten.

One person who hadn't forgotten about *Beggars*, though, was the perpetually contrary Wellman, who later called it "perhaps the best silent picture I ever made."[9] While some people were undoubtedly intrigued by the director's bold assertion, the film was not only forgotten by most people but, for decades, was considered lost. Even if the few people who even knew about the film wished to see it, they couldn't.

Then, in the 1960s, and well after Wellman's retirement, a murky 16-millimeter print was found and subsequently shown at the National Film Theatre in London. Among those in the audience was silent film historian Kevin Brownlow, who immediately saw it as a masterpiece and began to promote it. "*Beggars of Life* is brilliantly thought out and superbly made," he wrote in his 1968 book *The Parade's Gone By*. "[In it,] the rich, highly polished surface of technique gleamed through, revealing a style of astonishing elegance—an elegance that seemed out of place in such a picture...."[10]

Interest in the film grew in the 1980s, when Louise Brooks, long forgotten at this point, suddenly reemerged as a celebrated, even iconic figure among film historians and the art house set. Most of the attention centered on two films Brooks made in Germany for expressionist director G.W. Pabst shortly after *Beggars*: *Pandora's Box* and *Diary of a Lost Girl* (both 1929) and her more recent memoir writing. Eventually, people also began to look more closely at *Beggars*, both for Brooks' compelling performance and for the quality of the film overall.

Today, with the releases of both DVD and Blu-ray versions of *Beggars* and a higher quality 35-millimeter print from the George Eastman House that's shown periodically at silent film revival festivals, interest in the film continues to grow. Writing in 2012, for example, film historian Thomas Gladysz has called it "a film whose reputation is picking up steam."[11] And after seeing *Beggars* at the 2014 Giornate del Cinema Muto silent film

Oklahoma Red (Wallace Beery, left), Jim (Richard Arlen), and Nancy (Louise Brooks) all share the trials of vagabond life on the road and the rails in *Beggars of Life* (Paramount Pictures/Photofest).

festival in Pordelone, Italy, film writer Lokke Heiss concurred with Wellman, calling it "one of [the director's] greatest silent films."[12]

* * *

Considering the tantalizing brew of eccentrics involved, the making of *Beggars of Life* could, in itself, have been turned into a fascinating movie. In addition to the motley group of hoboes Wellman had enlisted to work as extras, some of the standouts in the cast and crew included Brooks, Wallace Beery, and the director himself.

Brooks (1906–1985) is a unique figure in film history. Although she made about two dozen films, most of them silent, her acting reputation rests almost entirely on her performances in just three: *Beggars* and her German films for Pabst, *Pandora's Box* and *Diary of a Lost Girl*. Of these, she is probably best known for at her mesmerizing Lulu, the seductive, amoral, and ultimately tragic prostitute in *Pandora's Box*. A dramatic departure from the sympathetic character she played in *Beggars* and many of her earlier flapper roles in silent comedies, her Lulu remains striking today and is often listed as one of the great performances by an actress in all of silent film. Forgotten for decades, Brooks has now also achieved near-cult status as a film industry figure famous for her beauty, charismatic screen presence, numerous romances and affairs (including, according to her, flings with both Charlie Chaplin and Greta Garbo), biting wit, and stylish and irreverent writing about films and filmmakers. Her most famous writing venture is probably her 1982 memoir about her years in the film business titled *Lulu in Hollywood*. A collection of anecdote-filled, gossipy, and often very insightful essays, the book includes her detailed and very entertaining account of the filming of *Beggars*. Devoting a full chapter of her book to the film's location shooting in and near the small California town of Jacumba near the Mexican border, she shares numerous anecdotes about Wellman, the rambunctious hobo extras, and her cantankerous co-star Wallace Beery.

Beery (1885–1949) was a larger-than-life character both on screen and off. In films, he specialized in playing colorful characters and usually dominated the scenes he was in. After *Beggars*, he was at the height of his popularity and acclaim for notable performances such as his brutal career criminal in the 1930 prison drama *The Big House*, Long John Silver in the 1934 screen version of Robert Louis Stevenson's *Treasure Island*, and an over-the-hill boxer attempting a comeback in King Vidor's 1931 drama *The Champ*, for which he won a Best Actor Academy Award. As a colleague, he was widely considered to be odd and difficult to work with. Often, he stole props from studio sets for no reason apparently other than the thrill of it. Several child actors also expressed their displeasure with working with him. The young Jackie Cooper, who made several films with Beery, claimed that the older actor was constantly trying to upstage him during scenes. And child actress Margaret O'Brien complained so often that Beery pinched her when they were on the set that special guards were assigned to protect her from him. Despite being such an annoyance, however, Beery worked regularly until his death. In all, he made about 100 films for numerous directors including, in addition to Wellman and Vidor, such major Hollywood figures as John Ford, George Cukor, Victor Fleming, Raoul Walsh, and Clarence Brown.

With the possible exception of Raoul Walsh, Wellman may be the most under-appreciated great American film director of all time. During his 35-year career, he made an amazing number of excellent-to-great films from silent classics such as *Wings* and *Beggars*, to enduring sound films such as 1931's *The Public Enemy* and *Safe in Hell*; 1932's *The Purchase Price*, *Heroes for Sale*, and *Frisco Jenny*; 1933's *Wild Boys of the Road* and *Midnight Mary*; 1937's *A Star Is Born*; 1943's *The Ox-Bow Incident*; 1945's *The Story of G.I. Joe*; and 1949's *Battleground*. Yet, he never received a Best Director Academy Award.[13]

Today, most film scholars generally regard him has a solid journeyman director without a singular artistic vision. Upon closer inspection, however, there is considerable unity in his work. For example, certain "Wellman-esque" characteristics that we see again and again in his films are deeply felt concerns about the nature and dispensation of justice, a special sensitivity toward the downtrodden or marginalized, an uncompromising emotional honesty, and a highly visceral, "in-your-face" directing style. Together, these attributes help to keep his films fresh and relevant many decades after their initial release. Reflecting his experience with, and great love for, aviation, he also returned to this subject repeatedly after *Wings*. Two notable later Wellman aviation films, for example, are 1953's *Island in the Sky* and 1954's *The High and the Mighty*. Not all of his efforts are distinctly "Wellman-esque," of course. Many, such as his contributions to 1936's *Tarzan Escapes* and 1944's *Buffalo Bill*, are routine studio work. *Beggars* and most of the films listed above, however, all possess the attributes and qualities that make Wellman's best work both distinctly his own and quite memorable.

* * *

The more closely we look at *Beggars of Life*, the more deeply one phrase of film criticism seems to resonate: Kevin Brownlow's comment that the film reveals "a style of astonishing elegance—an elegance that seemed out of place in such a picture." "Elegance" is certainly not the first word that comes to mind when the subject is a grim, gritty story about hoboes. The phrase "astonishing elegance" seems even more jarring. This is what *Beggars* possesses, however, and it is ultimately what makes it a great film.

We see this elegance throughout in the film's spare, eloquent visual artistry.

One of its most compelling and frequently discussed scenes, for example, is at the very beginning of the story. As the film opens, we see a man's legs and feet as he walks along a lonely road. As he happens on a farm house, we see that he is young and lean looking. He peers through a screen door, eyes an older man at a breakfast table, knocks, tries unsuccessfully to get the older man's attention, boldly enters asking for food and offering to work for it, and then realizes that the man is dead with a bullet hole in the side of his head. Immediately, he sees a young woman dressed as a boy looking down from upstairs. She comes down and readily admits to the murder, saying that, since he became her foster father two years before, he had constantly pawed and groped her. The camera moves in on her face, and, superimposed on it, are images of her serving him breakfast that morning; his grabbing her and tearing her dress; her breaking loose and taking a nearby rifle, shooting him, realizing in horror what she has done, and retreating to the upstairs. After this admission, the young man—seeming to understanding everything that's happened, the reasons for it, her sadness and desperation, and the various implications for both the woman and him—suggests that they leave so she can hop a freight train. As they depart, he grabs some food. Then the film cuts to two pairs of legs and feet walking along that lonely road.

This short sequence is quite impressive. It's told with a simplicity, directness, and emotional honesty that are breathtaking. It moves quickly and economically while also allowing the immense gravity of the situation to sink in fully with viewers. It conveys all the most critical details visually so viewers can more fully experience the young woman's pathetic, desperate situation as well as share the young man's empathy for her. As film historian Cliff Aliperti has noted, the whole experience is "absolutely phenomenal."[14]

Another example of this elegance occurs several minutes later in the narrative. On the road, the couple needs a place to sleep for the night. He spies a field dotted with haystacks, selects one, and hollows out a space in it large enough for the two to lie down. With Wellman's camera poised only on the two, Brooks and Arlen deliver a lovely, poignant scene, their characters, Jim and Nancy, each expressing personal feelings as well as a conveying a deepening sensitivity towards, trust in, and affection for, each other.

Noticing that she seems to be cold, Jim playfully covers Nancy's legs with his own and asks, "Warmer now?"

Then he asks if she is hungry. She licks her lips, suggesting that she is, but—so as not to concern him—says, "Not very."

Jim says that he is on his way to live with an uncle who is homesteading in Alberta, Canada, and that this might be a good place for Nancy as well. She would be out of the U.S. and safe from the law officers who will no doubt be pursuing her.

"I don't want to be no trouble to you," she replies.

"That's all right," he says.

Then, in a two-shot suggesting that a bond has just been forged, both appear happy and relieved. Now, they have a plan, and an essential part of it is that they remain together.

Next, the film cuts to a brief shot of the field of haystacks in a soothing blue filter suggesting both a calm night and that, at least for the moment, all is well in their world.

Rather than moving on to the next scene, the film cuts back to the couple inside the haystack as they share intimate thoughts.

"We're all beggars of life," Jim says. "Some begs for one thing and some for another—and me, I ain't found out yet what I want."

"I know what I want," Nancy says. "Just a place to be quiet in—a place to keep clean in—a place to call home. I never had it ... maybe I never will.... I guess that's why I want it so."

The two say good night, and, as she sleeps, he lovingly takes off his coat and lays it over her.

The film cuts to the shot of the hay field in blue filter once again as if to underscore the peace and contentment the two characters feel at that moment. Then the image fades to black.

This tranquil spell, however, is abruptly broken when a farmer with a pitchfork uncovers the two in the haystack the next morning and angrily chases them off his property. From this moment on, there will be no peace for the couple until the film's very last scene. Constantly, it seems, law officers, railroad guards, hoboes, or others are out to get them, and Nancy's dream of "a place to be quiet in" seems far from ever being fulfilled.

Again, the word "elegance" seems absolutely fitting to describe the inclusion of the haystack scene in the midst of such a grim narrative. This seemingly safe, nurturing, womb-like setting is a clear counterpoint to the hostile world on the outside—a world in which angry farmers, law officers, railroad guards, and hoboes are all after Jim and Nancy for one reason or another. Its presence, coming where it does in the story, magnifies everything that follows, increasing our empathy for the couple and making the people who threaten them seem even more unfeeling and cruel.

* * *

Another intriguing facet of *Beggars* is its preoccupation with a theme Wellman will come back to repeatedly in subsequent films such as *Heroes for Sale*, *Midnight Mary*, *Wild Boys of the Road*, and *The Ox-Bow Incident*: justice. Here, as well as throughout his work, he is clearly fascinated by such thorny questions as: What is justice? What constitutes a just verdict? In the real world, is such a thing even possible? Who, if anyone, has the right to judge or to dispense justice? Are these people truly interested in finding just solutions or merely in advancing personal (and sometimes very cruel) agendas? Should justice be tempered with mercy? If so, how do we do this?

One scene that vividly illustrates Wellman's interest in these ideas is the kangaroo court Beery's "alpha hobo" Oklahoma Red holds in the transient camp. The hoboes have discovered that Nancy, although in man's clothing, is really a woman, and the suggestion is that they would like nothing more than to gang rape her. As Red says, "Come on, baby, don't be so exclusive." Jim, however, is ready to protect her, whatever the personal cost. So Red convenes a mock trial to judge Jim that's filled with some very funny lines that twist legal jargon all around. Let's "dispense with justice," he says at one point. Later, he threatens a participant, telling him that he will not only be "disbarred" but also "dismembered." Well in advance of any verdict, he adds, "Before we go any further, the court will sentence the prisoner."

This scene—which bears striking similarities to the famous sequence in Fritz Lang's 1931 masterpiece *M*, when the local underworld puts Peter Lorre's serial murderer on trial—reveals Wellman's attitudes at their most cynical. Trials and verdicts are often just for show, he seems to be saying through Oklahoma Red—just pretexts for exerting one's control over another.

In addition to being highly entertaining, this hobo trial mirrors in a skewed way the much larger element in *Beggars* involving justice: the law's relentless pursuit of Jim and Nancy. Should, as Jim and Nancy both assume will happen if they are caught, she be hanged for shooting her abuser to protect herself from further abuse and he also be hanged for aiding her in her flight? Should the two receive lesser punishments? Or should the two simply be allowed to live quietly in Canada? Here, Wellman's sympathies are fairly clear, but he also reserves his judgment enough to nudge viewers into deciding for themselves. Is Canada the appropriate solution? Or are the two getting off too lightly? Most viewers, of course, would probably side with the Canadian option, but the verdict here is certainly not unanimous. For example, at least one 1928 review of the film—critic Harrison Carroll's in the *Los Angeles Evening Herald*—found the whole matter quite unsettling, calling film's morality "questionable" because it builds "sympathy for an escaping murderess."[15]

Finally, any appraisal of *Beggars* is incomplete without noting the acting, especially the two fine performances by Beery and Brooks.

Brooks, who was never one to mince words about fellow film performers, admired Beery's straightforwardness both as a person and as an actor, once calling his Oklahoma Red "a little masterpiece."[16] Her assessment is difficult to refute. Although Beery was a larger-than-life performer often guilty of being a "ham," his Oklahoma Red ably conveys the authority, humor, bravado, disdain for conventional morality, and fearsomeness that the character requires. We believe him when he essentially takes over a group of tough, hardened hoboes minutes after first meeting them. We even believe him when he seems so moved by the power of the love Jim and Nancy share, and so impressed by the courage this love has apparently given them, that he allows the two to escape. Because it involves such a radical change of heart for Red, this final feat is especially difficult to achieve. But Beery, largely by conveying Red's thought process so honestly and in such an understated way, manages to be quite credible. In itself, this character transformation is also "a little masterpiece."

As Nancy, Brooks is marvelous. In an era when exaggerated acting was widely practiced and accepted, she never betrays the truth of her character in a given situation. Her responses always seem real and natural, and many of them, especially when she expresses conflicting emotions, are conveyed with great subtlety. In fact, her character seems to inhabit her body so completely, that, as the saying goes, we rarely think of her as "acting." We can see an excellent example of this talent in the wonderful haystack scene. While Arlen competently conveys both the concerns that weigh the couple down and the surprising happiness Jim feels now that they have connected, Brooks—in her eyes, facial expressions, and other physical gestures—takes Nancy's feelings to another, more sublime, level. It's exciting how simply and beautifully Brooks expresses basic emotions such as disappointment and hopeful anticipation. As well as being a thoroughly captivating screen presence, Brooks was a terrific actress. It's a pity that she made so few films after she worked for Pabst in Europe.

* * *

After years when it was either considered lost or simply neglected, *Beggars of Life* is slowly but surely experiencing a rebirth. Whether it's at silent film festivals or on DVD or Blu-ray, more people are watching it and its critical reputation is on the rise. Some of these people, of course, have a special fondness for Brooks or a special interest in the chronically under-rated Wellman. But most of them may simply be drawn to it for the oldest—and best—reason of all: it's a timeless story well told. An uncompromising look at the harshness of life for the downtrodden, it is also a film of great humanity showing how the right human connections can give seemingly lost lives focus and purpose. Finally, it is a very satisfying artistic experience featuring fine writing, acting, cinematography, and editing under the watchful, endlessly resourceful direction of William Wellman. It's a great movie to see once, and, upon repeated viewings, it just gets better.

10

"Time was his; he owned it"
Erich von Stroheim and The Wedding March

> To those people who think that von Stroheim had no heart, no idealism, no sensitivity, one can only reply, "*The Wedding March.*" If he did not achieve genuine tragedy in this work, then no one has in the long history of film.—Arthur Lennig[1]

In 1920s Hollywood, a time and place filled with gifted, eccentric, ambitious, and larger-than-life film figures, perhaps no one person fits all these specifications more fully or emphatically than writer, director, and actor Erich von Stroheim. A master of self-invention and self-promotion, he spent much of his early film career seizing small opportunities through a combination of ingratiating charm, unmitigated gall, and outright lying. Once accepted in the industry, he pressed relentlessly for resources to produce grandiose, enormously expensive films and, in the process, infuriated producers and studio heads with his obsessive perfectionism and flagrant disregard for budgets and schedules. Several times he was removed from projects before they were completed; after just 13 years, he was blackballed from directing altogether; and for the remaining 25 years of his career, he could find work only as an actor.

Yet, during the first 10 of those 13 years, this man, who was determined to leave his mark on the film world in a big way, did exactly that. Two of his early directing efforts, 1919's *Blind Husbands* and 1922's *Foolish Wives*, offer superior production values and darker, more sophisticated takes on human motivations and behavior than most film audiences, especially those in the U.S., had seen up until that time. In addition, his 1924 masterpiece, *Greed*, one of the cinema's early examples of naturalistic drama that explores how environment and heredity control characters' fates, is widely considered to be one of the great landmarks in film history.

Though not as well-known as *Greed*, another exceptional von Stroheim effort is 1928's *The Wedding March*, a romantic drama that reveals even more growth in both the director's production acumen and his ability to effectively probe the inner workings of his characters.

Much like several other von Stroheim-directed efforts, the film's journey from conception to completion was long, chaotic, and bitterly contentious. The shooting and editing phases took months longer and were much more costly than planned. Then, after continued wrangling over budget, the story's excessive length (the director's first cut ran for eight hours), and other issues, von Stroheim was dismissed and others finished the project. Complicating matters even more, the October 1927 release of *The Jazz Singer* and the subsequent clamor for talking pictures made the process of selling this lengthy silent film even more daunting. Many more months of indecision and delay went by. Finally, on October 12, 1928, nearly two and a half years after shooting began, the film premiered. This version, however, dramatized only the first part of von Stroheim's original vision, and, running at just under two hours, it had been edited to the bone.

Yet, and especially in light of the film's deeply troubled production history, the finished product is surprisingly accomplished and satisfying. While only a fragment of what von Stroheim had initially planned, the

Beautiful commoner Mitzi (Fay Wray) is wooed by elegant nobleman Nicki (Erich von Stroheim) in one of several richly adorned romantic scenes in *The Wedding March* (Paramount Pictures/Photofest).

story that remains is, nevertheless, tightly focused, well-integrated, and easily able to stand on its own as a fully actualized work of art. It is, in every meaningful sense, whole. In addition, it is a work of very high quality—lovingly conceived, richly visualized, sensitively acted, psychologically sophisticated, and emotionally powerful—that superbly recreates a specific time and place with its distinctive manners and mores and convincingly portrays a broad spectrum of human experiences and perspectives. To this day, it remains one of the most remarkable releases in the remarkable movie year of 1928.

* * *

The man who shook up the 1920s film world with both his brilliant work and his extreme, often "off-the-rails" approach to filmmaking was born Erich Oswald Stroheim in Vienna in 1885. The elder of two sons in a middle-class Jewish family (his father was a hat maker), he was short, not especially attractive, and a poor student in school. From a young age he yearned to be someone quite different: a Catholic, an aristocrat, a romantic rogue, a military hero. But after repeated frustrations and failures (including a short, undistinguished military stint when he rose from private to corporal), he decided to cast himself in a new role. In November 1909, at age 24, he arrived in the U.S. in hopes of new opportunities and in possession of a new identity. Henceforth, he would be a Catholic Austrian aristocrat and army officer named Count Erich Oswald Hans Carl Maria von Stroheim und Nordenwall. For the rest of his life, he would play *this* role to the hilt.

The next five years, however, were as frustrating as his life in Austria had been. He held a series of low-level jobs, enlisted in the New York National Guard in 1911, and was dropped two months later. He married in February 1913, but his dissatisfaction with work led to heavy drinking and belligerent behavior. After he threatened to punch his wife in the face in May 1914, she filed for divorce.

Later in 1914, von Stroheim apparently met a group of actors working as movie extras who told him of opportunities in the fast-growing film industry in the Los Angeles area. Soon he was working as an extra and playing small parts. Then, most likely due to his talents as a self-promoter, he was hired as an assistant to John Emerson, a director at Majestic Studios, where D.W. Griffith was, at the time, the lead director. In his eagerness to please and advance in the ranks, von Stroheim took on more responsibilities in areas such as set decoration. Slowly but surely, he received larger and larger roles, often playing villainous Huns—typecasting that earned him the nickname "the man you love to hate."

By 1916, von Stroheim had made significant progress. Not only had he worked as an assistant to Emerson, but he had also assisted now-legendary director Allan Dwan. In addition, he had worked with three of the industry's top stars: Douglas Fairbanks, Norma Talmadge, and Mary Pickford.

After von Stroheim's well-received turn as the villain in the 1918 war propaganda melodrama, *The Heart of Humanity* (in which his character throws a baby out a second-story window), he was able to finagle a meeting with Carl Laemmle, the head of Universal Pictures. There are several differing accounts of this meeting, but, whatever the specifics, it is clear that von Stroheim's powers of persuasion, coupled with his willingness to work for very little money, soon captivated the shrewd, cost-minded studio head. The result was the green light for a film eventually called *Blind Husbands*: an effort that would be produced, directed, and written by—as well as star—none other than Erich von Stroheim. "Laemmle took the gamble," notes von Stroheim biographer Arthur Lennig, "and thus the stormiest career of any director in the whole history of movies was launched."[2]

Released in December 1919, *Blind Husbands* remains an intriguing film, especially considering that it is the work of a first-time director. While not a great advancement in filmmaking technique, it is significant for both its choice of subject matter, an emotionally neglected wife's flirtation with an extra-marital affair (scandalous stuff for 1919), and its insightful glimpses into the psychological motivations of its characters, which were virtually non-existent in films at the time. The film turned out to be a hit both with critics and audiences and made von Stroheim a force to be reckoned with in Hollywood.

In 1920, von Stroheim followed up with a now-lost film called *The Devil's Pass Key*. A domestic drama involving scandal and a couple of intriguing plot twists, von Stroheim again emphasized realism in all elements of production. Released in August 1920, the film was another critical and commercial hit for the director.

Building on the momentum of his back-to-back successes, von Stroheim then went to work on his most ambitious project yet, the story of a man (played, of course, by von Stroheim) who masquerades as an Eastern European count, seduces rich women, and then extorts money from them. Released in 1922 under the title *Foolish Wives*, the film's production history was, according to von Stroheim biographer Richard Koszarski, "a nightmare without precedent."[3] The director, who began insisting on more and more expenditures for the sake of production quality and greater storytelling realism, soon drove the project far over budget. In response, Laemmle promoted a 21-year-old staff producer named Irving Thalberg to head of production for the studio and charged him with overseeing the project and reining in the director's excesses. Thalberg eventually prevailed, ordering first a halt to shooting and, several months later, removing von Stroheim entirely from the production. Ultimately, *Foolish Wives* was a commercial and critical hit, but the cost—more than $1.1 million—made it both the first million-dollar film and by far the most expensive movie that had ever been made up until that time.

After running into many of the same problems in von Stroheim's next film, *The Merry-Go-Round*, Thalberg discharged the director before filming was completed. After four years, his tenure at Universal had ended.

Von Stroheim wasn't out of work for long, however. Because of the quality and commercial success of his first three Universal films, other studios showed great interest in his services. In November 1922, just six weeks after being fired by Thalberg, he signed with the Goldwyn Company, whose very pro-artist philosophy was to give its directors the autonomy to make each film, as Goldwyn executive Abe Lehr once put it, "a distinct entity breathing the spirit of its creator."[4] Factoring in von Stroheim's reputation for excessive spending, though, the Goldwyn contract, which called for three films in his first year, was very specific about stipulating the overall budget, the amount of film footage to be shot, and other parameters for each film.

As his first film with Goldwyn, von Stroheim chose to adapt Frank Norris's dark, sprawling 1899 novel about a commonplace couple's lust for wealth, *McTeague*, retitling the film version *Greed*. The film and the story behind its making are both the stuff of film industry legend and, in themselves, worthy fodder for entire books.

Very little about the making of the film went smoothly. The shoot was grueling and went far over budget, ending with two months of location shooting in California's Death Valley in mid-summer when temperatures often soared to more than 120° Fahrenheit. After months of editing, von Stroheim previewed an eight-hour version of the story to a dozen viewers. Several of them, including respected director Rex Ingram, called it the greatest film they had ever seen. The length, however, was deemed unmanageable, and further cuts were ordered. Then during the post-production, the Goldwyn Company was merged into the newly formed Metro-Goldwyn-Mayer, whose new production chief—and von Stroheim's new boss—was none other than Irving Thalberg, now working for MGM's Louis B. Mayer. Once again, von Stroheim and Thalberg clashed, the director was removed from the project, studio staff edited the film down to a running length of about two and a half hours, and most of the remaining footage was destroyed.

Finally released in December 1924, the film was mostly panned by critics, many of whom objected to its dark, depressing, often unsavory subject matter, and shunned by audiences. All totaled, it failed to make back even half of its $665,603 production costs at the box office, and for the rest of his life von Stroheim decried the butchering of film he fervently believed to be his masterpiece.

What remains of *Greed*, however, is still very highly regarded for its innovative storytelling techniques, uncompromising realism, superb acting, and other strengths. One striking example of innovative storytelling occurs in the wedding scene between two of the main characters, McTeague and Trina. The supposedly happy indoor ceremony is ironically contrasted with a funeral procession taking place outside the scene's window through the use of "depth of field," a photographic technique that clearly captures images placed at different distances from the camera's lens. Here it was used to great dramatic effect 17 years before it was applied in similar ways in the film often credited with pioneering the technique, Orson Welles's *Citizen Kane*. *Greed*'s realism is relentless, from the director's insistence on shooting at actual locations indicated in the story to the in-depth probing into the darker, more animal-like motivations of the characters. Also, performances of the actors involved, especially those of Gibson Gowland and ZaSu Pitts as the ill-fated McTeagues, are remarkable. Pitts especially, who specialized in comic roles for most of her 45-year Hollywood career, is a revelation as the miserly and ultimately tragic Trina. Von Stroheim, incidentally, thought very highly of her dramatic work and called upon her twice again, one of these times to play a pivotal role in *The Wedding March*.

Following the fiasco surrounding *Greed*, it seemed incredible that von Stroheim and Thalberg would ever agree to collaborate again. Despite his differences with the director, however, Thalberg believed he had great talent and could, if managed properly, direct a commercially successful film without going wildly over budget. Von Stroheim wasn't thrilled about the prospect, but, since he apparently needed money at the time, he had to be practical.

The project Thalberg had in mind was a silent version of the popular Franz Lehar operetta *The Merry Widow*. Once the two had agreed to terms, Thalberg kept the director, as the saying goes, "under his thumb," constantly reworking the script with him, preventing him from overshooting, insisting on the casting of certain actors, and essentially taking over the editing process. The result was a critical and popular success that adroitly blends von Stroheim's artistry with Thalberg's commercially savvy pragmatism. In terms of box office, the 1925 release would also be the most successful film of von Stroheim's directing career, bringing in $1.9 million from the box office, more than three times the film's estimated budget.

Apparently, though, even a joint venture as successful as this couldn't salvage the relationship between the equally strong-willed but diametrically opposed producer and director. In April 1925, the contract for future film projects involving von Stroheim and MGM was dissolved.

* * *

About the time the von Stroheim-MGM relationship was in its final death throes, the director began talking to Pat Powers, an independent producer who had worked with both Universal and the newly formed Disney Brothers Studio, and persuaded him to back a project that eventually became *The Wedding March*. Again, von Stroheim diligently developed a script that, if filmed to the letter, would run for many, many hours. Again, he was given a relatively free hand at filming and went far over budget. And again, he was ultimately removed and others (by this time, Paramount had become involved with the project) had to complete the film. This time, however, there were a couple of curious, and significant, differences. First, Paramount decided to make two films out of the story, one titled *The Wedding March* and the other, a sequel, titled *The Honeymoon*. Second, the studio assigned one of its most talented filmmakers, Josef von Sternberg, to help with the Herculean task of editing. Both films were eventually released, but *The Honeymoon*, due to contract restrictions, played only in South America and Europe and was never shown in the U.S. Then, in 1957, the only known copy of the film was destroyed in a fire.

All that remains today, of course, is only part of the first half of von Stroheim's original grand plan. But, because the film, in its current version, was designed as an evening's entertainment that could stand on its own and then edited with great intelligence and sensitivity, it—amazingly—succeeds quite well as a fully formed work of art.

The story takes place in Vienna in 1914, just before the beginning of World War I, and focuses mainly on Prince Nicki (von Stroheim), a free-spending playboy bachelor son of royal parents (George Fawcett and Maude George) whose family fortune is rapidly becoming depleted. When he asks each of his parents for money after a night of carousing, each tells him that the only real solution for him is to marry into wealth. Reluctant but practical, he tells his mother that, if an arrangement could be made with a suitably rich young woman, he would agree to it.

Later, Nicki, who is also an officer in the Austrian army, participates in pageantry to celebrate the religious holy day, the Feast of Corpus Christi, in front of Vienna's St. Stephen's Cathedral. There he notices and flirts with Mitzi (Fay Wray), the beautiful daughter of an innkeeper. The noise from a gun salute, however, startles Nicky's horse, and in a brief fracas the horse injures Mitzi, who is taken to the hospital. Schani (Matthew Betz), a crude and hot-tempered butcher who is with Nicki and her parents, goes into a rage, and Nicki has him arrested for disturbing the peace.

Feeling bad about the incident, as well as wanting to get to know this lovely young woman better, Nicki visits Mitzi in the hospital, bringing her a box of chocolates. She is charmed, and they begin to go on dates, several of them in gardens filled with apple blossoms, which they both associate with the feelings of love they quickly develop for each another. Learning about this, Mitzi's mother, who is deeply disturbed about her daughter's interest in this high-born ne'er-do-well, pushes for Mitzi to marry the unpleasant but gainfully employed Schani.

Meanwhile, Nicki's parents arrange a marriage between Nicki and Cecelia (ZaSu Pitts), the lame and melancholy daughter of an extremely rich and socially ambitious Viennese businessman. Schani is released from prison, learns about the relationship between Mitzi and Nicki, and shows Mitzi a newspaper article announcing the marriage of Nicki and Cecelia. Mitzi stands her ground, however, telling Schani that she hates him and still loves Nicki. Enraged, Schani tries to rape Mitzi, but at the last moment is prevented from following through. Schani now vows to murder Nicki.

Nicki and Cecelia are married with great pomp and pageantry in St. Stephen's, and during the ceremony Nicki presents Cecelia with a bouquet of apple blossoms. In the crowd of onlookers outside the cathedral, Schani, as promised, is waiting for Nicki with a gun. Just before Nicki and Cecelia exit the cathedral, a distressed Mitzi appears and promises to marry Schani if he does not kill Nicki. Schani relents but cruelly forces a now sobbing Mitzi to look at Nicki and Cecelia in their coach as it departs.

As they ride away, Cecelia asks Nicki about the sobbing woman and terrible man outside the cathedral. He stiffly says he doesn't have any idea who they are. Then, she comments, "How beautiful these apple blossoms are!" At this, Nicki wipes away a slight tear, and she continues, "Won't they *always* remind you … ?"

"Yes," Nicki says, "always."

* * *

Despite all the trials and tribulations that accompanied the making of *The Wedding March*, the finished product is an impressive achievement in terms of both conception and execution.

More than any of von Stroheim's previous films, including *Greed*, the story of *The Wedding March* captures the breadth of human experience in a mature and even-handed way. Unlike the world of *Greed*, where the emphasis is on characters who readily debase themselves for money, the world here encompasses a much broader spectrum of personalities, perspectives, and motives ranging from the kind-hearted Mitzi to the beastly Schani. Also, most of the main characters are complex and, as such, have a special authenticity and resonance about them. Nicki, who in many ways is a playboy and a parasite, quite unexpectedly experiences deep feelings of love for Mitzi. The sweet, innocent Mitzi, transformed by the love she feels for Nicki, finds the strength to stand up to Schani's threats and bullying. Far from being simply pathetic, Cecelia shows great insight and sensitivity in appraising the somewhat humiliating situation in which she finds herself. Even Nicki's money-hungry parents, Mitzi's practical but harsh mother, and Cecelia's socially ambitious father all—despite their own personal agendas—show at different times and in different ways great love for their children and concern for their children's well-being. The only character who lacks real complexity (and authenticity) is of course the vile Schani, making him perhaps the story's weakest character.

Although he had worked in film for only a decade before starting *The Wedding March*, von Stroheim also shows a level of mastery over the medium that only a relatively small percentage of directors are able to achieve in their lifetimes. His flair for art direction, first exhibited when he was an assistant to other directors, is very much in evidence here, especially in the scenes in the well-adorned home Nicki and his parents share, inside St. Stephen's Cathedral, and at the sites filled with apple blossoms where Nicki and Mitzi meet. He handles the big scenes, such as the Feast of Corpus Christi procession outside of St. Stephen's (which includes several minutes of two-strip Technicolor footage to highlight the colorful pageantry of the event) and Nicki and Cecelia's wedding with great finesse. Also, the acting, for the most part, is unusually realistic and restrained for a film of this time. Von Stroheim is quite convincing as Nicki, a good-natured but decadent and cash-strapped aristocrat, who, to his total surprise, falls deeply in love with one woman but then must accept the only practical solution for him and his parents: an arranged marriage to a rich heiress. As Mitzi, Fay Wray is a marvel. This was the breakout film for the actress who is best known today for her blood-curdling screams and revealing outfits in 1933's *King Kong*. Here, she does a wonderful job of giving Mitzi the combination of innocence, intelligence, emotional depth, and, when the time comes, courage that the story requires. In the supporting roles, other actors do fine work as well. As Cecelia, ZaSu Pitts is excellent at conveying the character's insight and sensitivity toward others as well as her own pathos. Finally, as Nicki's parents, character actors George Fawcett and Maude George are both quite effective in roles that begin as comical sniping and then shift to the more serious and subtle.

One of the miracles of the surviving version of *The Wedding March* is the film's editing, which is difficult to attribute to any single person: von Stroheim, who was involved early on; the talented Josef von Sternberg, who was committed to respecting von Stroheim's vision; long-time

Hollywood editor Frank E. Hull; or perhaps even others who are uncredited. Regardless of who deserves the accolades, however, the result is quite impressive. Despite the fact that the story, as it exists today, is only a part of what was originally intended, there are none of the continuity problems that, for instance, plague the existing, heavily edited versions of *Greed*. In addition, the main issues in the story are all resolved in the end, satisfactorily for Nicki and Cecelia's parents, but tragically for Nicki and even more tragically for Mitzi. The arranged marriage has been performed. Mitzi has made an enormous sacrifice to save Nicki's life. The consequences for everyone involved are crystal clear, and they must all now live with them.

When it was finally released in October 1928, *The Wedding March*, largely because talkies were all the rage by then, failed to attract audiences and quickly disappeared from theaters. It wasn't until the 1960s that significant numbers of people began to look at the film and appreciate its many fine qualities.

* * *

After *The Wedding March*, von Stroheim was involved as a director in only two more film projects. The first was the ill-fated *Queen Kelly*: an effort launched in 1928 as a "quality" starring vehicle for actress Gloria Swanson and produced by her lover at the time, financier and father-of-a-future-U.S.-President Joseph P. Kennedy. Hearing about von Stroheim's work history, the supremely confident Kennedy was certain he could handle him, but, when shooting went far over schedule and budget, he, too, was forced to cut his losses and fire the director. The second was a light romance called *Walking Down Broadway* that von Stroheim made for Fox Film Corporation in 1932. Filming was completed, but the studio, concerned about, as film writer Charles Stumph notes, the director's "sexual obsessions, neuroses, and other grim aspects of the film,"[5] rejected his version, fired him, rewrote and reshot about half the story, and released the film in 1933 under the title *Hello, Sister!* No one received directing credit.

Although *Queen Kelly* was conceived as a silent film when most of Hollywood was frantically adapting to talkies, the arrival of sound was not as damning for von Stroheim's directing career as were the increase in filmmaking costs that sound brought with it and the simultaneous encroachment of the studio system on the free-wheeling film auteurs of the 1920s. In an environment where tight shooting schedules, cost containment, and compliance were valued more and more, a person, no matter how talented, as dismissive of those concerns as von Stroheim was could no longer be tolerated. Unlike so many of his contemporaries whose careers crashed during or soon after 1928 because of the sound revolution, von Stroheim's career crash was, more than anything else, due to von Stroheim.

10. "Time was his; he owned it"

For the rest of his life, von Stroheim was able to work regularly in films but almost always only as an actor. In all, he appeared in more than 40 films produced both in Europe and the U.S. between 1929 and 1955. Of these, two performances are clear standouts. The first is as the elegant, wistful German military officer and aristocrat Captain (then Major) von Rauffenstein in Jean Renoir's 1937 masterpiece about World War I, *La Grande Illusion*. The second is as Max von Mayerling, the butler/chauffeur of a faded silent screen star, in Billy Wilder's 1950 film noir *Sunset Boulevard*, which (as noted earlier) stars faded silent film star Gloria Swanson as the faded silent film star. This role, which earned him an Academy Award nomination for Best Supporting Actor, is, when one knows anything about von Stroheim's silent era backstory, quite eerie. Now working as the Swanson character's servant, we learn that Max was once both her director and her husband. In fact, we are told that Max had once been widely regarded—along with D.W. Griffith and Cecil B. DeMille—as one of the three greatest directors of the silent film era. In one scene, Max even runs the projector for an at-home silent film screening for Swanson's character and her much younger current beau (William Holden) to watch. The footage we see are scenes of Swanson in, of all films, von Stroheim's *Queen Kelly*.

Why did von Stroheim take this role? It's always difficult to second-guess, but one possible explanation is that he wanted to draw attention to the humiliation he and other silent film artists had had to endure as the cold, heartless, money-grubbing world of Hollywood adapted to the talkies.

Von Stroheim married two more times after his short, ill-fated first marriage in the mid–1910s and had two children, one by each of these subsequent wives. Although he remained married to his third wife, whom he wed in 1920, for the rest of his life, he lived during his later years with French actress Denise Vernac, who was 30 years his junior. He died of cancer at age 71 in Maurepas, Seine-et-Oise (near Paris), France on May 12, 1957.

* * *

The early 20th Century literary figure Robert Sherwood, who, in addition to stage plays, screenplays, and books, wrote movie reviews, once commented, "Von Stroheim is a genius ... but he is badly in need of a stopwatch."[6] The remark is both flippant and quite telling. The writer/director had the artistic sensibility of a 19th Century novelist along the lines of a Dickens, George Eliot, or Tolstoy, and his grand, sprawling visions were, unfortunately, often incompatible with the relatively short feature film format he had to accommodate to survive as a filmmaker. He didn't sufficiently accommodate, so, ultimately, he didn't survive.

It's fascinating to ask what if von Stroheim had been born 50 years later and come into his own in the 1970s when the television miniseries had become a popular presentation form or even later than that when video streaming came into vogue in the 2010s. He would have had to make commercial compromises, many of them, in these mediums as well, and we won't ever know if he could have done this. At least, though, he would have had the benefit of longer formats to tell his stories the way he wanted to.

* * *

Although von Stroheim made many film industry enemies during his peak years in Hollywood, his idealistic, often-obsessive quest to create great art regardless of the consequences also earned him some staunch admirers. One of them was the young Fay Wray, who worked with him daily for months during the filming of *The Wedding March*. In a memoir written in the 1980s, she described the experience of seeing first-hand the commitment and passion with which von Stroheim approached his art:

> How impossible to relate the mood, the enormous capacity von Stroheim had for every minute detail of the setting, the costuming, the emphasis on symbolism, the richness of understanding about human behavior, the evident knowledge of old Vienna. *His* Vienna. There was never any sense of having to compete with time. Time was his; he owned it. He used it as it should be used by an artist. He ignored it.[7]

This may not have been the most practical, cost-efficient, or sustainable attitude for a Hollywood filmmaker in the 1920s to have, but, as Wray fervently believed, there is a great value in it, and perhaps even splendor about it, that is ultimately reflected in the art von Stroheim created. As a director, von Stroheim doomed himself, but perhaps his self-destructive approach was the only way he knew to create the kind of art that could satisfy his impossibly high standards and live on after him.

11

"I have a special confidence in you"

Lillian Gish, Victor Sjöström,[1] and The Wind

> To many, *The Wind* was an argument for the superiority of silent films over those with sound.... There are images in this film that are as poetic and as haunting as any that have ever been filmed.—Robert Osborne[2]
>
> What makes *The Wind* such an eloquent coda to its dying medium is Sjöström's and Gish's distillation of their art forms to the simplest, most elemental form: there are no frills. Sjöström was always at his best as a visual poet of natural forces impinging on human drama; in his films, natural forces convey drama and control human destiny. Gish, superficially fragile and innocent, could plumb the depths of her steely soul and find the will to prevail. The genius of both Sjöström and Gish comes to a climactic confluence in *The Wind*.... As a result, the film offers a quintessential cinematic moment of the rarest and most transcendentally pure art.—New York Museum of Modern Art[3]

While many films have proved wrong for the moment but right for the ages, few among them demonstrate this phenomenon more strikingly than MGM's *The Wind*, one of the last and—in the minds of many—one of the finest Hollywood films made during the silent era. For decades now, audiences at silent film festivals and other revivals have watched it with rapt respect and film historians have generously praised the work of both its star Lillian Gish and its director Victor Sjöström. When the film premiered in November 1928, though, critics were overwhelmingly negative and audiences generally unimpressed. The film lost money, a serious black mark for Gish, who, since 1925, had been MGM's highest paid female star.

Increasingly disenchanted with the industry that she—through her earlier work with director D.W. Griffith—had been instrumental in building, Gish would soon leave Hollywood and spend most of the next decade acting on the New York stage. The experience also soured Sjöström, who had additional concerns about the technical restrictions and increased studio meddling he saw coming with sound films. In April of 1930, he left Hollywood as well, returning to his native Sweden and eventually to working exclusively as an actor. Finally, both star and director were deeply saddened by the demise of the silent film medium, which had, for the previous 15 years, so well suited their artistic talents and aspirations.

But times were changing. Although Gish and Sjöström remained proud of *The Wind* and other films they had made at MGM, these two very serious artists now found themselves increasingly at odds with public tastes and corporate priorities. Hollywood had gone in a new direction, and neither of them could do much about it.

What survives from their time at MGM during the last years of the silent era, of course, is not only *The Wind* but also several other fine films each of them worked on, including their 1926 collaboration on the screen adaptation of Nathaniel Hawthorne's classic American novel of Puritan intolerance and repression, *The Scarlet Letter*. While it is regrettable that Gish and Sjöström were never able to work together again, it is also fortunate, considering all the vagaries of Hollywood, that they were ever able to work together at all and with some degree of artistic freedom. *The Wind*, especially, brought out the best in both of them. The continuing high regard today's classic film audiences and critics have for this film is a glowing testament to their talents. Their best was, in many respects, as good as it gets.

* * *

Only 33 years old when she completed her work on *The Wind* in the summer of 1927, Lillian Gish—petite, just five feet five inches tall, and often referred to as "delicate"—had already established herself as one of the few true giants of American cinema.

Born in Springfield, Ohio, on October 14, 1893, Lillian was the elder of two daughters of James Leigh Gish and Mary Robinson McConnell. Lillian's younger sister, Dorothy, would also become an actress and enjoy a long career in films. An alcoholic and carouser, James eventually deserted the family, causing Mary and the girls to move to East St. Louis, Illinois, to live with her brother and his wife. To support herself and the girls, Mary found work as an actress and supplemented her income by operating a candy shop that catered to patrons of a theater located next door. The girls also began acting, first in school plays and then in professional stage productions.

Letty (Lillian Gish) and Lige (Lars Hanson) play a couple who confront challenges arising from both the harsh natural elements around them and their seeming unsuitability for each other in *The Wind* (MGM/Photofest).

When Lillian and Dorothy were in their teens, Mary moved the three of them to New York where stage acting opportunities were much more plentiful. Soon, the girls became good friends with a next-door neighbor, another young actress named Gladys Smith. Gladys—who did some work in films for a director named D.W. Griffith just starting out in the young industry and would soon take the stage name Mary Pickford—eventually introduced the two sisters to Griffith and helped them secure contracts with Biograph Studios, where he then worked. In 1912, both Lillian and Dorothy made their film debuts in a 16-minute Griffith thriller called *The Unseen Enemy*, their work moving one reviewer to single out their "charming performances."[4]

Immediately sensing unusual potential in both these young actresses, Griffith featured them in dozens of short and feature-length films over the next couple of years. Seeing in Lillian's performances, especially, a keen intelligence and strong will that could offset her seemingly fragile physical frame, he cast her in increasingly challenging dramatic roles and she quickly became a star.

For the next decade, she would be indispensable to Griffith as he and his production team revolutionized filmmaking with such groundbreaking works as 1915's *Birth of a Nation*, 1916's *Intolerance*, 1919's *Broken Blossoms*, 1920's *Way Down East*, and 1921's *Orphans of the Storm*. For the rest of her life, though, she would have to contend with the barrage of criticism *Birth of a Nation* received (and continues to receive) for its overt racism. In film after film during this period, her brilliant performances captivated audiences. One highpoint is her deeply affecting turn as an abused young woman who is drawn to the kindness of a sensitive young Chinese man in *Broken Blossoms*, one of Griffith's best films. Another is the climatic sequence at the end of *Way Down East*, one of the most famous sequences in all of silent film, when her character lies unconscious on an ice block floating down a river toward a waterfall, her long hair and hand trailing in the bitterly cold water. To ensure realism, Gish did the scene on a real ice block under real-life conditions without the help of a stunt double or any special effects. In addition to making an unforgettable impression on audiences, the sequence remains compelling evidence of the lengths to which Gish would go to give a memorable performance.

Eventually, though, Gish's desire for more artistic control over films she starred in, Griffith's budget problems, and the director's growing interest in molding a younger actress named Carol Dempster into his next big star led to a professional break-up. In September 1922, she signed a contract with Inspiration Films, a small production company that gave her much more artistic control over film projects but that also required her to share in the financial risks of filmmaking. There she made two intriguing films, both for rising young director Henry King and both on location in Italy. The first was 1923's *The White Sister,* a romantic melodrama that would make her costar, the dashing young Ronald Colman, a major star in his own right. The second was a beautifully shot but quite expensive 1924 adaptation of nineteenth-century English writer George Eliot's sprawling historical novel *Romola*, which again featured Colman as the love interest along with a young William Powell and Lillian's sister Dorothy in key supporting roles.

Feeling the pressures of the costly production, Gish, now intent on working with an organization with "deeper pockets," signed with the newly formed and very well-resourced MGM in May 1925. Along with a handsome salary, she received the promise of a major voice in choosing her projects, directors, costars, and other key production personnel.

For her first MGM film, Gish and the studio settled on a silent version of the *La Bohème* story, which is probably best known as the inspiration for Puccini's popular 1896 opera. Quite impressed with scenes she'd watched from MGM's new World War I epic *The Big Parade*, she requested, and received, the services of its highly respected director King Vidor.

Writing about the experience many years later, Vidor was quite impressed with Gish's talent as an actress, knowledge of cinematography and other filmmaking arts, and dedication to delivering the best performance possible. To prepare for her character's death scene, for example, the director noted that Gish went for three days without drinking water and, even when she slept at night, kept cotton pads between her teeth and gums to soak up all her saliva. After doing this, Gish arrived on the set to shoot the scene with sunken eyes, hollow cheeks, and parched lips, and looked so ill herself that Vidor and others wondered if they might not only be filming the character's death scene but also their star's.[5] As she had done in *Way Down East* six years earlier, Gish again showed the extraordinary lengths to which she was willing to go to achieve an extraordinary result.

For Gish's next project, she and MGM agreed on an adaptation of *The Scarlet Letter*, starring Gish as the story's heroine Hester Prynne. As her director, she chose Victor Sjöström, a leading Swedish filmmaker who had come to the U.S. three years earlier to direct. Gish and Sjöström each sensed an artistic kinship with the other almost immediately and worked together quite harmoniously during the production. The result was a major critical and commercial success. A highlight of the film is Gish's performance as the strong and self-assured yet mercilessly persecuted Hester. Here, as in her other great silent work, she conveys the emotional essence of her character to the audience in an utterly honest and natural way. As one of her biographers, Charles Affron, notes about this performance, "Lillian goes beyond language to express that which words labor to convey. She provides an access, a point of entry, to an experience in all its many dimensions and temporalities."[6]

After Gish's next film, a drama called *Annie Laurie*, proved both a critical and commercial failure (and her relationship with MGM was beginning to show signs of strain), she found a property that excited her a great deal. It was *The Wind*, a 1925 novel by writer and literature professor Dorothy Scarborough that is set in 1880s Texas. To translate the novel into film, Gish once again requested, and received, the services of Victor Sjöström.

* * *

Fourteen years older than Gish, Victor Sjöström had, like the actress, also established himself as a leading figure in early silent films well before coming to MGM.

Born in Värmland, a province in west-central Sweden bordering Norway, Sjöström moved to the U.S. with his family when he was one year old. Then, when he was just seven, his mother died in childbirth, and he eventually moved back to Sweden and lived with relatives in Stockholm.

Victor Sjöström (right), shown here with actors Lars Hanson (left) and Greta Garbo on the set of the now-lost 1928 film *The Divine Woman*, returned to his native Sweden soon after talkies took over and concentrated on acting for the rest of his career (MGM/Photofest).

As a teenager, he loved the theater. But, when he completed his schooling, he made what seemed to be the more sensible career choice of going into business and became a doughnut salesman. He failed miserably at this, however, and soon turned his attention back to the stage where he quickly found success as an actor and then a director in a touring theater company.

In 1912, Sjöström moved from stage to film, going to work as an actor, director, and writer at the pioneering Swedish film company Swenska Bio. Over the next decade he made more than 40 films, most of them shorts. About three-fourths of these have been lost, but several of his later feature-length films—and, according to contemporary critics, his best efforts during this period—have survived. Among these are a few based on the work of Sweden's Nobel Prize-winning novelist Selma Lagerlof.

Although most of Swenska Bio's films during this period are forgettable melodramas, romances, and comedies, Sjöström managed to develop a strong personal voice. Increasingly, his efforts were noted for their focus on themes ranging from guilt and redemption to the role of women in society, complex portrayals of characters, intriguing use of flashbacks and

11. "I have a special confidence in you" 139

other storytelling techniques, and frequent use of the Swedish landscape to reflect different aspects of the psychological conflicts his films' characters experience. To link character and environment in the most realistic ways, he often shot films in actual wild, rural, and village locations, a practice unusual for the time.

Sjöström's first international hit and the film most frequently cited as his Swedish masterpiece is his 1921 adaptation of a Lagerlof story, *The Phantom Carriage*. A morality tale that blends elements of fantasy, naturalism, several excellent acting performances, intricate plotting, striking visual images, and (for the time) very inventive use of flashbacks and double-exposures into the mix, it remains gripping and thought-provoking even after a century. A highlight is Sjöström's own performance as David Holm, a thoroughly disreputable character who, as he faces death, undergoes an eerie and profound personal transformation.

Greatly impressed by *The Phantom Carriage*, Louis B. Mayer, then an independent producer, invited Sjöström to the U.S. in 1923 to make films for Goldwyn Pictures, which soon became part of the newly formed MGM. During the nearly seven years Sjöström worked as a director in the U.S., he made nine films, eight silent and one early and quickly forgotten talking picture. Of the silent films, only four survive in their entirety, and, of these, three—the two he made with Gish and a 1924 psychological melodrama he made with Lon Chaney, Norma Shearer, and John Gilbert, *He Who Gets Slapped*—remain highly regarded.

Based on a 1915 Russian play by the same name, *He Who Gets Slapped* is the dark, rather strange story of an obscure scientist whose wife and an unscrupulous baron conspire to steal, and take credit for, his earthshaking discoveries about the origins of human life. Devastated and humiliated, the scientist becomes a circus clown named "He who gets slapped" whose act is basically allowing himself to be slapped by other clowns as the audience roars with laughter.

Considering that—if not handled well—dark, strange subject matter such as this can quickly descend into farce, Sjöström did an excellent job of keeping a serious, grimly ironic, and sometimes poignant tone throughout by eliciting nuanced, psychologically credible performances from his actors. Especially effective are Chaney's masochistic scientist-turned-clown, Shearer's young circus performer, and character actor Marc McDermott's villainous baron. The director then bolsters the storytelling with vibrant, well-orchestrated staging; brisk pacing; and excellent use of cross-cutting both to drive the story forward and to heighten the drama. The result is an engaging, memorable film.

After making two more films, *Confessions of a Queen* and *The Tower of Lies* (both released in 1925 and, except for a few fragments of *Confessions*, both now considered lost), Sjöström began his two-film collaboration with Gish by accepting her invitation to direct 1926's *The Scarlet Letter*.

Gish's choice of Sjöström for this film was a savvy one, enabling him to work with subjects such as adultery, guilt, public intolerance, atonement, and the relationship between characters and their natural environment, which he had handled well in his Swedish films.[7] The finished product remains one of the best, if not *the* best, film adaptations of this iconic American novel. In addition to Gish's superb portrayal of the story's heroine Hester Prynne, the film delivers in scene after scene in multiple ways. One is the captivating imagery throughout. In one scene, for example, Gish's Hester loosens her long hair in a way that suggests both her sensual nature and her yearning to be free from Puritan sexual and social repression. In another scene, the sinister, web-like shadow of a spinning wheel is centered on Gish's womb to underscore the web of prejudice surrounding Hester's illegitimate pregnancy. Another way the film delivers is in the very effective staging of big crowd scenes. An excellent example of this is the film's finale in the town square when the public confession of the dying the Reverend Dimmesdale (Swedish actor Lars Hanson) deeply moves the townspeople who, until then, have been so merciless towards Hester. Still another, in light of the story's highly charged subject matter, is Sjöström's ability to draw well-modulated, understated performances, not only from Gish, but also from actors throughout his cast. This is a first-rate film.

* * *

In early 1927, both Gish and Sjöström then turned their attention to a film adaptation of *The Wind*. As had been the case with both *La Bohème* and *The Scarlet Letter*, she functioned as the film's *de facto* producer as well as its star, choosing (in addition to the property and her director) the screenwriter (the gifted Frances Marion), her leading man (again Lars Hanson), and other key production personnel.

The story of *The Wind* centers on Letty Mason, a refined but penniless young woman from Virginia who travels by train to Texas to live with her cousin Beverly (Edward Earle) and his family on their remote ranch. As her train nears her destination, she finds the constantly blowing wind more and more unnerving. Another passenger, a dapper but smarmy cattle buyer named Wirt Roddy (Montagu Love), appears to be attracted to her, makes her acquaintance, and strikes up a conversation about the region's incessantly blustery weather.

As soon as Letty arrives at Beverly's ranch, however, his wife Cora (Dorothy Cumming), sensing that Letty might represent a threat to her position, begins to pressure Letty to find another living arrangement, which, considering Letty's position, can only mean marriage to a local man. At first, Letty is drawn to the more urbane Wirt, who offers to take her away. When she learns that he is already married, though, she is appalled. Eventually, she settles on a well-meaning but roughneck rancher named Lige (Hanson), but put off by his coarse ways on their wedding night, she rejects him. Deeply hurt, Lige nevertheless reacts honorably, promising never to touch Letty again and to raise the money to send her back to Virginia.

With his ranch and other responsibilities, however, Lige is often gone from their isolated cabin, leaving Letty alone to cope with the ever-present wind, an experience that unnerves her more and more. Then, when Lige leaves to help round up wild horses to raise money for himself and other cattlemen, Wirt comes to the cabin and rapes her.

At her breaking point the next morning, Letty resists Wirt's demand to leave with him, shoots him, and then buries him in the sand outside the cabin. Later, she recoils in horror as she looks out the window and sees that, because of the wind, the sand has shifted, partially revealing Wirt's body. Running away from the window, she then sees two hands holding the cabin's door trying to force it open and assumes it is Wirt somehow still alive.

Instead, it is Lige who has returned. Greatly relieved and thrilled to see him, she kisses him. Then she confesses to killing and burying Wirt. When Lige looks outside, however, Wirt's corpse is nowhere to be seen. He shares with Letty a bit of local lore claiming that, when a killing is justified, the wind can remove all traces of it. Although Lige now has enough money to send Letty away, she says that she loves him, no longer wants to leave, and is no longer afraid of the wind or anything else.[8]

* * *

The Wind is widely regarded as one of the greatest of all American silent films for many reasons, and nearly all of them can be traced back to three factors critical to its creation. The first is Sjöström's great gift for visual storytelling, which, while present in his other silent films, reaches absolute mastery in this one. The second is Gish's rare talent as an actress, especially her ability to visually convey complex truths within emotionally charged situations with both honesty and economy and without—as so often happens in silent films—resorting to histrionics or other manipulative tricks. The third is their shared ability (along with other actors and contributors, of course) to fuse their individual contributions together fully and seamlessly to create moments of riveting cinema.

Sjöström reveals his gift for visual storytelling in numerous ways. Most obvious is the array of striking visual images we see throughout the film from the hanging animal carcass that the character of Cora carves up with a large, intimidating knife to Wirt Roddy's dead body partially revealed in the shifting sands. In every case, these images are telling us something that enhances the story in one way or another. The carcass, for example, gives emphasis to the harshness and rawness of the environment and how it has affected Cora. Also, Wirt's partially revealed body (which may be real or a figment of Letty's now near-paranoid mental state) suggests many things from the wind's power to bring even the dead back into the world to Letty's own tremendous fear and guilt. In addition, Sjöström employs a variety of more subtle visual touches to enrich the proceedings. One absolutely fascinating touch is the frequent absence of horizon lines in the outdoor scenes. In westerns, for example, horizon lines are standard establishing shots that have several uses, one of which is to help give a film's viewers a sense of geographic orientation—to visually reinforce where things are in relation to other things. In *The Wind*, however, the constant churning of the sand repeatedly blocks out horizon lines from outdoor scenes. Not only does this suggest Letty's personal disorientation, but it also creates a similar disoriented feeling in the minds of the viewers and, perhaps, gives them added insight into, and empathy for, Letty and her struggles.

Gish's abilities are also on full display in *The Wind*. In many respects, her performance is the summation of her work as an actress in silent film. Here, she takes the story, her character, and the hard task of conveying, even in the most melodramatic situations, emotional truths with the utmost seriousness and the highest level of commitment. And here, the transformation that her Letty goes through from sheltered young woman to worn-down wife, to crazed rape victim turned murderer is certainly executed as well as, if not better than, any transformation she had gone through in any of her previous films, including her great performances in *Broken Blossoms* and *La Bohème*.[9] Throughout *The Wind*, as Charles Affron eloquently puts it, "Her intentions are so vivid that she seems to be speaking without uttering a word."[10]

In addition, both Sjöström and Gish have an amazing knack for integrating their contributions (with each other's as well as those of other fine artists such as Lars Hanson) to seamlessly convey a complex, nuanced narrative almost entirely through visual means.

One of the best examples of this capability in *The Wind* is the 10-minute sequence depicting Letty and Lige's wedding night. From a minimalist wedding scene that focuses only on a sheriff/officiator, a book containing the marriage vows, and Lige's hand putting a ring on Letty's finger, the image dissolves to inside Lige's cabin where we see shots of a kitchen counter filled with dirty dishes and a cluttered table with uneaten food and uncleared dishes on it and then cuts to a reaction shot of a despondent Letty. After she and Lige say goodnight to Lige's friend Sourdough (William Orlamond), an excited Lige makes it known that he is anxious to kiss her. She complies, but with no enthusiasm. He takes her and her belongings into the bedroom and leaves to make a cup of coffee to help make her feel more comfortable. She finds the coffee impossible to drink and, when he isn't looking, pours her portion into a water pitcher by the bed. Sensing she is avoiding him, he leaves again, perhaps hoping that she will prepare herself for bed. The film then crosscuts between shots of him pacing in one room and her pacing in the other. The crosscuts then shift to close-ups of his boots and her shoes pacing in their respective rooms. Finally, the sexual tension is too much for Lige. He enters the bedroom and forcefully kisses her. The action repels her. In disgust, she wipes the taste of his lips off hers. "You've made me hate you," the intertitle reads. "Oh Lige—I didn't want to hate you." Deeply saddened and hurt, he promises both never to touch her again and to find the money to send her away. Then, walking near the bedside table, he notices the coffee Letty has poured into the pitcher. Both react to the additional humiliation, he with even greater feelings of rejection and sadness, she with embarrassment and some shame. He leaves her in the bedroom, and we see each alone in a different room as the wind continues to blow outside.

A defining characteristic of this sequence—and a key to its emotional power—is its scrupulous balance. Together, Sjöström, Gish, and Hanson create a natural flow of conflicting forces such as repulsion and attraction, conciliation and antagonism, and evasion and misunderstanding. They do this through multiple visual means such as gesture, movement, facial expression, camera placement, and camera movement.[11] The result, in addition to dramatizing both the increasing sexual tension of the moment and the seeming futility of Letty and Lige's relationship, is to move audience sympathy back and forth between the two characters in a way that never gives viewers a chance to side decisively with one character over the other. In turn, viewers are nudged to think in a more balanced, nuanced, and all-encompassing way and ultimately to adopt a greater understanding of, and empathy for, both characters' perspectives and frailties.

Another prominent characteristic is the sequence's unusual and imaginative ordering of shots, often for startling effect. The image of Letty and Lige's wedding, for example, dissolves directly to the images of uneaten food and dirty dishes in Lige's cabin, which in turn slowly dissolve to a forlorn Letty looking at the mess. Also, the medium shots of Letty and Lige both pacing in different rooms dissolve to close-ups of their pacing shoes and boots and then suddenly cut to a medium shot of Lige roughly, forcefully kissing Letty. As viewers, we find such arrangements of shots both jarring and disturbing, increasing the sequence's dramatic tension, our emotional response, and our sympathies for characters (Letty, especially, in these instances).

* * *

Although the reasons most often given for *The Wind*'s critical and commercial failure have been its downbeat subject matter and the rapidly declining audience interest in silent films, other factors also came into play. One was the decision by MGM executives to delay the film's release by more than a year. When it finally premiered (13 ½ months after the premiere of *The Jazz Singer*), audiences largely saw it as a relic. It's curious that, although MGM also held up the release of *The Crowd* for similar reasons, it premiered just four months after *The Jazz Singer* and (surprisingly) made money. A second factor was a soundtrack with music and sound effects added after the fact in hopes of enhancing *The Wind*'s commercial value. To try to make things more upbeat, the soundtrack included a theme song written especially for the film called "Love Brought the Sunshine," which was as comically inappropriate for this story as it might be for a film noir from the 1940s. A third factor could very well have been several negative reviews attacking Gish, whose acting (although it was actually evolving and expanding in very exciting ways) was increasingly seen as dated. Finally, a fourth factor was Gish's overall silent screen image, which like Mary Pickford's, was not seen as "modern" in the way younger actresses such as Norma Shearer, Greta Garbo, and Joan Crawford were. In any case, it appeared that this chapter in Gish's, Sjöström's, and Hanson's (who had no future in Hollywood talkies because he couldn't speak English) professional lives, was coming to an end.

* * *

After the disappointing release of *The Wind*, Gish's relationship with the Hollywood-based film industry changed considerably. She made two lackluster talkies in the early 1930s, and, after a series of well-received New York stage performances during that decade, returned to movies periodically beginning in the 1940s to perform mostly in supporting roles. One of these performances, her role as the long-suffering Laura Belle McCanles in King Vidor's 1946 epic western *Duel in the Sun*, earned her a Best Supporting Actress Academy Award nomination. Another was her brilliant turn as Rachel Cooper, a strong, tough-as-nails older woman who cares for homeless children, in Charles Laughton's classic 1955 thriller *Night of the Hunter*.

Based mainly in New York for the rest of her life, Gish divided her time among many interests. From the late 1940s to the early 1980s, she

11. "I have a special confidence in you" 145

performed on a variety of television shows from early anthology series such as the Philco Television Playhouse to made-for-TV movies, to TV series ranging from the legal drama *The Defenders* to the romantic comedy *The Love Boat*. As the names of more and more other leading silent film figures were forgotten over the decades, her reputation only seemed to grow. In 1971, she received an Academy Honorary Award for her artistry and contributions to the development of the motion picture medium. Then, in 1984, at age 90, she became only the second female (after Bette Davis) to receive the American Film Institute's Lifetime Achievement Award. Along the way, she also picked up the unofficial title "The First Lady of American Cinema," and she often used her unique position to champion silent films and advocate for their preservation.

She ended her film career in grand style exactly 75 years after she had begun, starring, at age 93, in director Lindsay Anderson's 1987 drama *The Whales of August*, a story of two elderly sisters (the other played by Bette Davis) who spend their summers on an island off the coast of Maine. Although the film received mixed-to-positive reviews, Gish's performance was widely praised, and that year she received the National Board of Review Award for Best Actress. There was much talk of Gish's also receiving a Best Actress Academy Award nomination, and, when she was passed over, people throughout the film world expressed their displeasure. Gish, however, responded to the news with the droll remark, "Well, now I won't have to go and lose to Cher."[12] (Cher eventually did win the Oscar for Best Actress that year for her performance in Norman Jewison's *Moonstruck*.)

Gish, who was extremely close to both her mother Mary and sister Dorothy throughout their lives, never married or had children. She was, however, linked romantically to several men at various times, including the legendary New York theater critic George Jean Nathan. Gish died in New York of heart failure on February 27, 1993. She was 99 years old.

* * *

Although he did direct three now-forgotten sound films, Sjöström's serious directing career essentially ended with *The Wind*. He spent the rest of his professional life acting, both on the Swedish stage and in Swedish films.

His silent film work both in Sweden and the U.S. has since had a profound impact on many directors. One of them was his fellow Swede, Ingmar Bergman, who would later direct Sjöström in two films, most notably Sjöström's final film appearance at age 78 in the 1957 drama *Wild Strawberries*. Cementing Bergman's international reputation, the film won numerous awards and is regularly included on lists of the greatest films ever made. One of the major contributing factors for the film's enduring appeal has been almost universal praise for Sjöström's performance as an elderly professor who is forced to look back at, and reevaluate, his long life. At the time of the film's release, Sjöström also received many honors for this work on it, including that year's National Board of Review's Best Actor Award in the U.S.

In an interview nearly 25 years after working with Sjöström on *Wild Strawberries*, Bergman generously praised his older colleague, saying how much he valued "being granted the opportunity to talk to such a great master of his craft, to listen to him and absorb his words." Concluding, Bergman added how this had made him feel that he was "a part of a grand tradition."[13]

After two unsuccessful marriages, Sjöström went on to lead a very happy—and private—life for many years with his third wife Edith Erastoff, who died in 1945. The two had one daughter, Guje Lagerwall, who also acted in Swedish films. Sjöström died on January 3, 1960, at age 80.

* * *

About 30 years after they had worked together on *The Wind* and just a few years before he died, Sjöström, not a person who easily expressed affection or admiration, sent a letter to Gish, with whom he apparently hadn't communicated in some time. "I know I have quite a few very good friends," he wrote, "but you have in a special way come so close to my heart. I have a special confidence in you, feel that you understand me thoroughly. Rather strange after all these years."[14] Although it is highly unusual for comments such as these to arrive in the mail decades after two people had last worked together, they reflect a level of trust, respect, and affection between professional colleagues that is rare under any circumstances.

The feelings were reciprocated, too. Gish also spoke fondly about her old director, once saying, "I never worked with anyone I liked better."[15]

Neither Sjöström nor Gish was a victim of the sound revolution in the tragic way that so many other silent film luminaries were. Both could and did continue to have productive and fulfilling careers as actors on the stage, in sound films, and, in Gish's case, television. For both of them, however, something very special was lost when the reason they had come together—the opportunity to make silent films—had died. Both possessed talents that meshed extremely well with this medium and a deep appreciation for its unique strengths as an art form. Both also had, as Sjöström's quote certainly affirms, an especially close personal connection, that "special confidence" in each other as partners in the pursuit of great collaborative art. The two films they made together, especially *The Wind*, emphatically reflect this rare and inspiring reality.

12

Partners in Perversity

Lon Chaney, Tod Browning,
and West of Zanzibar

From John Ford and John Wayne to Tim Burton and Johnny Depp, film history is liberally peppered with examples of long-running and extremely fertile director-star collaborations. The reasons for this intriguing phenomenon are numerous, and among them two seem to be cited most often. First, a director and a star share similar worldviews and artistic preoccupations. Second, a director sees in a particular star the potential to serve as an onscreen alter ego, perhaps even a muse. Sometimes, when both these factors are in play, the results can be spectacular. We see this, for example, in the nine films director Martin Scorsese and actor Robert De Niro made together between 1973 and 2020. Both New Yorkers of Italian descent, both fascinated by social misfits, and both preoccupied by the negative, sometimes violent sides of male behavior, the two were driven to delve deep into the same dark subjects and themes. In addition, De Niro often proved to be the ideal muse for Scorsese, the actor who could convey what the director was trying to express better than perhaps anyone else.

Something very similar was also at work during the 1919–1929 collaboration between actor Lon Chaney, Sr., and director Tod Browning. Much less well-known today than other classic partnerships such as Scorsese-De Niro, this very creative, and often very strange, alliance was still hugely successful and influential in its own right. The two collaborated on 10 films, all silent, and most of them so steeped in various kinds of human perversity that film scholar Gregory William Mank once described them as conveying "the most incredible catalogue of vengeance, cruelty, deformity, and sexual aberration in horror history."[1] During a decade when films were dominated by the wholesome likes of Pickford, Chaplin, and Lloyd, this duo and their work seem odd indeed. Their films are remarkable for dwelling on the dark side of the human psyche in ways that were unthinkable to most of their filmmaking contemporaries. Yet, their films are also so credible and compelling that audiences flocked to them and were absolutely mesmerized.

Of their collaborations, one of the best is their second to last, a film version of the lurid 1926 Broadway melodrama *Kongo*, which was retitled *West of Zanzibar*. Opening on November 24, 1928, the film is a marvelous showcase both for Chaney, who was clearly drawn to the story's profoundly twisted but still very human central character, and for Browning, a former carnival and circus performer who had lifetime fascinations with freakish people and things as well as abhorrent behavior. While there was some pressure to produce *West of Zanzibar* as a sound film, Chaney and Browning, who both disliked the idea of working in the new medium, won out, and the film was made as a silent and released as a hybrid, with a soundtrack and some sound effects. Once released, much of the initial critical response was fiercely negative. One trade journal, *Harrison's Reports*, even went as far as to call the film "An outpouring of the cesspools of Hollywood!" adding, "How any normal person could have thought that this horrible syphilitic play could have made an entertaining picture ... is beyond comprehension."[2] Outrage at the film also drove various guardians of morality to lead a fierce campaign against it. Despite such efforts, however, the film was a major popular success both in the U.S. and in Europe in late 1928 and 1929, and, for both years, Chaney was voted America's top male box office draw.

* * *

By far the better-known part of the Chaney-Browning partnership today is Chaney. Often called "The Man of a Thousand Faces," he is recognized both as one of the most riveting and versatile actors of the silent era and as a pioneer and absolute master of make-up for film roles. Appearing in more than 300 films (mostly shorts and most of them now lost) between 1913 and 1930, he played an extraordinarily wide variety of people and physical types. Of these, a relatively small number were horror roles, but the impact of these roles was immense. He especially relished the chance to play lost, tortured souls, whose disabled or disfigured bodies reflected a past misfortune, festering emotional pain, or inner ugliness, and, in playing these kinds of characters, to find their intense, and usually conflicting, emotions and basic humanity. "Drop Chaney into the most operatic of situations," film historian and critic Mick LaSalle has noted, "and he will find the truth in it."[3]

Perhaps even more than most actors, Chaney's upbringing influenced his work. Born in 1883 to a mother and father who were both deaf mutes, the young Chaney learned to communicate with them through

Crane (Lionel Barrymore, left), Phroso (Lon Chaney), and Maizie (Mary Nolan) form a strange and deeply troubled triumvirate in *West of Zanzibar* (MGM/Photofest).

pantomime. This led him to the stage and vaudeville in the early 1900s and finally to films in the 1910s. Of his many silent films, perhaps his two most famous non–Browning efforts are 1923's *The Hunchback of Notre Dame* directed by Wallace Worsley and 1925's *The Phantom of the Opera* directed by Rupert Julian. He only made one talkie, a lackluster 1930 remake of a 1925 hit he'd made with Browning called *The Unholy Three*.

Unlike many of his film industry colleagues during the high-flying 1920s, Chaney went to great pains to keep his private life private, once stating, "Between pictures, there is no Lon Chaney."[4] Chaney's first marriage ended unhappily. But it produced his one child, a son named Creighton (who later acted as Lon Chaney, Jr., in scores of films, including 1939's *Of Mice and Men*, 1941's *The Wolfman* and 1952's *High Noon*). When Chaney married again in 1915, he and his second wife, Hazel, raised young Creighton. According to the limited information available about them, all three lived amicably together. Near the end of 1929, however, Chaney was diagnosed with bronchial lung cancer. The disease gradually worsened. Then, in late August 1930, he died of a throat hemorrhage. He was 47 years old.

* * *

Although Browning is not as well known today as Chaney, he had quite a fascinating life and career of his own. A major force in creating and refining the horror genre in American film, he has also received a colorful name from film writers: "The Edgar Allan Poe of Cinema."

Born Charles Albert Browning, Jr., to a well-to-do family in Louisville, Kentucky, in 1880, he ran away from home at age 16, changed his first name to Tod, and for more than a decade worked extensively in circuses and carnivals. Drawn to the bizarre and freakish facets of these operations, he performed in a live burial act for a time in which

Nicknamed the "Edgar Allan Poe of Cinema," Tod Browning usually focused on the dark, macabre side of human experience in his films (Photofest).

he was billed as "The Living Corpse." Reportedly, he also had numerous affairs with women who performed in freak show acts. In 1913, he met D.W. Griffith and began acting in many of the director's films. Then, in 1915, an automobile he was driving hit a railroad train, and, while Browning and one passenger suffered serious injuries, another passenger, fellow Griffith actor Elmer Booth, was killed instantly. Devastated both physically and emotionally by the experience, Browning spent the next two years recovering from his injuries, writing scripts, and plotting his next moves in film. In 1917, he began directing. One of his earliest efforts, a drama for Metro Studios called *The Jury of Fate*, impressed studio executives with its use of double-exposure techniques, which were especially innovative for the time

When his father died in 1919, however, Browning went into a dark, alcoholic period. He was released by Universal, where he had been working and had briefly collaborated with Chaney. He didn't find work until 1923 when he signed a one-picture deal with Samuel Goldwyn to make a drama called *The Day of Faith*. The film was successful, and he was again in demand.

This led to a 1925 reunion with Chaney at the newly formed MGM and their collaboration on the film *The Unholy Three*. This story of three circus performers, a cross-dressing ventriloquist, a midget, and a strongman who steal jewels from rich people using cons and disguises, this film possesses much of what we now associate with Browning's very personal brand of filmmaking: the plight of outliers, perverse characters, and a bizarre plot. It was, as film historian Alfred Eaker has written, the first time Browning was "able to craft a film which attractively resonated with the aberration of his soul."[5] It was also a huge hit. With the strong support of MGM production head Irving Thalberg, Browning and Chaney made seven more films together over the next four years.

In addition to *West of Zanzibar*, two of these are of special note. One is their excellent 1927 effort *The Unknown*, another eerie tale involving carnival performers that also features a young Joan Crawford in one of her most memorable silent film roles. In the film, Chaney plays Alonzo, an armless (or so it seems) carnival knife thrower who uses his feet to throw with pinpoint accuracy and who is obsessed with his partner in the act, the beautiful Nanon (Crawford). Because other men have groped her relentlessly, Nanon has a phobia about men's arms and hands. Since Alonzo is armless, she feels relaxed and comfortable with him because, as she sees it, at least with him she won't be pawed. Unknown to her and others, though, Alonzo actually has arms, which he has previously used to strangle a man to death and which he now hides by binding them tight to his body. Hoping to win Nanon for good, and to avoid being suspected of the murder, he blackmails a surgeon into amputating his arms. In the meantime, Nanon has fallen for another, younger man, whom she trusts, and has moved beyond her phobia. At learning this, Alonzo becomes wildly jealous, and, as we might suspect, tragedy follows.

As well as giving Chaney the opportunity to play one of his creepiest and simultaneously most poignant roles, *The Unknown* also shows off Browning's growing skills as a creator of mood, director of actors, and stager of scenes. Another important collaboration, *London After Midnight* (also 1927), is Browning's first venture into vampire films. Although the last known print of the film burned in a 1967 MGM vault fire, Turner Classic Movies aired a fascinating reproduction in 2002 that drew from both the script and still photographs of the film that have survived. While not the actual film, this reproduction does give audiences an absorbing glimpse into what the viewing experience may have been like.

After 1929's *Where East Is East*, in which Chaney plays a wild animal tamer whose face bears the scars of animal attacks, Browning and Chaney began planning for a film version of *Dracula*. During pre-production, however, Chaney died, and Browning reluctantly turned to Hungarian actor

Bela Lugosi to play film's title role. Browning was not pleased with Lugosi's performance, and the film, which was finally released in 1931, is plodding and visually uninspired. This was due to the limitations of early sound technology as much as with Browning's discomfort with sound. *Dracula*, nevertheless, turned out to be an enormous hit. As a result, Lugosi became a major horror genre star and Browning's professional capital soared.

Taking advantage of the success of *Dracula*, Browning began work on a film that would ultimately prove to be both his supreme masterpiece and his professional undoing. The film, released in early 1932 and aptly titled *Freaks*, delved more deeply into the experience of carnival life and human freakishness than any of his previous efforts. Focusing entirely on a troupe of carnival performers, Browning cast both professional actors and real-life carnival freaks. Even to today's audiences, the wide array of freakish and deformed people from conjoined twins to people with no legs, deformed heads, and other abnormal features is quite unsettling to watch. As the film unfolds, though, Browning's theme of tolerance becomes apparent as we gradually see the physically deformed "freaks" as decent, honorable people and that two of the so-called "normal" people—conspirators plotting to murder one of the performers for his substantial inheritance—as the real monsters. The idea is brilliant, and, even though *Freaks* is often promoted as a conventional horror film, it is nothing of the sort. Unfortunately, though, critical reception and audience response were overwhelmingly negative, the film lost money, and Browning's career, although he did make four more films during the 1930s, was effectively over.

Officially announcing his retirement from films in the early 1940s, Browning lived, largely forgotten, until his death at age 82 in 1962. He was a victim of a throat cancer similar to the kind that had killed his great collaborator, Lon Chaney, 32 years before.

After his death, however, a new generation of cult film fans in the 1960s and 1970s reacted to *Freaks* with great enthusiasm. Since then, it has received considerable interest and praise for its truly unique take on human experience. Several film writers, in fact, have called it a subgenre of one. Curiously, too, the reemergence of *Freaks* has also led cult film fans as well as film historians back to the best of the Browning-Chaney collaborations, most notably, the 1925 version of *The Unholy Three*, *The Unknown*, and their great joint venture of 1928, *West of Zanzibar*.

* * *

"How did God ever put a thing like you on this Earth?" a young prostitute named Maizie (Mary Nolan), disgustedly asks mid-way through the film *West of Zanzibar*. She is addressing Phroso (Chaney), a former magician who has lost the use of his legs and now lives deep in the African jungle. For reasons Maizie does not know, he has had her brought to this seedy outpost and, since her arrival, has treated her with hateful disdain.

To Maizie, Phroso is simply a cruel and sadistic monster, but for those who've watched the film to his point, there is far more to the story. Once married and very much in love, Phroso, a successful magician, learns that his wife, Anna, is in love with another man named Crane (Lionel Barrymore) and plans to run away with him. In an ensuing argument, Crane pushes Phroso over a railing, crippling him, and then Crane and Anna disappear. A year later, however, Anna returns. She is near death, and she has a baby (presumably Crane's) with her. When Anna dies, Phroso vows revenge, both on Crane and the child.

The story moves forward 18 more years. Phroso, or "Dead Legs," as those at the outpost call him, makes arrangements for the child, who has been living for all this time in "the lowest dive in Zanzibar," to come to the outpost. Now a young woman, Maizie journeys there only to be appalled by a custom she soon witnesses: local natives forcing the wife or daughter of every man who dies onto his funeral pyre. She is also appalled by Dead Legs and is relieved to hear that he is not her father. Her father, Dead Legs tells her, is Crane, who is now an ivory hunter and is located nearby. Dead Legs has also arranged for Crane to come to the outpost. Unknown to Maizie, however, Dead Legs has also fixed it so that Crane will be killed and Maizie, in compliance with local native practice, thrown upon his funeral pyre.

When Crane arrives and the plot is put into motion, though, Dead Legs unexpectedly learns that Anna never ran away with Crane and that Maizie is not Crane's daughter but his. He is stunned and filled with remorse. Soon, the natives kill Crane and demand that Dead Legs turn over Maizie so they can put her on Crane's funeral pyre. Wanting to make at least partial amends, Dead Legs cleverly uses his magic skills to trick the natives into thinking that he has turned Maizie into a skeleton. This ruse, he hopes, will give her the opportunity she needs to escape. The natives, however, see through the deception, and, although Maizie manages to get away, Dead Legs goes to the pyre instead.

* * *

Commenting on *West of Zanzibar* in 2013, film writer Fritzi Kramer noted, "Sleazy doesn't even begin to describe it."[6] It's difficult to disagree: the story is about as sordid and melodramatic as they come. Dead Legs is a man so crazed and deranged by his wife's adultery that he wants to kill both the other man and the child he presumes resulted from that union. Sickened by Dead Legs, Maizie sinks into despair and alcoholism. The

African natives are treated in the most demeaning, stereotypical terms imaginable. But, as Kramer also notes, "no one could do sleazy quite as well as Chaney and Browning."[7]

Central to the film's success is Chaney's performance, which, film writer Jay Seaver has astutely noted, is, "shockingly charismatic for the character who is basically the villain, with Chaney adding the right hint of pathos underneath the rage and cruelty to get the audience to empathize with his evil plan while definitely not sympathizing...."[8]

Much of this Chaney charisma comes from his ability to demonstrate amazing command over both his character's outward presence and internal state of mind. After we briefly see him as the happily married and then suddenly betrayed Phroso, he emerges 18 years later as the thoroughly odious Dead Legs. His physical transformation is startling. Not only is he nearly two decades older, but, as his new name clearly states, he is completely without the use of his legs. In the very first scene that we see him as Dead Legs, he demonstrates this with great physical skill: crawling out of his bed on the second story of his jungle outpost, slithering down a rope to the ground floor, crawling to his wheelchair, and then pulling himself up into the seat. In every move he makes, he is utterly credible. We believe that his legs are now no more than dead weights he must drag along with him, that he is also in great physical pain, and that both his wife's betrayal and the loss of his legs have profoundly hardened his soul. This tortured, loathsome man is light years away from the happy magician we saw in the film's very first scenes. Yet, as Chaney does in many of his great roles, he also conveys his character's long-buried humanity with great conviction. An amazing moment in *West of Zanzibar* is when Dead Legs learns that Maizie is not Crane's daughter, but his. As he allows himself to absorb this new information, we can see in Chaney's face a variety of emotions: his horror as the recalls the terrible ordeal he's put Maizie through, his sympathy for the suffering she's endured, and the enormous sense of sadness and remorse he feels. Looking into his eyes, we can see his heart breaking. In lesser hands, of course, the scene would not have been nearly as effective. In Chaney's, however, a kind of emotional truth emerges that enables the film to soar above its melodramatic plotting.

In addition to Chaney's masterly work, two other performances in *West of Zanzibar* deserve praise. One is the contribution of actress Mary Nolan as Maizie. Her character could have easily been played as a one-dimensional "woman-as-victim" or "woman-in-jeopardy" stereotype. Nolan, however, infuses the role with the kind of intelligence and emotional depth that gives it added complexity and distinctiveness. After learning that Dead Legs is her father and that, to save her own life, she must also separate from him, for example, she ably expresses a range of conflicted feelings from relief in knowing that she will be safe to profound sadness in realizing that she will know her father so briefly. It's a very mature, thoughtful effort. The other is Lionel Barrymore's relative brief performance as Crane. In the film's first scenes, Crane seems to be little more than a charming philanderer. When we see Crane again as an ivory hunter in Africa, however, Barrymore brings a level of menace and cruelty to his character that serves to strengthen audience sympathies for Dead Legs. One example of this is the scene when he takes a dark delight in telling Dead Legs whose daughter Maizie really is. As a sadist, his capacity rivals, and perhaps even surpasses, Dead Legs. Again, this brings greater complexity and ambiguity to the situation, helping to lift the proceedings above melodrama.

Equally, if not more, critical to the film's success than Chaney's tour-de-force performance is Browning's direction.

In part because of Chaney's on-screen dominance, many film historians have not fully appreciated Browning's contributions to their joint efforts. They've generally acknowledged Browning's ability to infuse films with his distinctive personal stamps: a preoccupation with bizarre subject matter and his identification with freaks and outliers of various kinds. Yet, notes film historian Brian Darr, they've also labeled his work as "undistinguished" and him as "not a true filmmaker at all but a primitive, a showman who happened to make his name in the mass medium of his time."[9]

Darr, one of a growing number of film historians who takes issue with this stance, has countered, saying that "the most lucid arguments for [Browning's] mastery are his great silent films, especially those starring Lon Chaney," and adding that "*West of Zanzibar* may be the greatest of these."[10]

Looking closely at *West of Zanzibar*, we can acquire a greater appreciation for this point of view: it's clear that Browning has enriched the material in numerous ways.

Perhaps the most obvious is the way that Browning has, in a Hollywood studio, created a jungle atmosphere that brilliantly complements the nasty nature of the human story. Everything about the setting seems run-down, squalid, foul, and oozing with sweat. As Fritzi Kramer has noted, "You can practically feel the heavy, humid jungle air waft out of the screen."[11]

Darr has also suggested another artistic strategy that Browning employs not only in *West of Zanzibar* but also in several other of his silent films: using "the convention of silent cinema's voicelessness to engage the viewer's aural imagination in a crucial moment of [a story's] narrative."[12] In *West of Zanzibar*, one moment we see this is when Dead Legs tells Crane that Maizie is his daughter. At first, Crane's face is hidden from us. We see his body making heaving motions, and we assume that he is overcome with grief and sobbing. Then, when Crane finally shows us his face, we see that he hasn't been sobbing but convulsing with laughter. Maizie, as he has known all along, is Dead Legs' daughter, not his. The effect, Darr adds, results in a surprise that "has an emotional impact unapproached by the corresponding scene in [the play] *Kongo*" and is entirely Browning's doing.[13]

In addition, Darr discusses how artfully Browning routinely "arranges his actors' bodies in positions that hide or disclose secrets both narrative and psychological." As he elaborates:

> It's fascinating to take note of the many instances when one character approaches another from behind. A general pattern emerges: when characters meet each other face-to-face, it signals their meeting as congruent to the unfolding of Chaney's magician character's manipulative schemes. When one comes up on another from the back it invariably indicates that his plans are going awry. Sometimes we come into a scene between two characters after it has already begun to play out, and we have no way of knowing whether their approach was head-on or from behind. In these instances, it is as if the camera itself has snuck up on the characters and is recording them unguarded.[14]

Clearly, Browning is far more of a cinematic artist than his detractors contend. His skills—ranging from his ability to create evocative, suggestive settings to his ability to arrange and photograph actors in ways that heighten drama and reinforce meaning—are quite sophisticated and impressive. He may not have been F.W. Murnau or Josef von Sternberg, but he was certainly not a primitive.

West of Zanzibar is not without its shortcomings. Perhaps the most glaring of these is its stereotypical, and highly negative, depiction of the African natives. As one of the white characters remarks at one point, "We'll end up being a mess of chops for those cannibals!" While this kind of treatment is unacceptable by today's standards, it was typical of the times and dates the film somewhat. In the larger scheme of the story, however, the natives collectively play the relatively small role of a menacing plot device. So, while this depiction detracts, it doesn't cause irreparable harm. It is a shortcoming in a film filled with many strengths.

* * *

West of Zanzibar, Lon Chaney and Tod Browning's superb contribution to the great film year of 1928, is a last hurrah for one of the silent era's most successful director-actor partnerships. Within two years of the film's release, Chaney of course was dead, and Browning, always uncomfortable with sound, was struggling to express himself in the new medium. While their careers were cut tragically short, however, their influence, especially on the emerging Hollywood horror movie genre, was enormous. We can see Chaney and Browning's imprint on the highly successful Universal horror films of James Whale and others in the 1930s, in the haunting films of producer Val Lewton at RKO during the 1940s, and even, as film writer Bret Wood contends, "in such contemporary [horror] anti-heroes as Chucky (*Child's Play*, 1988), Freddy Krueger (*A Nightmare on Elm Street*, 1984), and Jason (*Friday the 13th*, 1980)."[15] Together, Chaney and Browning brought a strange and alluring horror sensibility to the screen: one that didn't exist before them, and one that continues to inspire filmmakers and captivate audiences well into the 21st century. Without these two kindred souls, we can honestly say, horror films as we know them would simply not exist.

13

"To reach for the moon one last time"

Douglas Fairbanks and The Iron Mask

In the late 1970s, the set designer and art director Laurence Irving recalled a few moments he shared with Douglas Fairbanks in early 1928 in the new sound stage United Artists was building at its Hollywood studios. Instead of the large, brightly lit shooting stages filled with happy bustling workers that had energized both men when they worked on silent films, the scene before them struck Irving as a "ghastly sort of cave."[1] There were no lights. Blankets to muffle noise hung all about. Wires and cables covered the floors. And Irving made a special point of noting "these menacing microphones"[2] that many actors at the time dreaded like the plague. Then, as the two men were taking in this strange, unsettling scene, Fairbanks laid his hand on Irving's arm and said, "Laurence, the romance of motion picture making ends here."[3]

The addition of sound may not have ended the romance of motion picture making forever, but, for Douglas Fairbanks, the coming of sound stages, microphones, and all the severe production restrictions that initially came with it meant the end of the kind of motion picture he loved and excelled at. Things would never be same. While his wife Mary Pickford immediately prepared to meet the new challenge head on, and his close friend Charlie Chaplin vowed to keep on making silent films, he accepted the hard facts of change with the wistful stoicism of some of the dashing, swashbuckling heroes he had played for years. Yes, at best his career was winding down. In addition to all the restrictions that sound would impose on the big, visually dynamic action-adventure films he specialized in, he was now well into his 40s, and his ability to dazzle audiences with his athletic feats and balletic grace, an ability he had once so easily exhibited, was in decline.

So, in early 1928, as Pickford forged ahead with sound and Chaplin

13. "To reach for the moon one last time" 159

stubbornly resisted it, Fairbanks chose a third course. He would do one more signature Fairbanks silent film, sparing no expense, pulling out all the stops, putting every ounce of himself into the effort. If indeed his time had come, he would go out, not just on his terms, but in the grandest style possible.

The project he chose for his valedictory to the silent era was a sequel to his 1921 hit *The Three Musketeers*. Titled *The Iron Mask*, it is based on The *Vicomte de Bragelonne*, the third and last of the Alexandre Dumas novels to feature d'Artagnan and the three original musketeers, Athos, Porthos, and Aramis. For most of 1928, Fairbanks poured his heart into the production. And, when the film premiered on February 21, 1929—a full 16 ½ months after *The Jazz Singer* had shaken the filmmaking world— it was well received by both critics and audiences. In every respect from its beautifully conceived set designs and grand spectacle scenes to its clever writing, vibrant acting, and brisk pacing, it is a swashbuckler of the first order. As Fairbanks biographer Jeffrey Vance noted about the actor-writer-producer and his production team, "They had dared to reach for the moon one last time, and they had captured it."[4]

* * *

Douglas Fairbanks, the man who transformed movie swashbuckling into a high art and set the standard for all swashbuckling films that followed, was born Douglas Elton Thomas Ullman in Denver, Colorado, on May 23, 1883. When he was five years old, his father Charles abandoned the family, leaving his mother Ella to bring up both Douglas and his older brother Robert. Soon afterwards, Ella, most likely in response to her estranged husband's action, changed her two sons' surname to Fairbanks, the surname of her first husband.

From an early age, Douglas was attracted to the stage and for several years acted in amateur productions in the Denver area. Then, after dropping out of high school at age 15, he joined the acting troupe of Frederick Barkham Warde, an English actor who toured in the U.S. and later played prominent roles in early silent films. Fairbanks stayed with Warde's company for two years and then moved to New York, where, in early 1902, he opened in his first Broadway production, a moderately successful drama titled *Her Lord and Master*. In addition to acting during his early New York years, he took various jobs between shows to make ends meet. These ranged from working in a hardware store to clerking in a Wall Street office. But, as he continued to impress producers and audiences with his performances, especially ones where he could show off his gifts for comedy and acrobatics, he was better able to support himself through the theater.

During this time, Fairbanks's life briefly veered in a decidedly

As an aging d'Artagnan in his final silent film, *The Iron Mask*, Douglas Fairbanks, Sr., still managed to provide audiences with the swashbuckling thrills that had become his on-screen trademark (United Artists/Photofest).

different direction. He fell in love with Anna Beth Sully, the daughter of industrialist Daniel J. Sully. The two wished to wed, but her father, unhappy about the prospect of his daughter marrying an actor, would agree to the union only if Fairbanks quit the theater and come to work at his soap company. After carefully considering these terms, Fairbanks agreed. On July 11, 1907, he and Anna Beth were married. Then, on December 9, 1909, their only child (and future Hollywood star), Douglas Fairbanks, Jr., was born. Soon, however, it became apparent that Fairbanks had far more potential as an actor than a soap salesman, and, by 1910, he had returned to acting for good. While this perturbed his father-in-law, his wife, always a great supporter of his acting, was thrilled. For the next several years, Fairbanks's stage career, now under the management of the famed Broadway producing team of George M. Cohan and Jed Harris, flourished.

Then, in 1914, while strolling in New York's Central Park with his wife and son, Fairbanks had a chance encounter that changed his life. A motion picture crew asked him to mug a bit for their camera. The crew was captivated by the actor's vibrant personality and acrobatic movements. Eventually, an informal "screen test" was shown to Harry Aitken of the newly formed Triangle Film Corporation. Aitken was also impressed. This led to an offer of much more money than Fairbanks could ever hope to make acting on Broadway. Even though he voiced concerns about entering the less prestigious art of the movies, it was clear that he was eager to set foot on what potentially could be a much bigger stage.

Arriving in Hollywood in 1915, Fairbanks quickly adapted to the new work environment. He began making films for Triangle that showcased his comic and athletic skills, and his very first outing, a comedy called *The Lamb*, turned out to be a major hit. Understanding the economic and artistic benefits of being his own producer, he also started his own production company in 1916. By 1918, after just three years in the business, he had joined Mary Pickford and Charlie Chaplin as one of the industry's top three box office draws. In 1919, he—along with Pickford, Chaplin, and director D.W. Griffith—formed United Artists, a company that created distribution channels for their films, enabling them greater independence from the major studios and complete control over the profits generated from their films.

In 1916, Fairbanks also began an affair with Pickford that led to his divorce from Anna Beth; Pickford's divorce from her husband, actor Owen Moore; and their eventual marriage in 1920. Although their affair had caused some scandal, the public generally embraced their marriage and the idea that "America's Sweetheart" had found true love with the dashing actor who would soon be known as "The King of Hollywood." The two would be known worldwide as "Hollywood Royalty," and they would regularly host now-legendary gatherings of celebrities and dignitaries at their Beverly Hills mansion, "Pickfair," which *Life Magazine* once described as "a gathering place only slightly less important than the White House … and much more fun."[5]

By 1920, Fairbanks was ready to embark on another career adventure, one that would drastically alter his screen image, catapult him to new heights of stardom, and ultimately define his professional legacy. He would integrate his comic and acrobatic flair into the action-adventure-romance costume drama, a genre which was then out of fashion. In his quest to present superior entertainment, he would invest liberally in every element of production.

As his first offering, he and writer Eugene Miller wrote a screenplay called *The Mark of Zorro*. Based on a story called *The Curse of Capistrano* that had been published only a year before, the film is the now-famous story of Don Diego Vega, the wealthy young man who, through his secret identity as the masked Zorro, becomes a champion of the downtrodden and oppressed in early California. An enormous hit upon its release, *The Mark of Zorro* became the template not only for most of Fairbanks's subsequent films but also for numerous swashbuckling films that have followed up to the present day. In addition, it was hugely influential in the creation of the story of Batman, the comic book, film, and television superhero. In fact, in DC Comics continuity, *The Mark of Zorro* is the film that the young Bruce Wayne sees in a movie theater just before he witnesses his parents' deaths at the hands of an armed thug.

Spurred on by the success of *The Mark of Zorro*, Fairbanks followed up with a series of more and more grandiose epics: 1921's *The Three Musketeers*, 1922's *Douglas Fairbanks in Robin Hood*, 1924's *The Thief of Bagdad*, 1926's *The Black Pirate*, and 1927's *The Gaucho*. In every one of these films, great care and creativity were put into every facet of production, and the endlessly energetic Fairbanks supervised it all, working closely (and by most accounts, quite harmoniously) with his co-writers, directors, cinematographers, lighting technicians, set and costume design staff, editors, and virtually everyone else associated with the effort. In fact, decades later, when director Allan Dwan, who had worked with Fairbanks on 10 of his films, including *Douglas Fairbanks in Robin Hood* and *The Iron Mask*, was asked what Fairbanks was like to work with, he replied without hesitation, "Oh, great, because he was very creative and on-the-ball all the time.... It was a real pleasure to work with him."[6]

Although several of the early and mid–1920s Fairbanks' swashbucklers are still absorbing and fun to watch today, the supreme achievement among them is *The Thief of Bagdad*, directed by Raoul Walsh. An epic based on several of the Arabian Nights tales, it blends fantasy and stunning, state-of-the-art visual effects (such as a "magic" rope and both a flying horse and a flying carpet) with Fairbanks's usual mix of humor, acrobatics, action, adventure, and romance. The sets are large and lavish, often dwarfing the actors in their grandeur. The story is extremely well executed, fast-moving, endlessly inventive, often humorous, and always engaging. With a running time of nearly two and a half hours, it is on the lengthy side for a silent film, but the viewing experience never seems long. Much like the airborne carpet Fairbanks's title character rides, the film flies wondrously by.

Another captivating adventure is *The Black Pirate*, which, in addition to offering all the trimmings audiences were used to seeing in Fairbanks's films, is presented entirely in high-quality two-strip Technicolor, an extreme rarity for the time. This process doesn't deliver quite the true color of the three-strip Technicolor process introduced in the 1930s. Considering that *The Black Pirate* was made in 1926, though, seeing an entire silent feature film in color is a fascinating experience.

In addition to his films, Fairbanks made another important contribution to the film industry during this time. Along with Louis Mayer of MGM and more than 30 other film industry executives and artists, he co-founded the Academy of Motion Picture Arts and Sciences in May 1927. Between then and October 1929, he also served as the organization's first president. In May 1929, as one of his presidential duties, he also hosted the very first presentation of the organization's Academy Awards at the Hollywood Roosevelt Hotel.

* * *

As Hollywood's film industry experienced tumultuous change in 1928, and Fairbanks was considering options for his silent film farewell, the story of *The Iron Mask* rapidly emerged as the ideal choice. It would be a continuation of one of his most successful swashbucklers, his 1921 version of *The Three Musketeers*. It would be perhaps his last opportunity to play one of his favorite swashbuckling characters, d'Artagnan. Especially as he sensed the end of his life's best years, the story of an older d'Artagnan and his Musketeer compatriots saving France for one last time resonated deeply within. "It is," Jeffrey Vance wrote, "as if Fairbanks is bidding farewell not only to the art form he had pioneered and perfected, but also the best part of himself and his work."[7]

The story of *The Iron Mask* begins in 1638. King Louis XIII of France is delighted that the queen has given birth to a son, the future King Louis XIV. Unknown to the king, however, the queen delivers a twin, a second son. Hearing this news, Cardinal Richelieu, France's manipulative secretary of state, views the second son as a potential threat to France's future political stability and sends the newborn off to Spain to be raised in secret. Meanwhile, the villainous Count de Rochefort learns of these developments and kidnaps the second child, planning to raise the boy to be loyal to him. Then, at the right time, the Count will replace the rightful king with his twin and seize the throne. Fearing great danger ahead for France, Richelieu enlists the fearless and patriotic d'Artagnan to look after the older brother and rightful heir.

Many years pass, both Louis XIII and Richelieu have died, and a hearty, good-natured young Louis XIV (ably mentored by d'Artagnan) sits on the throne. Deciding that the time is ripe, de Rochefort sets his scheme in motion, kidnapping the real king and cruelly imprisoning him in a castle in an iron mask to assure that no one discovers his true identity. In the king's place, he puts his brother, who, due to de Rochefort's tutelage, has become mentally unbalanced.

Learning of the plot, the aging d'Artagnan calls on his great comrades-in-arms, Athos, Porthos, and Aramis, to help him rescue the true king, remove the insane twin, deal with de Rochefort, and put the real Louis XIV back on the throne. All this is accomplished, of course, but in the process each of the original three Musketeers and finally d'Artagnan all fall in the line of duty in service to, as several intertitles note, "the greater glory of France."

While this ending seems quite bleak with respect to the four heroes, it is, in true Fairbanks fashion, spun in the most upbeat and romanticized way possible. After d'Artagnan falls, his spirit leaves his body and rises to the heavens to join the spirits of his three friends, and the four jauntily march off into the clouds to seek, as the final intertitle reads, "greater adventures beyond." Then, instead of concluding with the customary "The End," the final words displayed on the screen are "The Beginning."

* * *

One of the attributes of Fairbanks's best films is the commitment to quality in every facet of production, and in *The Iron Mask*, we see this in almost every frame of the film.

Perhaps the film's most striking feature is its production design. Fairbanks had not been happy with the look of his 1921 *The Three Musketeers*, believing that it lacked the historical accuracy that would have made it more compelling to audiences. So, as he prepared *The Iron Mask*, he went to great lengths to give the film both a more authentic look and added visual grandeur. To help in this effort, he assembled an impressive team of design specialists that included French artist and set designer Maurice Leloir and British painter and set designer Laurence Irving. Leloir, an authority on the period of Louis XIV as well as the illustrator of an edition of the book of *The Three Musketeers*, was Fairbanks's consultant for all things visual starting with film's costume design and properties. In addition, he helped to bring the twentieth-century actors up to speed on seventeenth-century French etiquette and social mores. Irving was the film's lead art director, and Fairbanks assigned him the formidable task of designing 54 different sets that reflected the authenticity of the period while also conveying the romanticism that Fairbanks was aiming for. Fairbanks's older brother Robert, who worked as the production manager on his younger brother's films, and his team then had the challenging job of building the sets.[8] One person particularly impressed with the entire design achievement was Fairbank's son Douglas Jr. who, in an interview many years later, said, "*The Iron Mask* is second only to *The Thief of Bagdad* in terms of design. In fact, it may have been a more daunting task than *Bagdad*. *The Thief of Bagdad* was pure fantasy. *The Iron Mask* attempts to authentically recreate a specific time and place."[9]

Another highlight is the cinematography by Henry Sharp, a favorite cameraman of Fairbanks, whose Hollywood career spanned from 1920 to 1959. As well as ably capturing the visual grandeur of the palaces and other settings, Sharp was marvelous at using shadow and light to heighten the emotion of certain scenes. An excellent example is a scene when the villainous de Rochefort captures the young King Louis XIV and puts him in the hideous iron mask. Against the high castle walls, we see gigantic shadows of the evildoers accompanied by what appears to be the silhouettes of gallows ropes. It is, to say the least, a chilling, ominous sight.

Still another excellent contribution is the screenplay, which is credited to Elton Thomas. Fairbanks enjoyed in-jokes, and Elton Thomas, who receives writing credit in many Fairbanks films, is a pseudonym based on (as noted earlier) his two middle names. The reality, though, was that, in Fairbanks's movies, Fairbanks and many others contributed to the final draft. In *The Iron Mask* this highly collaborative process resulted in a tight, fast-paced, and often very creative script. The story, which is darker than nearly all of Fairbanks's other films, carefully balances the tragic and poignant moments with comic ones so that nothing seems contrived or forced. Also, clever flashbacks are occasionally inserted that dramatically convey crucial past events so that the film doesn't need to depend on long intertitles to tell us about them.

Finally, Fairbanks's performance deserves special notice. Throughout his career, he was considered more a personality than a "real" actor such as Emil Jannings or John Barrymore, and *The Iron Mask* is clearly a swashbuckling film in which acting is almost always secondary to action. In the film, however, Fairbanks creates a fully realized d'Artagnan who relishes life but must also cope with great personal loss, accept the aging process and the loss of physical prowess that comes with it, and ultimately come to terms with his own mortality. Though often underappreciated, it is a fine, thoughtful, well-modulated performance—a worthy farewell by a great star.

While *The Iron Mask* was shot entirely as a silent film, Fairbanks did make a concession to sound, agreeing to release one version with a music soundtrack, some sound effects, and two brief speeches which he delivers at the beginning of the film and then mid-way through the story. The speeches, especially, are superfluous, but Fairbanks agreed to them, believing that the film would attract more people if it were marketed as a picture with dialogue.

* * *

Although he had now completed his silent film farewell, the robust, restless, 45-year-old Fairbanks was by no means ready to retire. Like d'Artagnan and his Musketeer friends, he harbored hopes, at least for a time, that the end of this chapter of his life could also be the beginning of something else, perhaps even "greater adventures beyond." Then, in early 1929, as he was preparing for *The Iron Mask's* premiere, he thought he may have found an answer.

One evening that January, Fairbanks and Mary Pickford went to see a production of Shakespeare's *The Taming of the Shrew* in Los Angeles. Like Fairbanks, Pickford was eager to reinvent herself for a new era, and, at the moment, she was putting the finishing touches on her first all-talking picture, a film version of the hit Broadway drama *Coquette*, and considering future projects. Watching *The Taming of the Shrew* sparked both their imaginations. Their fans had long wanted to see the couple act together in a film. The play had great male and female lead roles that they could identify with. With the help of the best production team they could muster, they could make the first all-talking feature film of a play by the English language's greatest writer. It would be Fairbanks, Pickford, and Shakespeare himself all contributing to one magnificent motion picture experience!

Soon, however, their great expectations clashed with a number of unpleasant realities. From the moment the film began shooting in June 1929, Fairbanks seemed resentful of working in the new medium of sound and the constraints it put on him. Instead of the friendly, enthusiastic, highly creative person director Allan Dwan and so many others remembered from silent film productions, Fairbanks was tense, frustrated, and disagreeable. He soon developed an intense dislike for the film's director, Sam Taylor. As the production proceeded, he was increasingly at odds with Pickford as well, sometimes arguing openly with her in front of the production crew. All this greatly saddened Pickford, who later wrote, "I saw a completely new Douglas, a Douglas who no longer cared apparently about me or my feelings...."[10]

Despite all the on-the-set friction, filming and post-production were completed without any serious delays, and *The Taming of the Shrew* opened in New York in November 1929. Most of the initial reviews were favorable, especially for Fairbanks, whose performance is generally regarded today as much more effective than Pickford's. Although the film made money, it was not the hit with audiences that Fairbanks and Pickford had assumed it would be. Reasons ranged from the catastrophic stock market crash that had occurred just a month before the film's opening to the story's lack of romance, to the public's desire for new stars for a new era of movies.[11] Perhaps all these factors contributed.

In any case, the first all-talking film of a Shakespearian play, a project that began with the highest hopes of its two great stars, was a major step leading to the demise of their careers and their marriage. Fairbanks starred in only three more films, all of which were poorly received. As noted earlier, Pickford starred in only two that were released, neither of which was commercially successful.[12] The two divorced in 1936.

Long before the Fairbanks-Pickford divorce was official, the two had begun leading separate lives. Fairbanks had begun an affair with Sylvia Ashley, an English model, actress, and socialite best known today for her numerous marriages to noblemen and movie stars.[13] The two would marry in March 1936, just two months after the Fairbanks-Pickford divorce had been finalized.

Only peripherally involved in the film business during the 1930s, Fairbanks spent more and more time playing golf and traveling. A long-time chain smoker, his health also began to decline during this time. Then, on December 12, 1939, just two days and a few hours after helping his son Douglas Jr. celebrate his 30th birthday, Fairbanks died in his sleep after experiencing a heart attack. He was 56 years old.

A couple of hours earlier, when a male nurse attending him asked how he was feeling, Fairbanks, in his characteristic upbeat way, answered, "I've never felt better."[14] Those, according to the nurse, were Fairbanks's last words.

* * *

Although Douglas Fairbanks had also distinguished himself on the New York stage, he and silent film—the artist and the art form—shared an almost mystical connection. The wonder is that they found each other at exactly the right time and then thrived together for a decade and a half, producing several undisputed masterpieces along the way.

Many explanations have been given for Fairbanks's inability to make the leap to dialogue movies, ranging from a voice that didn't quite fit his screen persona to the public's growing perception of him and silent films as anachronisms. Perhaps the explanation that reverberates more deeply than all the others, though, is that his heart simply wasn't in it anymore. For him, sound not only meant major new production restrictions, but it also killed what he loved most about the movies—that magical spell he felt that only silent films could provide. When the opportunity to cast that spell on audiences had been taken away, so too had an essential reason for his being. He had, in his mind, become a magician without an audience or an art. And where does someone in that position go from there?

14

Twenty-Eight Other Notable U.S. Silent and Hybrid Films Released During the Long 1928

The films discussed in the preceding chapters represent only a handful of the notable silent or hybrid U.S. features released during the Long 1928. Dozens of other intriguing films also remain, and, for those who wish to delve more deeply into this subject, this chapter offers a list of 28 additional silent or hybrid productions. The selections here are quite diverse and were chosen for a wide assortment of reasons ranging from production quality to significant performers and performances, to historical interest.

They are listed chronologically by their release dates.

* * *

November 1927

The Gaucho, United Artists, produced by Douglas Fairbanks, directed by F. Richard Jones, starring Douglas Fairbanks and Lupe Velez, released November 21, 1927.

The Gaucho is the story of an Argentine bandit leader El Gaucho (Fairbanks) who becomes an unlikely hero after a ruthless strongman takes over the Andean village that El Gaucho has used as his group's base. Then, after winning the village back, El Gaucho experiences a spiritual transformation. A fascinating departure from Fairbanks's trademark swashbuckling roles, film historian Jeffrey Vance has called *The Gaucho* "a near masterwork" and noted its especially dark tone. "The spirit of adolescent boyish adventure, the omnipresent characteristic of [Fairbanks's] prior films, is noticeably absent," observes Vance. "It has been replaced by a spiritual fervor and an element of seething sexuality the likes of which has never been seen before in one of his productions."[1] Fairbanks excels in this (for him) unusual role, and one can't help but wonder what he could have done as an actor if he had cast himself against type more often. The production is lavishly mounted, and giving an added luster to the film's "spiritual fervor," audiences get to see Mary Pickford play the Blessed Virgin Mary in a cameo.

* * *

December 1927

Get Your Man, produced by Adolph Zukor and Jesse Lasky, directed by Dorothy Arzner, starring Clara Bow and Buddy Rogers, released December 7, 1927.

Get Your Man is a charming light comic romance about a coquettish American woman and young European nobleman who fall in love and then must find a way for him to break a commitment he'd made to an arranged marriage when he was a small child. It is also a chance to see what a bright, charismatic presence Clara Bow was on the silent screen. Unfortunately, the four films Bow made that were released in 1928—her last silent efforts—are all lost, and, although a few scenes are also missing from *Get Your Man*, it stands as her last mostly in tact still-existing silent film. For viewers who wish to see more of Bow, she is also excellent in William Wellman's 1927 World War I aerial epic *Wings* and in Clarence Badger's 1927 *It*, the film that established her as "the it girl," the woman with "it"—the quality that only some possess that draws all others with its magnetic force. Finally, *Get Your Man* is a chance to see the work of its director Dorothy Arzner, an exceptionally talented early-1920s film editor who went on to became the only woman to direct films for major Hollywood studios between the late 1920s and early 1940s.

* * *

January 1928

Leave 'Em Laughing, MGM, produced by Hal Roach, directed by Clyde Bruckman, starring Stan Laurel and Oliver Hardy, released January 28, 1928.

The legendary comedians Stan Laurel and Oliver Hardy were able to translate their distinctive brand of farce from the last decade of silent films into the first two decades of dialogue films with great success, a truly rare accomplishment among silent film comics. While not a full-fledged feature film, *Leave 'Em Laughing* is both a good example of the work they did in the last years of silent films and a chance to see how well they worked together in this medium. The story, which involves Stan's suffering from a toothache at home and then going with his long-suffering friend Ollie to the dentist's office, is silly but filled with clever comic bits. Also, the film's cameraman was George Stevens, who would graduate to directing in the 1930s and go on to be one of Hollywood's most celebrated directors over the next 30 years, winning Best Director Academy Awards for his work on 1951's *A Place in the Sun* and 1956's *Giant*.

* * *

February 1928

Four Sons, Fox, produced by William Fox and John Ford, directed by John Ford, starring Margaret Mann, released February 12, 1928.

A big hit for Fox and John Ford when it came out (bringing in $1.5 million at the box office), *Four Sons* is the story of a kind, loving Bavarian widow (Mann), who helps pay for one of her sons to emigrate to the U.S. before World War I, and, when war breaks out, endures as her three remaining sons fight, and all ultimately die, for Germany. The film features an early appearance of the steadfast, long-suffering mother, an archetypal character Ford would develop to perfection in such later films as 1940's *The Grapes of Wrath* and 1941's *How Green Was My Valley*. Another highlight includes the dark and ominous World War I battle scenes, beautifully photographed by cinematographer George Schneiderman and heavily influenced by such films as F.W Murnau's 1927 expressionistic masterpiece, *Sunrise*.

* * *

A Girl in Every Port, Fox, produced by William Fox, directed by Howard Hawks, starring Victor McLaglen and Louise Brooks, released February 26, 1928.

Howard Hawks' fifth film, this is often considered the most significant of the director's silent films because it is the first to incorporate the strong male "buddy" relationships and other themes he would return to again and again during his 45-year career. Specifically, this focuses on two sailors who compete for the attentions of various women but who seem to have the most fun when they banter and brawl with each other. A highlight is the all-too-brief appearance by Louise Brooks as one of the women the two men compete for. Reportedly, her role in this film led to German director G.W. Pabst's casting her in the part she is best remembered for today, Lulu in Pabst's 1929's classic *Pandora's Box*.

* * *

March 1928

The Matinee Idol, Columbia, produced by Harry Cohn and Frank Capra, directed by Frank Capra, starring Bessie Love and Johnny Walker, released March 14, 1928.

Considered lost until a print was found in Paris in the 1990s, *The Matinee Idol* is a romantic comedy about a vacationing Broadway star who meets a spunky young woman who helps her father manage a rustic theater company. One of the first films the young Capra directed for Columbia, it is little more than a situation comedy with solid performances by Love and Walker. It also has some elements that will make today's audiences a bit squeamish such as a white actor performing in blackface and an exaggerated gay stereotype. For fans of Capra, however, this also has some of the elements, from fast-paced editing to highly entertaining visual gags, to a deep feeling for underdogs, that we see in his great films of the 1930s and 1940s.

* * *

The Trail of '98, MGM, produced and directed by Clarence Brown, starring Dolores del Rio and Ralph Forbes, released March 20, 1928.

Based on a 1910 novel by Robert W. Service, *The Trail of '98* focuses, like much of Service's other writing, on the terrible things greed and the lust for gold can do to one's soul. Several groups of people, including two brothers from South Carolina, prospectors from Nevada, and others all head north to Alaska to seek their fortunes after the Klondike gold strike of 1897. The journey is extremely taxing and often dangerous, complete with blizzards, rivers swollen by melting ice, and human threats such as claim jumping. Originally released in an experimental and short-lived widescreen process called Fantom Screen, the film offers some stunning visuals by cinematographer John F. Seitz.

* * *

April 1928

Street Angel, Fox, produced by William Fox, directed by Frank Borzage, starring Janet Gaynor and Charles Farrell, released April 9, 1928.

This romantic melodrama features Gaynor as a young woman who

Frank Borzage's *Street Angel*, a moving romance starring Janet Gaynor and Charles Farrell as a couple struggling against formidable odds, was one of 1928's critical and popular successes (Fox Film Corporation/Photofest).

does shady things to buy medicine for her dying mother, gets caught, escapes, finds her mother dead, runs away, joins a traveling carnival, and falls for an itinerant painter (Farrell). Ultimately, though, she must come to terms with her past. Gaynor's performance in this film is one of the three performances for which she received the first Academy Award for Best Actress (the others were F.W. Murnau's *Sunrise* and Borzage's *Seventh Heaven*). This is also a fine example of the work of Borzage, one of the premiere directors of the late silent and early sound film eras and a specialist in romances with well-developed characters and mature themes. For those who may be interested, an excellent example of Borzage's early sound work is 1933's *A Man's Castle*, a depression-era drama featuring stellar performances by Spencer Tracy and Loretta Young.

* * *

Laugh, Clown, Laugh, MGM; produced by Irving Thalberg; directed by Herbert Brenon; Starring Lon Chaney, Loretta Young, and Nils Asther; released April 14, 1928.

14. Twenty-Eight Other Notable U.S. Silent and Hybrid Films

Film critic Leonard Maltin once called *Laugh, Clown, Laugh* "the perfect example of Chaney's unmatched talent for turning tearjerking melodrama into heartbreaking tragedy."[2] It's difficult to disagree. The story of a traveling clown who raises an abandoned girl and, as she grows into a beautiful young woman, realizes that, although he is decades older, he is deeply, romantically in love with her, is definitely the stuff of melodrama and may also make modern viewers a bit uneasy. But the superb performances by the great Lon Chaney, the radiant Loretta Young (in her first significant role at age 14), and the underappreciated Nils Asther along with Herbert Brenon's excellent direction and the striking cinematography by the legendary James Wong Howe help to make this film an enthralling experience from beginning to end.

* * *

The Patsy, MGM; produced by Marion Davies, William Randolph Hearst, and King Vidor; directed by King Vidor; starring Marion Davies and Marie Dressler; released April 22, 1928.

Next to *Show People*, *The Patsy* may well be Marion Davies' best silent film. Based on a hit Broadway play, this modern Cinderella story is about Patsy Harrington (Davies), the drudge of her social-climbing family. Secretly in love with the boyfriend of her irresponsible but irresistible sister Grace, Patsy yearns to be a "personality girl." Rather than cultivate her looks, she decides to become the "intellectual" of her family, which outrages her mother (Dressler), who believes that beauty and brains don't mix. Meanwhile, Patsy's sister begins cheating on her boyfriend with a millionaire named Bill. For the boyfriend's sake, the "new" Patsy throws herself at Grace's new beau, hoping to break up the romance. The whole affair ends in a predictable but still quite satisfying manner. Best scene: sitting by a mirror, Davies impersonates fellow silent film stars Lillian Gish, Mae Murray, and Pola Negri. Reportedly, this wonderful bit of business greatly annoyed Murray and Negri but delighted Gish.

* * *

Across to Singapore, MGM; produced and directed by William Nigh; starring Ramon Navarro, Joan Crawford, and Ernest Torrence; released April 30, 1928.

This romantic melodrama is mainly about two brothers in a seafaring Massachusetts family—one a tough, towering middle-age ship's captain (Torrence) and the other a much younger and inexperienced seaman (Navarro)—who both fall in love with the same woman (Crawford). The woman clearly prefers the younger brother, but, without her knowledge, her father gives her hand in marriage to the older one and the banns are announced. Then, before any of this messy relationship business is sorted out, lots of action ensues, including two dramatic voyages to Singapore, a mutiny masterminded by a jealous crewmember, and dark doings on Singapore's seedy streets. Crawford shines, especially in scenes when she visually conveys complex, conflicted emotions. The real star, however, is the towering character actor Torrence as the man in love with the younger woman who realizes that she doesn't love him, descends into drink, and hallucinates obsessively about her. Some of the visual effects in these scenes are very clever and engaging.

* * *

May 1928

Hangman's House, Fox, produced and directed by John Ford, starring Victor McLaglen, released May 13, 1928.

Victor McLaglen plays Denis Hogan, an Irishman with a price on his head serving in the military in Algiers who returns to Ireland, disguises himself as a holy man, and ultimately uncovers skullduggery while also aiding a couple of young lovers. This film is noted for its fine cinematography by George Schneiderman, a rousing larger-than-life performance by McLaglen, a riveting horse race action sequence near the end of the film, and two brief and uncredited appearances by a very young John Wayne. According to Ford biographer Joseph McBride, this is the first confirmed appearance by Wayne in a Ford film.

* * *

Ramona, Inspiration Pictures/United Artists, directed by Edwin Carewe, starring Dolores del Rio and Warner Baxter, released May 20, 1928.

Ramona is a moving drama of a woman (del Rio), half Native American and half Mexican, who has been raised by a Mexican family. She faces prejudice from her community that leads to tragic consequences when she marries a Native American (Baxter) and has a child by him. Part Chickasaw, the film's director, Edwin Carewe, was committed to exposing the U.S. Government's mistreatment of Native Americans and was widely applauded for his honest and sensitive handling of the subject. Partially shot in Utah's Zion National Park and Cedar Breaks National Monument, the film's cinematography is often stunning. The performances by del Rio and Baxter are also quite poignant and affecting. Considered a lost film for eight decades, *Ramona* was rediscovered by film archivists in Prague in 2010, and a newly restored version had its world premiere at UCLA in 2014.

* * *

June 1928

Lonesome, Universal Pictures; produced by Carl Laemmle, Carl Laemmle, Jr., and Oskar Schubert-Stevens; directed by Paul Fejos; starring Barbara Kent and Glenn Tryon; released on June 20, 1928.

A young man and woman, both living in New York, both longing for a romantic connection, go to the beach one Saturday, meet, spark up an attraction, continue their encounter well into the evening at Coney Island, realize that they are in love, and then lose each other in the crowd. Only knowing each other's first names, can they ever reconnect? While the actors, Barbara Kent and Glenn Tryon, are not at the Garbo-John Gilbert level, they both excellently convey the pangs of loneliness and the hope that their characters have both found someone who they can be with and be happy with. The film itself, with its amazing double-exposures that provide resonance to the narrative and tinted scenes to accent certain highlights, has a real visual richness to it. A hybrid film, *Lonesome* does have a couple of clumsy dialogue scenes that detract a bit. But, overall, it is a delightful viewing experience.

* * *

August 1928

The Mysterious Lady, MGM, produced and directed by Fred Niblo, starring Greta Garbo and Conrad Nagel, released on August 4, 1928.

Based on a 1923 novel called *War in the Dark* by Ludwig Wolfe, *The Mysterious Lady* is a romantic drama set at the turn of the 20th Century involving a beautiful Russian spy (Garbo) who falls in love with a young Austrian officer (Nagel). After they become involved, he learns what she does for a living and is understandably shocked. When they meet again on a train, she tells him that she is in love with him, but he now rejects her. The next morning, he wakes to learn that important government plans in his possession have been stolen and receives a message from her saying that she'd come as a woman in love with him and has now left as his enemy. The officer is declared a traitor and imprisoned. Later, however, he receives an opportunity to clear his name, and both he and the beautiful spy must make several serious choices. Garbo is excellent playing the smoldering seductress who, much to her surprise, falls for the dashing officer.

* * *

September 1928

The Singing Fool, Warner Brothers, produced by Darryl F. Zanuck, directed by Lloyd Bacon, starring Al Jolson, released on September 19, 1928.

Al Jolson's hybrid follow-up to *The Jazz Singer*, *The Singing Fool* accounted for more than $5 million in U.S. box office, more than 12 times its $388,000 production cost. The runaway audience favorite in 1928, it also made more money than any other film of the 1920s and, by doing so, emphatically reinforced the contention that both movies with spoken dialogue and musicals were here to stay. The film has some fine moments, such as Jolson's spirited rendition of "I'm Sittin' on Top of the World." Most of it, however, is a plodding, poorly written, poorly acted melodrama that tugs shamelessly at the heart strings. All things considered, though, it is an intriguing curiosity for film enthusiasts who want to see, and hear, how powerful the lure of talking and singing pictures were for late-1920s audiences.

* * *

The Cameraman, MGM, produced by Buster Keaton and Lawrence Weingarten, directed by Edward Sedgwick, starring Buster Keaton and Marceline Day, released September 22, 1928.

In this film, the first Keaton made under his new contract with MGM, Buster, plays a portrait photographer who buys a broken-down movie camera in an attempt to find work at MGM Newsreels so he can be close to Sally (Marceline Day), a young woman he's sweet on who works there. No one else at MGM Newsreels takes him seriously, however, until he manages to get footage of a street war between rival Chinese gangs in Los Angeles. The film, which contains a good share of clever gags and other comic bits and remains highly regarded today, is one of the last times Keaton performs at the top of his game. One memorable highlight is a dressing room scene in which Buster and another man try to change for the beach while being pressed up against each other and getting tangled in each other's clothes. Very soon after *The Cameraman*'s release, however, MGM took artistic control of Keaton's films completely away from him, resulting in lasting damage to the great comic's career.

14. Twenty-Eight Other Notable U.S. Silent and Hybrid Films 177

* * *

A Woman Disputed, Joseph M. Schenck Productions/United Artists, produced by Joseph M. Schenck, directed by Henry King and Sam Taylor, starring Norma Talmadge and Gilbert Roland, released in September 1928.

The last silent film of Norma Talmadge, one of the medium's top stars during the 1920s, this is the story of an Austrian prostitute (Talmadge) who is lured into a romantic triangle just as World War I is breaking out. Knowing that the talkies were inevitable, Paramount spent lavishly on the look of the film, and the great cinematographer William Cameron Menzies obliged with some beautiful camera work. The film also includes an impressive star turn by Talmadge and an excellent performance in a supporting role by the dashing young Gilbert Roland. Sadly for Talmadge, however, her first two talking films failed with audiences, and, although she was just 35 at the time, she retired from acting.

* * *

October 1928

The Man Who Laughs, Universal Pictures, produced by Carl Laemmle, directed Paul Leni, starring Conrad Veidt and Mary Philbin, released October 5, 1928.

Based on the Victor Hugo novel of the same name, *The Man Who Laughs* is a superb but sadly overlooked historical romantic melodrama with horror elements. The story takes place in seventeenth-century England and focuses on Gwynplaine, whose mouth was purposely disfigured when he was a boy, leaving him with a strange, very disturbing looking rictus grin. Played by the brilliant Conrad Veidt, one of the great actors of German expressionistic films, Gwynplaine is a fascinating figure who responds to many challenges and yearns for the woman he loves while constantly feeling great shame for his disfigurement. In the years that followed its release, *The Man Who Laughs* had an immense impact on many of the much more famous Universal horror films of the 1930s and 1940s such as *Dracula*, *Frankenstein*, and *The Wolfman*. In addition, Gwynplaine's disfigurement was an inspiration in the development of the Joker, the now-iconic villain who first appeared in Batman comics in 1940.

* * *

The Power of the Press, Columbia, produced by Jack Cohn, directed by Frank Capra, starring Douglas Fairbanks, Jr., and Jobyna Ralston, released October 31, 1928.

Fans of vintage Frank Capra films such as 1936's *Mr. Deeds Goes to Town*, 1939's *Mr. Smith Goes to Washington*, and 1940's *Meet John Doe* will especially appreciate *The Power of the Press*, which introduces many of the stylistic flourishes (fast-paced editing, wonderful visual touches) and themes (political corruption, media manipulation) that Capra explores in greater depth in those later films. The story of an ambitious young reporter (Fairbanks) who at first suspects a big city mayoral candidate's daughter of murdering the city's district attorney and then tries to prove her innocence, it has many fine moments. A sequence in which the newspaper editor "stops the presses" to create a new front page and all the ramifications of his decision are shown is pure, exhilarating filmmaking. Fairbanks Jr., only 18 when he played this role, exhibits great confidence, charm, and wit in this film.

* * *

November 1928

The Racket, The Caddo Company/distributed by Paramount Pictures; produced by Howard Hughes; directed by Lewis Milestone; starring Thomas Meighan, Louis Wolheim, Marie Prevost, and Sam De Grasse; released November 1, 1928.

Based on the 1927 Broadway play of the same name, *The Racket* is a taut, intelligently directed, and well-acted story about a fearsome and politically well-connected Chicago bootlegger (Wolheim) and the honest police captain (Meighan) and district attorney (De Grasse) who want to put him behind bars. Along with Josef von Sternberg's 1927 hit *Underworld*, it played a major role in inspiring many of the hard-hitting gangster films of the 1930s. It was highly praised when released and nominated for Best Picture at the first Academy Awards in 1929. For decades, *The Racket* was considered a lost film. A copy, however, was eventually discovered in the film collection of its producer, Howard Hughes, after his death and has been preserved since 2016 at the Academy Film Archive.

* * *

Noah's Ark, Warner Brothers, produced by Darryl F. Zanuck (uncredited), directed by Michael Curtiz, starring Dolores Costello and George O'Brien, released November 1, 1928.

Noah's Ark is an intriguing grand-scale disaster melodrama that moves back and forth between two thematically connected stories: the great flood described in the Bible story of Noah, and events depicting, as one character puts it, "the flood of blood" unleashed by World War I. To reinforce the connection, many of the film's actors play similar roles in each story. An enormous hit at the time, the film is best known today for an epic flood sequence that reportedly required 600,000 gallons of water to film and, because of the overwhelming force of the water, caused three extras to drown and many more to be injured. At one point 35 ambulances were on the scene attending to casualties. Despite the disaster that occurred on the film set, however, the disaster sequence is quite well-orchestrated and thrilling to watch—a tribute to ingenuity of Hollywood's special effects technicians before the introduction of computer-generated images and other technologies.

* * *

White Shadows in the South Seas, MGM; produced by Irving Thalberg, Hunt Stromberg, and William Randolph Hearst; directed by W.S. Van Dyke; starring Monte Blue and Raquel Torres; released November 10, 1928.

Filmed in Tahiti, a rarity at the time, *White Shadows in the South Seas* is a sumptuously photographed adventure tale. Matthew Lloyd (Blue), an alcoholic doctor, is disgusted by the way the white traders exploit the native pearl divers on a Polynesian island. When a diver is gravely injured, Sebastian, a leading trader, is indifferent, demanding the other divers keep working. When Lloyd objects, Sebastian threatens him, demands that Lloyd leave the island, and swings a punch at him. Later, the diver dies despite Lloyd's treatment, but the traders have a party all the same. Sebastian then tricks Lloyd to board an arriving ship, saying that the passengers have measles. His men tie the doctor up and send the ship off unmanned. Eventually, Lloyd is washed ashore on an island where none of the natives has ever seen a white man, and his adventures continue. For his efforts on the film, cinematographer Clyde De Vinna picked up an Academy Award for Best Cinematography at the second Academy Award ceremonies in 1930.

* * *

Show People, Cosmopolitan Pictures/MGM; produced by Marion Davies, King Vidor, and Irving Thalberg; directed by King Vidor; starring Marion Davies and William Haines; released November 20, 1928

A light and lively look at the Hollywood movie business in 1928, *Show People* is the story of Peggy Pepper, a young woman who leaves her home in Georgia and travels to Hollywood in hopes of becoming a movie star. After some initial frustration, and with the help of comic actor Billy Boone (Haines), she breaks in doing slapstick comedy and becomes a hit. She presses on with dreams of becoming a serious actress, though, and eventually signs with prestigious High Art Studios. Unfortunately, complications

Billy Boone (William Haines) and Peggy Pepper (Marion Davies) take in a picture in one of the very entertaining movies about the movies, King Vidor's *Show People* (MGM/Photofest).

emerge that Peggy, Billy, and others must grapple with before we get to the requisite happy ending. Davies, a very under-appreciated comic talent, had a major impact on other comediennes who followed her, most notably the great Lucille Ball. In the absolutely wonderful performance Davies delivers here, perhaps the best of her career, we see much of the inspired visual comedy that Ball and others have imitated. As an added attraction, viewers are treated to cameo appearances by numerous silent film stars such as Charlie Chaplin, Douglas Fairbanks, Sr., John Gilbert, William S. Hart, Mae Murray, and Norma Talmadge.

* * *

December 1928

A Lady of Chance, MGM, produced and directed by Robert Z. Leonard, starring Norma Shearer and Johnny Mack Brown, released December 1, 1928.

In her last silent film, Norma Shearer plays a con-woman who thinks good people are chumps and marries an unwitting businessman (Brown) for his money. Soon, however, she finds out that, while he's not nearly as wealthy as she'd assumed, he and others in his family are genuinely kind and caring. Although the plot is predictable, Shearer, best known for her dramatic roles, shows real flair as a sophisticated comedienne. Contemporary critics thought Shearer, who usually played much more genteel heroines, was badly miscast in this part, but she pulls the whole thing off quite well.

* * *

The Barker, Warner Brothers; produced by Al Rockett and Richard A. Rowland; directed by George Fitzmaurice; starring Dorothy Mackaill, Milton Sills, Betty Compson, and Douglas Fairbanks, Jr.; released December 9, 1928.

A romantic drama, *The Barker* tells the story of Lou (Mackaill), a dancing girl who comes between Nifty (Sills) and his estranged son Chris (Fairbanks). Nifty is a carnival barker, or pitchman, who is in love with Lou and also has ambitions for Chris to become a lawyer. Chris, however, has other ideas, and during his vacation he hops a freight train, joins the carnival, and weds Lou. Eventually, Chris fulfills his father's dream and becomes a lawyer. All the leads give fine performances, especially the little-known Sills, who plays the world-weary, self-indulgent Nifty. For her portrayal of another dancer who specializes in Hawaiian numbers, the talented Betty Compson received a Best Actress nomination the second year the Academy Awards were presented.

* * *

A Woman of Affairs, MGM, produced by Irving Thalberg, directed by Clarence Brown, starring Greta Garbo and John Gilbert, released December 15, 1928.

Based on a lurid 1924 novel called *The Green Hat* by Michael Arlen that dealt with an array of (for the time) taboo subjects from heroin use to homosexuality, to syphilis, *A Woman of Affairs* was only released after MGM agreed to several changes made by the film industry's censors. The story, which revolves around a husband who commits suicide during his honeymoon, his friend's descent into alcoholism, the new widow's (Garbo) attempts to deal with despair by pursuing meaningless affairs, and much more, is pure soap opera. Still, with the fine direction of Clarence Brown; the contributions of MGM's two biggest stars, Greta Garbo and John Gilbert; the wonderful cinematography by William Daniels (Garbo's favorite cameraman); and an Academy Award nominated script by Arlen and Bess Meredyth; it was both a critical and commercial hit. Despite the story's contrivances and sensationalism, many elements of the film, especially the terrific on-screen chemistry between Garbo and Gilbert, are great fun to watch.

* * *

January 1929

The Flying Fleet, MGM; produced and directed by George W. Hill; starring Ramon Novarro, Ralph Graves, and Anita Page; released on January 19, 1929.

An action film with romance, *The Flying Fleet* is the story of two young U.S. Navy flyers (Novarro and Graves) who compete, sometimes in less-than-gentlemanly ways, for the love of the same woman (Page). A highlight of the film, and quite thrilling to watch even today, is a series of stunt sequences featuring an acrobatic team called the Three Seahawks. This film was also based on a story (his first to be translated to the screen) by Frank "Spig" Wead, a U.S. Navy Commander and authority on early aviation who turned to writing after a crippling injury in 1926. In the 1930s and 1940s, he wrote a number of navy-and-aviation-oriented film scenarios and screenplays for such top Hollywood directors as Frank Capra, Victor Fleming, King Vidor, Michael Curtiz, Howard Hawks, and John Ford. Perhaps the most memorable of these is his screenplay for *They Were Expendable*, Ford's 1945 salute to the Navy's PT boat efforts during World War II.

Afterthoughts
Requiem and Reemergence

By 1933, just five years after the Long 1928, a new, greatly changed Hollywood stood in the place of the old. Fashions were quite different, with more women preferring shorter bobbed hair and more men sporting narrow pencil-thin mustaches. The environments in which the movies were made were greatly altered as well. The large studios—the film factories with their assembly line production models and cost-conscious business practices—had swallowed up many of the independent production companies and now dominated the scene. To accommodate the needs of sound technology, much new building construction had occurred. Hordes of film industry newcomers, many from Broadway and other theater hubs, had come to town and quickly become some of the industry's leading directors, writers, and stars. Meanwhile, many of the film pioneers who, just two decades before, had transformed the sleepy little village of Hollywood into the movie capital of the world—once-towering figures such as D.W. Griffith, Mary Pickford, and Douglas Fairbanks—had quietly faded into semi-obscurity. One of most telling signs that the torch had been passed was the transfer of an unofficial royal title. Throughout the 1920s, the undisputed "King of Hollywood" had been Fairbanks. By the mid-1930s, the crown had passed to an actor virtually unknown to film fans in 1928, an MGM contract player named Clark Gable.

Audience expectations had shifted dramatically as well. With many of the technical difficulties initially associated with sound resolved, films had become an entirely different experience. Many of these new films were filled with snappy wise-cracking dialogue adapted directly from stage plays. The new comedies had become far less visual and far more verbal, with the inspired sight gags of Keaton and Lloyd giving way to the witty one-liners of Groucho Marx and Mae West. An entirely new film genre, the musical, had also come into being, routinely enthralling audiences with lavish song and dance numbers.

All things considered, though, the transition to sound had not been pleasant, easy, or kind. As film historian Scott Eyman has written, rather than a "gentle grafting," it was more of "a brutal, crude transplantation."[1] "As a result," Eyman has also noted, "many of cinema's roots withered and died, and much native strength was lost. The culture of Hollywood itself grew harsher, more Darwinian."[2]

Even many of the silent era veterans who had managed to survive the transition and then thrive for decades in the sound medium lamented what had been lost. One of them was director Clarence Brown, whose career extended into the 1950s and included such highly praised films as 1943's *The Human Comedy* with Mickey Rooney, 1944's *National Velvet* with Elizabeth Taylor, and 1946's *The Yearling* with Gregory Peck. Throughout his long life he maintained a preference for silent film, once noting: "I think that silent pictures were more of an art than the talkies have ever been. No matter how you manage it, talkies have dialogue and dialogue belongs to the stage; too many people let dialogue do the thinking for them, do the plot exposition for them, do everything for them. Silents were ... subtler."[3]

Another person who experienced the silent-to-sound transition and spoke forcefully about the subject was British journalist and film critic Cedric Belfrage. In an interview he made in the late 1970s for the 1980 documentary series *Hollywood: A Celebration of the American Silent Film*, he commented, often with great emotion in his voice, on the change. "The thing that made me so sad, really, was that the international language was over," he said. "This was really a thing which nobody seemed to notice very much, but [silent film had given people] a language in which they could all speak to each other, which could be shown anywhere, and which everyone could understand. We just blew it up. And it was really rather sad."[4]

By the late 1930s, even the stubborn Charlie Chaplin had retired his beloved Tramp character and pivoted to talkies. As a living art, silent films were no more.

* * *

Although silent films were no longer being made, the opportunity to see them (or at least to see the ones that hadn't been lost or destroyed) still remained. At first, the challenges were awareness and accessibility: the films simply weren't available. As time passed, however, new generations of audiences discovered these films, appreciated their unique qualities, and embraced them. The "doomed art," in perhaps the greatest testament to its value and power, proved that it could speak across the decades to new generations of viewers.

This process of reemergence began in earnest during the 1950s. Film revival theaters, especially in large cities, occasionally included silent films on their schedules. Film festivals began to include silents as part of tributes to old film masters. Local television stations, always hungry for content, began to run silents in late-night and other less-popular time slots. During the decade, the annual Academy Awards ceremonies even gave the silent era much-needed attention and recognition when special Academy Honorary Awards were presented to Lloyd, Keaton, and pioneer silent film cowboy star Bronco Billy Anderson.

From the 1960s to the 1990s, interest in silent films continued to grow on several fronts. More film revival theaters opened across the U.S., Europe, and elsewhere. More tributes honored aging silent film masters at film festivals throughout the world. At events such as the annual Academy Awards ceremonies silent film luminaries from Mary Pickford and Lillian Gish to Charlie Chaplin and King Vidor were also recognized. More colleges and universities included courses in their curricula that studied silent films. Major film festivals devoted exclusively or mainly to silent films sprouted up around the world. One of the first, most prestigious, and most popular of these is the Giornate del Cinema Muto. Founded in 1982, it is held each fall in the town of Pordenone in Northern Italy. In the U.S., one of the most popular is the San Francisco Silent Film Festival. Founded in 1996, it now draws approximately 25,000 attendees each year.

Since 2000, recognition for, and interest in, silent films has continued to grow even more. In 2010, film historian Kevin Brownlow was given an Academy Honorary Award for his decades of work chronicling the silent film era and advocating the great value of these films and the need to preserve them for future generations. In addition, scores of other festivals devoted exclusively or largely to silent films have been founded and are now held each year in Europe, Asia, and North America in locales ranging from Warsaw, Poland, to Topeka, Kansas.

Technological accessibility has also played a role in enabling interest in silent films to grow. In the 1980s and 1990s, new technologies such as Video Home System (VHS) tape cassettes and Digital Video Discs (DVDs) and player/recorders first made it possible for people to view silent films at home without having to depend on television programming. Since the early 2000s, various online streaming platforms have also offered the same opportunity. Although the main focus of the Turner Classic Movies (TCM) cable channel is classic sound films, it regularly airs silent films along with helpful commentary and background for viewers. Its *Silent Sunday Nights* program, for example, has been a fixture in its weekly lineup since 1994.

All of this ably demonstrates, of course, that, even though people don't make silent films anymore, many of these films remain vital, continue to speak to us in ways that other arts cannot, and continue to attract new audiences. All totaled, these audiences might not comprise anywhere near the number of people who went to theaters each week in the mid–1920s, but they are loyal, and they are growing. While no longer a living art, silent films are still very much with us.

* * *

For those of us who wish to know more about what these films have to say, how they say it, and why they continue resonate with us today, one excellent place to start is by watching some of the great films of perhaps the most accomplished period in the history of the silent medium, the Long 1928.

When we watch, we'll be amazed again and again by what we see.

There is, for example, the moment in Josef von Sternberg's *The Docks of New York* when a crestfallen Mae bravely tries to thread a needle to repair the torn shirt pocket of Bill, the man who has just rejected her love. Suddenly, we see the image she is focused on, image of the thread and needle, blur, and we immediately understand that her eyes have now welled up with tears of grief.

There is the shot that pans up a New York City skyscraper in King Vidor's *The Crowd*, stops at a single window, and goes through the window into a huge open office filled with long, straight rows of identical desks. Once inside, the camera keeps moving forward, finally zeroing in one desk where young, hopeful John Sims (designated here as employee number 137) sits, looking like little more than a single ant in an enormous ant colony.

There is the 14-minute cyclone sequence of *Steamboat Bill, Jr.*, when Buster Keaton, in complete daredevil mode, rides on the trunk of a tree that's flying like a bullet through the air, jumps up multiple levels of a steamboat "Douglas Fairbanks style," and stands perfectly still as two tons of housing façade fall all around him, leaving him standing calmly within the small frame of the house's open attic window.

And there is so much more—all of it part of the Long 1928, that very short-lived time when a great but dying art lived its glorious last days.

Where to Find the Films Featured in This Book

While scores of U.S. silent and hybrid films released in the Long 1928 are readily available in DVD, streaming, and both formats through both major and niche distribution channels, it can sometimes be challenging to find just the one you want when you want it.

Fortunately, when writing this book, I could obtain or stream all the films I wanted to see. I ordered most films available on DVD through Amazon and went to eBay as a back-up. If you can't find what you want on the major distribution channels, a variety of niche DVD sites such as DVD Lady or Oldies.com are also worth checking out.

If DVD or streaming quality is a key consideration, any films you buy or stream through Criterion will more than meet your expectations. Also, short documentaries, interviews, and other "extras" that often accompany Criterion films can add greatly to the viewing experience.

If money or convenience is a consideration, streaming films available on YouTube might be the way to go. The challenge on YouTube, though, can be quality. For example, several different prints of some films (such as von Stroheim's *The Wedding March*) are available, but, before you start watching one of them, it might be prudent to check out two or three posted options to see which offers the best visual quality and musical score.

Two other options are television and theaters that play silent films or host silent film festivals. The Turner Classic Movies (TCM) channel plays silent films regularly, and, depending on your good fortune, the film you may be looking for may be on the upcoming TCM schedule. Also, several of the films spotlighted in this book have played at silent film festivals around the U.S. in recent years and will likely be showing up again in the not-too-distant future.

One final note: if at first you don't succeed, don't despair. All of the films discussed in this book are available in some form, somewhere.

Where to Find the Films Featured in This Book

Here is a list of the films spotlighted in each chapter and places where you can access them:

Chapter:
1. *My Best Girl*. DVD, The Milestone Collection.
2. *Sadie Thompson*. DVD, Kino.
3. *The Circus*. DVD, Criterion. Streams on the Criterion Channel and YouTube.
4. *The Last Command* and *The Docks of New York*. DVD, Criterion. Both stream on YouTube.
5. *The Crowd*. DVD available through eBay, DVD Lady, other outlets. Streams periodically on the Criterion Channel.
6. *Speedy*. DVD, Criterion. Streams on Criterion Channel.
7. *Steamboat Bill, Jr.* DVD, Kino. Streams on Amazon and YouTube
8. *Our Dancing Daughters*. DVD, Warner Archive. Streams on Amazon.
9. *Beggars of Life*. DVD, Grapevine Video. DVD and Blu-ray, Kino. Streams on YouTube.
10. *The Wedding March*. Streams on YouTube.
11. *The Wind*. DVD available through eBay.
12. *West of Zanzibar*. DVD, NOSE-SILO VIDEO. Steams on YouTube.
13. *The Iron Mask*. DVD, Kino and other distributors. Streams on Amazon and YouTube.
14. The 28 additional films discussed here are available either on DVD or through Amazon, YouTube, or other streaming services.

Chapter Notes

Introduction

1. Peter Bogdanovich, "1928: The Last and Greatest Year of the Original Motion Picture Art, B.S. (Before Sound)," *IndieWire*, January 30, 2011.
2. *Ibid.*
3. Gerald Mast and Bruce F. Kawin, *A Short History of the Movies, Ninth Edition* (New York: Pearson Longman, 2006) p. 226.
4. *Ibid.*, p. 227.
5. "Father of Film" is a nickname for D.W. Griffith that was also used as the title for the 1993 documentary about him, *D.W. Griffith: Father of Film*, by David Gill and Kevin Brownlow.
6. Among these "up-and-coming" directors were Cecil B. DeMille, King Vidor, John Ford, Raoul Walsh, Erich von Stroheim, Josef von Sternberg, Henry King, Allan Dwan, Clarence Brown, William Wellman, Charlie Chaplin, Buster Keaton, and Frank Capra. While some of them began directing in the 1910s, all of them found their artistic "voices" during the 1920s and several of them, including Ford, Walsh, King, Dwan, Capra, and Chaplin, enjoyed directing careers that extended into the 1960s.
7. Mast and Kawin, p. 230.
8. Scott Eyman, *The Speed of Sound: Hollywood and the Talkie Revolution, 1926–1930* (New York: Simon & Schuster, 1997) p. 160.
9. William K. Everson, *American Silent Film* (New York: Da Capo Press, 1998) p. 335.
10. *Ibid.*
11. Eyman, p. 160.
12. David Gill and Kevin Brownlow, *Harold Lloyd, The Third Genius* (London: Thames Television, 1989).

Chapter 1

1. Kevin Brownlow, *The Parade's Gone By...* (Berkeley: University of California Press, 1968) p. 120.
2. Eileen Whitfield, *Pickford: The Woman Who Made Hollywood* (Lexington: University Press of Kentucky, 1997) p. 259.
3. *Ibid.*, pp. 259–260.
4. *Ibid.*, p. 260.
5. *Ibid.*, p. 146.
6. Shari Kizirian, "My Best Girl," San Francisco Silent Film Festival, 2013.
7. Brownlow, p. 128.
8. Whitfield, p. 256.
9. Promotional poster for *Coquette*, 1929.
10. Whitfield, p. 260.
11. *Ibid.*, p. 253.
12. For the Second Academy Awards, the eligibility period was from August 1, 1928, to July 31, 1929. Later, the Academy's rules were changed so that films released during a certain calendar year would be eligible to be nominated for that year's awards.
13. Brownlow, p. 135.

Chapter 2

1. Marilyn Ann Moss, *Raoul Walsh: The True Adventures of Hollywood's Legendary Director* (Lexington: University Press of Kentucky, 2011) p. 100.
2. Gloria Swanson, *Swanson on*

Swanson (New York: Simon & Schuster, 1981) p. 307.
  3. *Ibid.*
  4. *Ibid.*
  5. *Ibid.*
  6. *Ibid.*, p. 308.
  7. *Ibid.*
  8. "The Hays Office" was industry shorthand for the film industry's self-censorship body that administered its much-despised Production Code (which determined what was morally appropriate for audiences to see) and was overseen by a former U.S. Postmaster General named Will Hays. After several scandals rocked the film industry in the 1920s, the office tightened up its censorship, leading to headaches for people such as Swanson and Walsh in 1927. Later, the office relaxed its restrictions somewhat, leading to a relatively brief period between 1929 and 1934 when films openly tested the boundaries of propriety, breaking new ground in the depiction of sex, violence, and other controversial subject matter. This in turn led to a conservative backlash and, beginning on July 1, 1934, the strict enforcement of a very restrictive code of morality for the next 30 years. Although it is a misnomer, this period of openness is usually referred to as the "Pre-Code Era." A fine book on this subject is Mick LaSalle's *Complicated Women: Sex and Power in Pre-Code Hollywood* (New York: St. Martin's Griffin, 2000).
  9. Swanson, p. 309.
  10. *Ibid.*
  11. Eric Sherman, ed., *Directing the Film: Film Directors on Their Art* (Los Angeles: Acrobat, 1976) p. 294.
  12. Swanson, pp. 397–398.
  13. Michael Henry Wilson, *Raoul Walsh: A Man and His Time*, short-subject documentary (Cloverland, 2013).
  14. Swanson, front matter.
  15. *Ibid.*, back cover.
  16. *Ibid.*
  17. Moss, p. 106.
  18. William K. Everson, *American Silent Film* (New York: Da Capo Press, 1998) p. 336.
  19. Mordaunt Hall, "The Screen: Gloria Swanson," *The New York Times*, February 6, 1928.
  20. *Ibid.*

Chapter 3

  1. Mordaunt Hall, "The Gold Rush," *The New York Times*, August 17, 1925.
  2. "Film Reviews," *Variety*, July 1, 1925.
  3. David Robinson, *Chaplin: His Life and Art* (New York: McGraw-Hill, 1985) p. 361.
  4. *Ibid.*, p. 360.
  5. Andrew Sarris, *You Ain't Heard Nothin' Yet: The American Talking Film—History and Memory, 1927–1949* (New York: Oxford University Press, 1998) p. 139.
  6. Pamela Hutchinson, "The Circus: The Tramp in the Mirror," The Criterion Channel, September 27, 2019.
  7. Robinson, p. 465.
  8. Roger Ebert, "Tightrope Walking with Monkeys in His Face," rogerebert.com, October 20, 2010.
  9. Hutchison.
  10. David Weddle, "Nothing Obvious or Easy: Chaplin's Feature Films," *Variety*, April 28, 2003, p. 6.
  11. Just a couple of the other projects Chaplin focused on during this period were a re-release of his 1921 film *The Kid* and a film script called *The Freak*, the story of a winged girl found in South America, which was to star his daughter Victoria. The film was never produced.

Chapter 4

  1. The seven films were *The Blue Angel* (1930), *Morocco* (1930), *Dishonored* (1931), *The Shanghai Express* (1932), *Blonde Venus* (1932), *The Scarlett Empress* (1934), and *The Devil Is a Woman* (1935).
  2. David Thompson (director), "Von Sternberg: The Man Who Made Dietrich," British Broadcasting Corporation, 1994.
  3. Andrew Sarris, *The Films of Josef von Sternberg* (New York: The Museum of Modern Art/Doubleday, 1966) p. 6.
  4. *Ibid.*, p. 18.
  5. Charles Silver, "Joseph von Sternberg's *The Docks of New York*," *Inside/Out* (a publication of the New York Museum of Modern Art), May 11, 2010.
  6. Ed Howard, "The Docks of New York," *Only the Cinema* (website), March 8, 2012.
  7. Eddie Muller, "The Docks of New

York," *San Francisco Silent Film Festival* (website), 2012.
   8. *Ibid.*
   9. "AN ENTERTAINING PICTURE: *Docks of New York*, With Bancroft and Miss Compson, Well Acted," *The New York Times*, September 17, 1928.
   10. Josef von Sternberg, *Fun in a Chinese Laundry: An Autobiography* (New York: Collier Books, 1965) p. 219.

Chapter 5

   1. Peter Bogdanovich, "1928: The Last and Greatest Year of the Original Motion Picture Art, B.S. (Before Sound)," *IndieWire*, January 30, 2011.
   2. King Vidor, *A Tree Is a Tree* (London: Longmans, Green, 1954) p. 98.
   3. *Ibid.*
   4. The American Dream is a term used to describe the widespread belief that equality of opportunity and the happiness that naturally comes with success are available to all in the U.S.
   5. Jason Fraley, "*The Crowd* (1928)," *The Film Spectrum*, November 16, 2013.
   6. Vidor, p. 3.
   7. *Ibid.*, p. 73.
   8. *Ibid.*, p. 77.
   9. Charles Silver, "King Vidor's *The Big Parade*," *Inside/Out* (a publication of the New York Museum of Modern Art), February 23, 2010.
   10. Vidor, p. 100.
   11. "*The Crowd*," *Variety*, February 15, 1928.
   12. Mordaunt Hall, "The Screen: Don Juans of the Deep," *The New York Times*, February 20, 1928.
   13. Tim Dirks, "*The Crowd* (1928)," filmsite.org.
   14. Many filmmakers have paid homage to Vidor for this sequence. One famous example is Billy Wilder in his Academy Award–winning 1960 film *The Apartment*. Early in the film, he introduces his clerical worker lead character played by Jack Lemmon in a similar fashion.
   15. Vidor, p. 104.
   16. Davies was Hearst's mistress and the frequent hostess at events held at Hearst Castle.
   17. Vidor, p. 114.
   18. *Ibid.*, pp. 114–115.
   19. Vidor's four other Best Director Academy Award nominations were for 1929's *Hallelujah*, 1931's *The Champ*, 1938's *The Citadel*, and 1956's *War and Peace*. In addition, he was credited as the producer of *The Champ*, which was also nominated for Best Picture.

Chapter 6

   1. Jeffrey Vance and Suzanne Lloyd, *Harold Lloyd: Master Comedian* (New York: Harry N. Abrams, 2002) p. 161.
   2. *Ibid.*
   3. Peter Kobel, *Silent Movies: The Birth of Film and the Triumph of Movie Culture* (New York: Little, Brown, 2007) p. 61.
   4. David Thomson, as quoted in Phillip Lopate's "The Comic Figure of the Average Man," an essay included in the Criterion DVD of *Speedy* released in 2015.
   5. "Harold Clayton Lloyd (1893–1971)," Harold Lloyd website.
   6. Kevin Brownlow, *The Parade's Gone By* ... (Berkeley: University of California Press, 1968) p. 459.
   7. *Ibid.*, p. 460.
   8. *Ibid.*
   9. *Ibid.*, p. 462.
   10. *Ibid.*, p. 464.
   11. Vance and Lloyd, p. 152.
   12. James Agee, as quoted in Lopate.
   13. Richard Griffith, as quoted in Lopate.
   14. Vance and Lloyd, p. 9.
   15. Kobel, p. 61.
   16. Harold Lloyd website.

Chapter 7

   1. Edward McPherson, *Buster Keaton: Tempest in a Teapot* (New York: Newmarket Press, 2004) p. 203.
   2. Roger Ebert, "The Films of Buster Keaton," rogerebert.com, November 10, 2002.
   3. Nicholas Barber, "Deadpan But Alive to the Future: Buster Keaton the Revolutionary," *Independent*, January 5, 2014.
   4. Marion Meade, *Buster Keaton: Cut to the Chase: A Biography* (New York: Open Road Media, 2014) p. 19.
   5. Gerald Mast and Bruce F. Kawin, *A*

Short History of the Movies, Ninth Edition (New York: Pearson Longman, 2006) p. 160.

6. *Variety* Staff. "*The General,*" *Variety*, December 31, 1926.

7. Mordaunt Hall, "THE SCREEN: A Civil War Farce." *The New York Times*, February 8, 1927.

8. Anon., "*The General,*" *New York Herald Tribune*, February 1927.

9. Orson Welles (archive interview), Blu-Ray edition of *The General*, Kino, November 10, 2009.

10. Adam Gopnik, "Silent Treatment: The Case for Buster Keaton," *The New Yorker*, January 31, 2022, p. 64.

11. Citation on Keaton's Oscar statuette.

Chapter 8

1. Bob Thomas, *Joan Crawford* (New York: Simon & Schuster, 1978) p. iiv.

2. Donald Spoto, *Possessed: The Life of Joan Crawford* (New York: HarperCollins, 2010), p. 58.

3. Sheila O'Malley, "World Class Acting: On Joan Crawford and *Sudden Fear,*" rogerebert.com, March 27, 2017.

4. Crawford's birth year has long been a subject of dispute. Various sources have put it as 1904, 1905, 1906, and 1908.

5. Mick LaSalle, *Complicated Women: Sex and Power in Pre-Code Hollywood* (New York: Thomas Dunne, 2000) p. 123.

6. Lawrence J. Quirk and William Schoell, *Joan Crawford: The Essential Biography* (Lexington: University of Kentucky Press, 2002) p. 29.

7. Spoto, p. 47.

8. Quirk and Schoell, p. 29.

9. Langdon W. Post, review of *The Unknown*, *New York Evening World*, June 5, 1927.

10. Pre-Code Hollywood (see note #8 from Chapter 2 for a brief description of this subject).

11. Bland Johaneson, review in *New York Mirror*, September 1928.

12. *Motion Picture Magazine*, September 1928.

13. Review in *New York World*, September 1928.

14. The 1947 film *Possessed* shares the same title as Crawford's 1931 film *Possessed* with Clark Gable, but it is an entirely different story.

15. More commonly known as "box office poison." This phrase was from an ad titled "WAKE UP! Hollywood Producers," taken out by Harry Brandt, the president of the Independent Theater Owners of America posted in the *Hollywood Reporter* and other film trade publications on May 4, 1938.

16. "*Trog* and *Taste Blood of Dracula*," *The New York Times*, October 29, 1970.

Chapter 9

1. William Wellman, Jr., *Wild Bill Wellman: Hollywood Rebel* (New York: Pantheon Books, 2015) p. 219.

2. Ibid.

3. Thomas Gladysz, "*Beggars of Life* with Louise Brooks Screens in New York," *Huffington Post*, February 17, 2012 (updated April 18, 2012).

4. Ibid.

5. Ibid.

6. Ibid.

7. Ibid.

8. Ibid.

9. Wellman, p. 226.

10. Kevin Brownlow, *The Parade's Gone By...* (Berkeley: University of California Press, 1968) p. 169.

11. Gladysz.

12. Lokke Heiss, "King Hearts and Cruel Comforts," the 32nd Pordenone Silent Film Festival, 2014,

13. Although he never received an Oscar for Best Direction. Wellman was nominated in this category three times: for 1937's *A Star Is Born*, 1949's *Battleground*, and 1954's *The High and the Mighty*. He did, however, receive an Oscar for his work on the screenplay of *A Star Is Born*.

14. Cliff Aliperti, "Louise Brooks stars in William Wellman's *Beggars of Life* (1928)," *Immortal Ephemera*, June 22, 2009.

15. Gladysz.

16. Louise Brooks, *Lulu in Hollywood* (Minneapolis: University of Minnesota Press, 2000) p. 23.

Chapter 10

1. Arthur Lennig, *Stroheim* (Lexington: University Press of Kentucky, 2000) p. 272.

2. *Ibid.*, p. 58.
3. Richard Koszarski, *The Man You Loved to Hate: Erich von Stroheim and Hollywood* (Oxford: Oxford University Press, 1983) p. 72.
4. Lenning, p. 222.
5. Charles Stumpf, *ZaSu Pitts: The Life and Career* (Jefferson, NC: McFarland, 2010) pp. 53–54.
6. Phillip Lopate (editor), *American Movie Critics: An Anthology from the Silents Until Now* (New York: The Library of America, 2006) p. 30.
7. Fay Wray, *On the Other Hand* (New York: St. Martin's Press, 1989) p. 72.

Chapter 11

1. The Swedish surname "Sjöström" was changed to the more anglicized spelling "Seastrom" when the director worked at MGM in the 1920s to make his name more relatable to American audiences, and he apparently had no objection to this. References to him in articles and books continue to use either one or the other of these spellings depending on the specific author's preference. I chose the original because it appears to be the predominant spelling in most recent writing.
2. Robert Osborne, introducing a showing of *The Wind* on Turner Classic Movies, December 28, 2003.
3. *MoMA Highlights* (New York: The Museum of Modern Art, 1999) p. 174.
4. "The Biograph Collection," *Still Moving: The Film and Media Collections of The Museum of Modern Art* (New York: The Museum of Modern Art, 2006) p. 41.
5. King Vidor, *A Tree Is a Tree* (London: Longmans, Green, 1954) pp. 88–89.
6. Charles Affron, *Lillian Gish: Her Legend, Her Life* (Berkeley: University of California Press, 2001) pp. 216–217.
7. Graham Petrie, *Hollywood Destinies: European Directors in America, 1922–1931* (Detroit: Wayne State University Press, 2002) p. 143.
8. The film adaption of *The Wind* was originally planned to end tragically, as the novel had, with a crazed Letty wandering alone and aimless in the windswept desert. Apparently, Gish, Frances Marion, and others were adamant that this ending be kept in the film version. But MGM executives overruled them, and the happy ending that audiences see today prevailed. For the rest of her life, Gish maintained the original, tragic ending had been filmed, and then, after the executives viewed it, changed and reshot. Gish biographer Charles Affron, however, disputes this claim, making a compelling case that the decision to go with a happy ending had been finalized earlier and that the tragic ending had never been filmed.
9. Affron, pp. 229–230.
10. *Ibid.*, p. 230.
11. Petrie, p. 155.
12. James Caryn, "Film: Eye on the Prize, Foot in the Mouth," *The New York Times*, March 28, 1993.
13. Ingmar Bergman (in interview), *Victor Sjöström: A Portrait*, 1981 television documentary, Gosta Werner (director).
14. Affron, p. 215.
15. *Ibid.*

Chapter 12

1. Brian Darr, "*West of Zanzibar*, 1928," San Francisco Silent Film Festival website, December 2009.
2. *Ibid.*
3. Mick LaSalle, "The Lon Chaney and Tod Browning Film Festival of 1994," *San Francisco Chronicle*, August 8, 2016.
4. E.J. Fleming, *Paul Bern: The Life and Famous Death of the Metro-Goldwyn-Mayer Director and Husband of Harlow*. (Jefferson, NC: McFarland, 2009) p. 167.
5. Alfred Eaker, "Tod Browning: A Retrospective," *The Blue Mahler*, January 26, 2016.
6. Fritzi Kramer, "*West of Zanzibar* (1928) A Silent Film Review," *Movies Silently*, February 4, 2013.
7. *Ibid.*
8. Jay Seaver, "*West of Zanzibar*," eFilmCritic.com, November 6, 2015.
9. Brian Darr, "*West of Zanzibar*," *Senses of Cinema*, July 2010.
10. *Ibid.*
11. Kramer.
12. Darr, *Senses of Cinema*.
13. *Ibid.*
14. *Ibid.*

15. Bret Wood, *West of Zanzibar* (1928), Turner Classic Movies website.

Chapter 13

1. Interview with Laurence Irving for the documentary *Hollywood: A Celebration of the American Silent Film*, Episode 13 (1980), David Gill and Kevin Brownlow, producers.
2. *Ibid.*
3. *Ibid.*
4. Jeffrey Vance, *Douglas Fairbanks* (Berkeley: University of California Press, 2008) p. 267.
5. "*Life* Visits Pickfair," *Life Magazine*, November 17, 1947.
6. Peter Bogdanovich, *Allan Dwan: The Last Pioneer* (New York: Praeger, 1971)
7. Vance, pp. 250–25.
8. *Ibid.*, pp. 253–254.
9. *Ibid.*, pp. 256–257.
10. Mary Pickford, *Sunshine and Shadow* (Garden City, NY: Doubleday, 1955) p. 311.
11. Vance, pp. 271–280.
12. In addition to the two films released during this time, 1931's *Kiki* and 1933's *Secrets*, Pickford also started and then abandoned a 1930 project directed by Marshall Neilan called *Forever Yours*. Apparently, she had been unhappy with her performance and the film's overall quality.
13. Lady Sylvia Ashley's other well-known movie star husband was Clark Gable, another King of Hollywood. Their marriage lasted between 1949 and 1952.
14. Vance, p. 306.

Chapter 14

1. Jeffrey Vance, *Douglas Fairbanks* (Berkeley: University of California Press, 2008) p. 227.
2. Leonard Maltin, *Classic Movie Guide: From the Silent Era Through 1965* (New York: Penguin Publishing Group, 2015) pp. 380–381.

Afterthoughts

1. Scott Eyman, *The Speed of Sound: Hollywood and the Talkie Revolution, 1926–1930* (New York: Simon & Schuster, 1997) p. 377.
2. *Ibid.*
3. *Ibid.*, p. 378.
4. Interview with Cedric Belfrage for the documentary *Hollywood: A Celebration of the American Silent Film*, Episode 13 (1980), David Gill and Kevin Brownlow, producers.

Bibliography

Acker, Ally. *Reel Women: Pioneers of the Cinema, 1896 to the Present.* New York: Continuum, 1991.
Affron, Charles. *Lillian Gish: Her Legend, Her Life.* Berkeley: University of California Press, 2001.
Aliperti, Cliff. "Louise Brooks Stars in William Wellman's *Beggars of Life* (1928)." *Immortal Ephemera,* June 22, 2009.
Barber, Nicholas. "Deadpan but Alive to the Future: Buster Keaton the Revolutionary." *Independent,* January 5, 2014.
Bogdanovich, Peter. *Allan Dwan: The Last Pioneer.* New York: Praeger, 1971.
_____. "1928: The Last and Greatest Year of the Original Motion Picture Art, B.S. (Before Sound)." *IndieWire,* January 30, 2011.
Brooks, Louise. *Lulu in Hollywood.* Minneapolis: University of Minnesota Press, 2000.
Brownlow, Kevin. *The Parade's Gone By...* Berkeley: University of California Press, 1968.
Caryn, James. "Film: Eye on the Prize, Foot in the Mouth." *The New York Times,* March 28, 1993.
Colman, Juliet Benita. *Ronald Colman: A Very Private Person.* New York: William Morrow, 1975.
Darr, Brian. "*West of Zanzibar,* 1928." San Francisco Silent Film Festival website, December 2009.
_____. "*West of Zanzibar.*" *Senses of Cinema,* July 2010.
Dirks, Tim. "*The Crowd* (1928)." filmsite.org.
Eaker, Alfred. "Tod Browning: A Retrospective." *The Blue Mahler,* January 26, 2016
Ebert, Roger. "The Films of Buster Keaton." rogerebert.com, November 10, 2002.
_____. "Tightrope Walking with Monkeys in His Face." rogerebert.com, October 20, 2010.
Everson, William K. *American Silent Film.* New York: Da Capo Press, 1998.
Eyman, Scott. *Empire of Dreams: The Epic Life of Cecil B. DeMille.* New York: Simon & Schuster, 1997.
_____. *The Speed of Sound: Hollywood and the Talkie Revolution, 1926–1930.* New York: Simon & Schuster, 1997.
Fleming, E.J. *Paul Bern: The Life and Famous Death of the Metro-Goldwyn-Mayer Director and Husband of Harlow.* Jefferson, NC: McFarland, 2009.
Fraley, Jason. "*The Crowd* (1928)." *The Film Spectrum,* November 16, 2013.
Gill, David, and Brownlow, Kevin. *Harold Lloyd, The Third Genius.* London: Thames Television, 1989
_____, and _____. *Hollywood: A Celebration of the American Silent Film.* London: Thames Television, 1980.
Gish, Lillian. *The Movies, Mr. Griffith, and Me.* Englewood Cliffs, NJ: Prentice-Hall, 1969.
Gladysz, Thomas. "*Beggars of Life* with Louise Brooks Screens in New York." *Huffington Post,* February 17, 2012.
Gopnik, Adam. "Silent Treatment: The Case for Buster Keaton." *The New Yorker,* January 31, 2022.

Hall, Mordaunt. "THE SCREEN: A Civil War Farce." *The New York Times*, February 8, 1927.
―――. "*The Gold Rush*." *The New York Times*, August 17, 1925.
―――. "The Screen: Don Juans of the Deep." *The New York Times*, February 20, 1928.
―――. "The Screen: Gloria Swanson." *The New York Times*, February 6, 1928.
Heiss, Lokke. "King Hearts and Cruel Comforts." The 32nd Pordenone Silent Film Festival website, 2014.
Howard, Ed. "*The Docks of New York*." Only the Cinema website, March 8, 2012.
Hutchinson, Pamela. "*The Circus*: The Tramp in the Mirror." The Criterion Channel, September 27, 2019.
Kizirian, Shari. "*My Best Girl*." San Francisco Silent Film Festival website, 2013.
Kobel, Peter. *Silent Movies: The Birth of Film and the Triumph of Movie Culture*. New York: Little, Brown, 2007.
Koszarski, Richard. *The Man You Loved to Hate: Erich von Stroheim and Hollywood*. Oxford: Oxford University Press, 1983.
Kramer, Fritzi. "*West of Zanzibar* (1928) A Silent Film Review." *Movies Silently*, February 4, 2013.
LaSalle, Mick. *Complicated Women: Sex and Power in Pre-Code Hollywood*. New York: Thomas Dunne, 2000.
―――. "The Lon Chaney and Tod Browning Film Festival of 1994." *San Francisco Chronicle*, August 8, 2016.
Lennig, Arthur. *Stroheim*. Lexington: University Press of Kentucky, 2000.
Lopate, Phillip. "The Comic Figure of the Average Man." Criterion DVD of *Speedy*, 2015.
―――, ed. *American Movie Critics: An Anthology from the Silents Until Now*. New York: Library of America, 2006.
Maher, Karen Ward. *Woman Filmmakers in Early Hollywood*. Baltimore: Johns Hopkins University Press, 2006.
Maltin, Leonard. *Classic Movie Guide: From the Silent Era Through 1965*. New York: Penguin Publishing Group, 2015.
Mast, Gerald, and Bruce F. Kawin. *A Short History of the Movies, Ninth Edition*. New York: Pearson Longman, 2006.
McPherson, Edward. *Buster Keaton: Tempest in a Teapot*. New York: Newmarket Press, 2004.
Meade, Marion. *Buster Keaton: Cut to the Chase: A Biography*. New York: Open Road Media, 2014.
Moss, Marilyn Ann. *Raoul Walsh: The True Adventures of Hollywood's Legendary Director*. Lexington: University Press of Kentucky, 2011.
Muller, Eddie. "*The Docks of New York*," San Francisco Silent Film Festival website, 2012.
O'Malley, Sheila. "World Class Acting: On Joan Crawford and *Sudden Fear*." rogerebert.com, March 27, 2017.
Peary, Danny. *Alternate Oscars*. New York: Dell, 1993.
Petrie, Graham. *Hollywood Destinies: European Directors in America, 1922–1931*. Detroit: Wayne State University Press, 2002.
Pickford, Mary. *Sunshine and Shadow*. Garden City, NY: Doubleday, 1955.
Post, Langdon W. "*The Unknown*." *New York Evening World*, June 5, 1927.
Quirk, Lawrence J., and William Schoell. *Joan Crawford: The Essential Biography*. Lexington: University of Kentucky Press, 2002.
Robinson, David. *Chaplin: His Life and Art*. New York: McGraw-Hill, 1985.
Sarris, Andrew. *The Films of Josef von Sternberg*. New York: The Museum of Modern Art/Doubleday, 1966.
―――. *You Ain't Heard Nothin' Yet: The American Talking Film—History and Memory, 1927–1949*. New York: Oxford University Press 1998.
Seaver, Jay. "*West of Zanzibar*." eFilmCritic.com, November 6, 2015.
Sherman, Eric, ed. *Directing the Film: Film Directors on Their Art*. Los Angeles: Acrobat, 1976.
Silver, Charles. "Joseph von Sternberg's *The Docks of New York*." *Inside/Out* (New York's Museum of Modern Art), May 11, 2010.

Bibliography

_____. "King Vidor's *The Big Parade.*" *Inside/Out* (New York's Museum of Modern Art), February 23, 2010.
Spoto, Donald. *Possessed: The Life of Joan Crawford.* New York: HarperCollins, 2010.
Stumpf, Charles. *ZaSu Pitts: The Life and Career.* Jefferson, NC: McFarland, 2010.
Swanson, Gloria. *Swanson on Swanson.* New York: Simon & Schuster, 1981.
Thomas, Bob. *Joan Crawford.* New York: Simon & Schuster, 1978.
Thompson, David. *Von Sternberg: The Man Who Made Dietrich.* London: British Broadcasting Corporation, 1994.
Vance, Jeffrey. *Douglas Fairbanks.* Berkeley: University of California Press, 2008.
Vance, Jeffrey, and Suzanne Lloyd. *Harold Lloyd: Master Comedian.* New York: Harry N. Abrams, 2002.
Vidor, King. *A Tree Is a Tree.* London: Longmans, Green, 1954.
Von Sternberg, Josef. *Fun in a Chinese Laundry: An Autobiography.* New York: Collier Books, 1965.
Weddle, David. "Nothing Obvious or Easy: Chaplin's Feature Films." *Variety*, April 28, 2003.
Wellman, William, Jr. *Wild Bill Wellman: Hollywood Rebel.* New York: Pantheon Books, 2015.
Whitfield, Eileen. *Pickford: The Woman Who Made Hollywood.* Lexington: University Press of Kentucky, 1997.
Wilson, Michael Henry. *Raoul Walsh: A Man and His Time* (short-subject documentary). Cloverland, 2013.
Wood, Bret. "*West of Zanzibar* (1928)." Turner Classic Movies website.
Wray, Fay. *On the Other Hand.* New York: St. Martin's Press, 1989.

Index

Numbers in **_bold italics_** refer to pages with illustrations

Abbott, George 110
Academy Awards 21, 25, 29, 30, 44, 49, 55, 58, 66, 75, 85, 99, 100, 108, 112, 115, 131, 144, 145, 163, 170, 172, 178, 179, 185
Across to Singapore 173–174
Adoree, Renee 68
Affron, Charles 137, 142
Agee, James 83
Aitken, Harry 161
Aliperti, Cliff 117
American Dream 15, 66, 72; films about 72
American Film Institute's Lifetime Achievement Award 145
Annie Laurie 137
Arbuckle, Roscoe "Fatty" 91
Arlen, Richard 112, ***114***
The Artist 5
Arzner, Dorothy 169
Ashley, Sylvia 167
Astaire, Fred 107
Asther, Nils 173

Bachonova, Olga 60
Ball, Lucille 98
Bancroft, George 54, 55, 60, 62
Banky, Vilma 12
Barber, Nicholas 89–90
The Barker 181
Barnes, George 37
Barrymore, Lionel 36, 37, ***149***, 155
Beaumont, Harry 16, 102
Beery, Wallace 62, 112, 114, 115, 119–120
Beggars of Life 15, ***110-120***
Belfrage, Cedric 184
Bergman, Henry 40
Bergman, Ingmar 145–146
Besserer, Eugenie ***7***
The Big Parade 65
The Big Trail 31
Biograph Studios 135
Birth of a Nation 136
The Black Pirate 162–163

Blind Husbands 121, 124
The Blue Angel 59, 64
Boardman, Eleanor 66, 69, 70, 73–75
Bogdanovich, Peter 5, 65, 99
La Bohème (1926 film) 136
Borzage, Frank 171–172
Bow, Clara 21, 169
Brenon, Herbert 172–173
Brent, Evelyn 54, 55, 57, 58
Broken Blossoms 136
Brook, Clive 54, 55
Brooks, Louise 112, 113, 114–115, 119–120, 170–171
Brown, Clarence 2, 115, 171, 181–182, 184
Brown, Johnny Mack 105, 106
Browning, Tod 16, ***147-157***
Brownlow, Kevin 17, 76, 86, 99, 113, 116, 185
Buster Keaton: A Hard Act to Follow 99
Buster Keaton Productions 88, 91, 94
Byron, Marion 95

The Cameraman 16, 97–98, 176
Capra, Frank 171, 177–178
Carewe, Edwin 174
Carne, Marcel 55
Carroll, Harrison 119
The Case of Lena Smith 53, 63
Chaney, Lon 16, 104, ***147-157***, 172–173
Chaney, Lon, Jr. 149
Chaplin, Charlie 5, 6, 15, 17, 18, ***40-50***, 53
Chicago Tribune 112
Children of Divorce 53
Christy, Ann ***78***, 82
The Circus 15, ***40-50***
Citizen Kane 126
City Lights 5, 48
Cohan, George M. 161
College 94
Compson, Betty 60, 62
Coney Island 70, 73, 83, 85
Cops 92
Coquette 24, 25

199

Index

The Countess from Hong Kong 49
Crawford, Joan 16, 38, **100–109**, 151, 173–174
Cromwell, John 110, 111
The Crowd 15, **65–76**, 186
Cukor, George 110, 111

Dancing Lady 107
Darr, Brian 155, 156
Davies, Marion 16, 173, **179–180**
Davis, Mildred 85
Day, Richard 102, 105
The Day of Fate 150
De Niro, Robert 147
depth of field 126
The Devil's Pass Key 124
Diary of a Lost Girl 113, 114
Dietrich, Marlene 51–52, 64
Dirks, Tim 72
The Docks of New York 15, 53, 54, **59–63**, 64, 186
Don Juan (1926 film) 8–9
Dracula (1931 film) 151–152
Dreier, Hans 55, 58, 62
Duel in the Sun 144
Durante, Jimmy 98
Duvivier, Julien 55
Dwan, Allan 123, 162

Eagels, Jeanne 28
Eaker, Alfred 151
Ebert, Roger 43, 89
Edison Company 7
Emerson, John 123, 124
Everson, William 11, 36
expressionism 61–62, 66, 69, 72–73
Eyman, Scott 184

Fairbanks, Douglas 13, 14, 18, 19, 25, **158–167**, 168–169
Fairbanks, Douglas, Jr. 160, 164–165, 177–178
Fantom Screen 171
Fawcett, George 129
Fields, W.C. 13, 79
Film Daily 113
Fitzgerald, F. Scott 103
The Flying Fleet 182
Foolish Wives 121, 124
For Heaven's Sake 82
Ford, John 170, 174
Four Sons 170
Fox Film Corporation 8
Freaks 152
Fred Karno company 43
The Freshman 78, 82
Fun in a Chinese Laundry 51

Galveston, TX 66–67
Garbo, Greta **138**, 175–176, 181–182
The Gaucho 168–169
Gaumont, Leon 7

Gaynor, Janet 171–172
Gehrig, Lou 84
The General 93–94
George, Maude 129
Get Your Man 169
Gibbons, Cedric 102, 105
Gilbert, John 68, 69, 104
Gill, David 76, 86, 99
Giornate del Cinema Muto 185
A Girl in Every Port 170–171
Girl Shy 78, 82
Gish, Dorothy 134, 135
Gish, Lillian 15, 107, **133–146**
Gladysz, Thomas 113
Glennon, Bert 55, 58
Godard, Jean-Luc 66
Goddard, Paulette 49
The Gold Rush 40
Goldwyn, Frances 11
Goldwyn, Samuel 68
Goldwyn Company 125, 126
Gowland, Gibson 126
Grande Illusion, La 131
Grandma's Boy 78, 81
The Great Buster: A Celebration 99
The Great Dictator 48
Greed 121, 125–126
Greenacres 85
Grey, Lita 40, 44
Griffith, D.W. 7, 8, **12–13**, 18, 76, 135, 150
Griffith, Richard 86

Haines, William 104, **179–180**
Hall, Mordaunt 37, 38, 40, 69, 94, 113
Hangman's House 174
Hanson, Lars 135, **138**, 140, 142
Harbaugh, Carl 95
Hardy, Oliver 169–170
Harold Lloyd: The Third Genius 86
Harold Lloyd's World of Comedy 85
Harris, Jed 161
Harris, Mildred 43–44
Harrison's Reports 148
Hawks, Howard 170
Hays Office 28, 29
He Who Gets Slapped (1924 film) 139
The Heart of Humanity 124
Hecht, Ben 53, 55
Heiss, Lokke 114
The High Sign 91
Hollywood: A Celebration of the American Silent Film 76
Hollywood Reporter 108
The Honeymoon 127
Houdini, Harry 90
Howard, Ed 61
Howe, James Wong 173
Hull, Frank E. 130
The Hunchback of Notre Dame (1923 film) 149

Index

Huston, Walter 38
hybrid film 11-12

In Old Arizona 30
Inspiration Films 136
The Iron Mask (1929 film) 6, 14, **158-167**
Irving, Laurence 158, 164
It 21

Jannings, Emil 12, 56, 58
The Jazz Singer (1927 film) 1, 5, **6-7**, 8-9, 11, 19, 23, 44, 122
John Barkam Reviews 34
Jolson, Al 9, 176
The Jury of Fate 150

Kawin, Bruce F. 92
Keaton, Buster 13, 15, **88-99**, 176; Great Stone Face character 89
Kennedy, Joseph P. 130
The Kid 46
The Kid Brother 82
King, Henry 136
Kino Video 34
Kobel, Peter 79, 87
Kongo 148
Koszarski, Richard 124
Kramer, Fritzi 153-154, 155
Kurrle, Robert 35

A Lady of Chance 180-181
Laemmle, Carl 124
Lagerlof, Selma 138
The Lamb 161
LaSalle, Mick 148
Lasky, Jesse 110, 111
The Last Command 15, 53, 54, **56-58**, 64
Laugh, Clown, Laugh 16, 172-173
Laurel, Stan 169-170
Leave 'Em Laughing 169-170
Lehr, Abe 125
Leloir, Maurice 164
Lemmon, Jack 86
Lennig, Arthur 121, 124
Life Magazine 161
Limelight 46, 49
Littlefield, Lucien 22
Lloyd, Harold 13, 15, **77-87**; "glasses" character 80-81
Lloyd, Suzanne 82, 86
London After Midnight 151
Lonesome 175
Long 1928 1-3, 6, 11, 14, 16, 168
Loring, Hope 21
Los Angeles Times 34
The Love of Sunya 27
Lugosi, Bela 152
Lulu in Hollywood 115
Lundin, Walter 83, 85

M (1931 film) 119
Maas, Frederica Sagor 104
Maltin, Leonard 173
The Man Who Laughs 177
Mank, Gregory William 147
A Man's Castle 172
The Mark of Zorro (1920 film) 162
Marsh, Oliver 35, 37
Martin, Quinn 113
Marx, Groucho 13, 79
Mast, Gerald 92
The Matinee Idol 171
Mayer, Louis B. 67-68, 139, 163
McLaglen, Victor 174
McPherson, Edward 88
Menzies, William Cameron 37
The Merry Widow 126
Metro-Goldwyn-Mayer (MGM) 8, 68, 88, 89, 98, 108, 110 126, 136
Miss Sadie Thompson 38
Modern Times 5, 48-49
Mommie Dearest 109
Moore, Colleen 76
Moore, Owen 19
Morocco 54, 64
Motion Picture Magazine 106
Movietone 8
Muller, Eddie 62
Murray, James 66, 69, 70, 73-74, 75
Mussolini, Benito 7
My Best Girl 14, **17-26**
The Mysterious Lady 175-176

National Film Registry (of U.S. Library of Congress) 57, 99
The Navigator 89, 91-92, 93
New York Herald Tribune 94
New York Mirror 106
New York Museum of Modern Art 133
New York Times 108
New York World 106
Newmeyer, Fred 81
nickelodeon 67
Night of the Hunter 144
Noah's Ark 178-179
Nolan, Mary **149**, 154-155
Norris, Eleanor 98, 99
Novarro, Ramon 104

O'Malley, Sheila 101
One Week 89, 91-92
O'Neill, Oona 49
Osborne, Robert 133
Our Blushing Brides 107
Our Daily Bread 74
Our Dancing Daughters 16, **100-109**
Our Hospitality 92
Our Modern Maidens 107

Index

Page, Anita 105
Pandora's Box 113, 114, 171
The Parade's Gone By 113
Paramount Pictures 8, 53, 55, 57, 110–111, 127
Parsons, Louella 113
The Passion of Joan of Arc 1, 36
The Patsy 173
Peg 'o My Heart 67–68
The Phantom Carriage 139
The Phantom of the Opera (1925 film) 149
Philadelphia Inquirer 34
Pickfair 19, 25, 161
Pickford, Mary 13, 14, **17-26**, 53, 107, 135, 161, 166–167
Pitts, ZaSu 126, 129
Post, Langdon W. 104
Powell, William 56
The Power of the Press 177–178
Powers, Pat 127
Pre-Code period 105
Production Code (film industry) 28, 38
The Purple Rose of Cairo 92
Purviance, Edna 53

Queen Kelly 30, 130

The Racket 178
Rain 38
Ramona 174–175
Rapf, Harry 103
Reisner, Charles 95
Roach, Hal 80–81, 82
Robinson, David 42
Rogers, Charles ("Buddy") **20**, 22, 25
Rohauer, Raymond 98
Romola (1924 film) 136
Rosher, Charles 21–22, 24
Rosher Kino Portrait Lens 22
Rosson, Harold 62
Ruth, Babe 79, 83–84

Sadie Thompson 15, **27-39**
Safety Last! 78, 81–82
The Salvation Hunters 53
San Francisco Silent Film Festival 185
Sarris, Andrew 42, 52, 57–58
The Scarlet Letter (1926 film) 134, 137, 140
Schenck, Joseph 27–28, 88, 89, 91, 94
Schneiderman, George 170, 174
Schulberg, B.P. 53
Scorsese, Martin 147
Scriven, Mae 98
Seaver, Jay 154
Sebastian, Dorothy 105
The Secret Life of Walter Mitty (short story) 92
Secrets 25
Sedgwick, Edward 67, 98
Sharp, Henry 165

Shaw, George Bernard 7, 65
Shearer, Norma 180–181
Sherlock, Jr. 92
Sherwood, Robert 131
Show People 16, **179-180**
Shriners 85
Sight and Sound Magazine 94
silent film musicians 13–14
Silent Movie 5
Silent Sunday Nights 185
Silver, Charles 59, 69
The Sin of Harold Diddlebock 85
The Singing Fool 63, 176
Sjöström, Victor 14–15, **133-146**
Skelton, Red 98
sound film technology 9–10; benefits 9; liabilities 9–10
Speedy 15, **77-87**
Stallings, Laurence 68
Steamboat Bill, Jr. 15, **88-99**, 186
Street Angel 171–172
Stumph, Charles 130
Sturges, Preston 57
Sudden Fear 101
Sugar Blues 34
The Suicide Club 40
Sully, Anna Beth 160
Sunrise 1, 170
Sunset Boulevard 33, 36–37, 131
Swanson, Gloria **27-39**
Swanson on Swanson 34
Swenska Bio 138

Talmadge, Natalie 98
Talmadge, Norma 177
The Taming of the Shrew (1929 film) 25, 166–167
Taylor, Laurette 67
Taylor, Sam 21, 24, 166
Thalberg, Irving 9, 65–66, 68, 69, 74, 124–125, 126–127, 151
The Thief of Bagdad (1924 film) 27, 162
Thomson, David 79
Three Ages 92
The Three Musketeers (1921 film) 159
Thunderbolt 64
Torrence, Ernest 90, 95, 96, 173–174
The Trail of '98 171
transition to sound films 1–16, 30–31, 43, 183–184
The Trespasser 30, 33, 39
Triangle Film Corporation 161
Trog 109
Tully, Jim 112
Turrin, Joseph 35, 36
two-strip Technicolor film 8

Underworld 53, 54–56, 64
The Unholy Three 149, 151
United Artists 17, 43, 88, 161

Index

The Unknown 104, 151
The Unseen Enemy 135

Vance, Jeffrey 46, 82, 15, 163, 168–169
Variety 18, 40, 69, 75, 94
Veidt, Conrad 177
Vidor, Florence Arlo 67
Vidor, King 15, **65–76**, 136–137, 173
Vidor Village 67
Vitaphone 8
von Sternberg, Josef 15, **51–64**, 127, 129
Von Sternberg: The Man Who Made Dietrich 51
von Stroheim, Erich 15, 30, ***121–132***

Walking Down Broadway (Hello Sister!) 130
Walsh, Raoul 15, **27–39**
Warde, Frederick Barkham 159
Warner Brothers 8, 108
Way Down East 136
The Way of All Flesh 58
Wead, Frank ("Spig") 182
The Wedding March 15, ***121–132***

Welcome Danger 77, 79
Welles, Orson 94
Wellman, William 15, ***110–120***
West, Mae 13
West of Zanzibar 16, ***147–157***
The Whales of August 145
What Price Glory? (1926 film) 27
White Shadows in the South Seas 179
The White Sister 136
Wild Boys of the Road 72
Wild Oranges 68
Wild Strawberries 145–146
Wilson, Michael Henry 32
The Wind 14, ***133–146***
Wings 1, 21, 111
A Woman Disputed 177
A Woman of Affairs 181–182
A Woman of the Sea 53
Wood, Bret 157
Wray, Fay ***122***, 129, 132

Young, Loretta 173

Zukor, Adolph 110, 111

www.ingramcontent.com/pod-product-compliance
Lightning Source LLC
Chambersburg PA
CBHW032044300426
44117CB00009B/1185